P9-ASN-347

792.094
AL5t

126284

DATE DUE			

DISCARDED

Theatre In Europe

CARL A. RUDISILL LIBRARY
LENOIR RHYNE COLLEGE

John Allen

792.094

A L 5π

126284

Sept. 1983

First Published 1981

Copyright © John Allen

All rights reserved. No part of this publication may be recorded or transmitted in any form or by any means, including photocopying and recording, without the prior permission of the copyright owner, application for which should be addressed to the publishers. Written permission must also be obtained before any part of this publication is stored in any kind of information retrieval system.

ISBN 0 903931 40 0

CITY ARTS SERIES
General Editor: John Pick

John Offord (Publications) Ltd.
P.O. Box 64, Eastbourne, East Sussex.

Printed by Eastbourne Printers Ltd.

Acknowledgements

The author would like to express his thanks to the following people for help in a number of ways at various stages of a study that has been spread over four-and-a-half years. In many instances it has been impossible to distinguish between material derived from conversation and various kinds of printed material.

It need hardly be added that the author takes full responsibility for any construction he may have put upon the material or inaccuracies that may have occurred. Detailed aknowledgements are made at the end of each chapter.

M. Alfons van Impe; members of the staff of the Ministrie van Nederlands Cultuur, Brussels; M. Frank Lucas and M. Marc Quaghebeur of the Ministère de l'Education et de la Culture Française, Brussels; M. Marc Liebens; Representative and staff of the British Council, Brussels; General-Administrator of the Belgian National Theatre; Mm. Guy Brajot, François Miermont, Eric Westphal, Augustin Girard and A-C. Charpentier of the Ministère de la Culture et de la Communication; Representative and staff of the British Council, Paris, Madame Gabrielle Heller of the Centre Française du Théâtre; Madamoiselle Jeanne Laurent; M. Denis Maurey, President of the Syndicat des Directeurs de Théâtres de Paris et de la Région Parisienne; Madam Rose-Marie Moudoues of A.T.E.J.; M. Pierre Laville; M. Jean Darcante and staff of the French Centre of the International Theatre Institute.

Professor Mark Blaug; Mr John Whittaker of the Office of Arts and Libraries; Mr Stephen Mennell; Mr Roger Lancaster; the Editor of The Stage; the staff of British Actor's Equity Association; Mr Gerald Croasdell of the International Federation of Actors; Mr Bill Granger and Miss Christine Porter of the Polytechnic of Central London; The Secretary-General, Mr Rod Fisher and members of staff of the Arts Council of Great Britain; Mr Sean Sutton of the B.B.C.; Miss Margaret Ramsay; Miss Jane Hackworth-Young of the British Theatre Association; Mr Harvey Unna; Mr Peter Husbands of the Central Council for Amateur Theatre; Mr Robert Hutchinson; Mr David Conville and Mr Oscar Lewenstein; Mr Vincent Burke of the Theatrical Managers' Association.

Representatives and staff of the British Council in Rome and Milan; Signora Anne Guerrieri; Signora Barzetti of the Italian Institute, London; Dr Pietro Mauri of the Comune di Milano; Dr Giancarlo Sorini of the Associazione dei Teatri Italiani; Signor Franco Parenti.

Herr Joachim Werner Preuss of the Federal German Centre of the

International Theatre Institute; the Director of the Deutscher Bühnen-verein; Dr Brigitte Lohmeyer of the West German Embassy; Professor Dr W. Keim of the Bavarian Ministry for Education and Culture; Herr Wolfgang Zimmermann of the Münich Kammerspiel; Herr Jorg-Dieter Haas of the Bavarian State theatre; Internaciones, Münich; Herr and Frau Redmann of the Münich Children's Theatre; Secretary of the Standing Conference of the Länder Ministers of Culture; Secretary of the Union of German Amateur theatres.

Director of the Municipal Theatre, Utrecht; M. John Ytteborg, Secre-tary of International Amateur Theatre Association; Mr Max Wagener and staff of the Dutch Centre of the I.T.I.; Secretary of the Union of Dutch Theatre Companies; Director of United Dutch Dramatists; Secretary of the Dutch Actor's Trade Union; Director of the Mickery Theatre, Amsterdam; Cultural Attaché, Royal Netherlands Embassy, London; offices of the Ministry of Culture, Rijswijk.

M. J.O. Svensson, former Cultural Attaché, Royal Swedish Embassy, London; staff of the Swedish Arts Council; Secretary of the Swedish Centre of the I.T.I.; staff of the Swedish Institute, Stockholm; Secretary of Theatre Centre; Publicity Officer of the Stockholm City Theatre and the Royal Dramatic Theatre, Stockholm; Secretary of the Swedish Actor's Union; Secretary of the Swedish National Theatre Centre and Swedish Dramatic Institute.

Cultural Attaché, Swiss Embassy, London; Madame J.M. Favre, Federal Office of Cultural Affairs, Berne; Press Service, Pro Helvetia; the publishers of *Theater in der Schweiz*, Zürich, and of *Szene Schweiz*.

Especial thanks to M. Jean Raty who fostered this study when it was under the editorial aegis of the Council of Europe; Dr. John Pick of the City University and General Editor of City Arts who made possible and gave invaluable help to the present publication; to Mr John Offord, the most agreeable of publishers his assistant Mr Nicholas Wood, and the staff; and to the staff of Wordplus (Word-processing Bureau) who took pains to make a legible script of an illegible draft.

More precise aknowledgements and thanks are due as follows:

Heinemann Educational Books for permission to quote from J.S.R. Goodlad's *A Sociology of Popular Drama*; Messrs Faber and Faber for a passage from John Arden's *To Pretend the Pretence;* Stock, Paris, for a passage from M. Jean Dasté's *Le Voyage d'un Comédien*, and M. Christoph Campos of the British Institute, Paris, and the editor of Theatre Quarterly for various material.

Notes on sources at the end of each chapter and in particular Appen-dix One will give details of the vast amount of published and unpubli-shed material from which material has been drawn and to which reference has constantly been made. Those to whom the author is particularly indebted include: the Belgian Ministries of both Dutch and French Culture; the Service de l'Animation et de la Diffusion Culturelle, and the Belgian Centre of the International Theatre Institute; the French Ministry of Culture, together with the Service des Etudes et de la Recherche, the Association Technique pour l'Action Culturelle (ATAC), and the Association du Théâtre pour l'Enfance et la Jeunesse; the Deutscher Bühnenverein of the Federal Republic of Germany and the West German Centre of the ITI; the Editor of the Stage, London; in Italy, the Societa Italiana degli Autori ed Editori (SIAE); the Dutch Ministry of Culture, Recreation and Social Work, and the Dutch Centre of the ITI; in Sweden, the National Council for Cultural Affairs, the Swedish Institute in Stockholm, and the Swedish Theatre Union (ITI); the Swiss Federal Office of Cultural Affairs; Pro Helvetia; and the editors of the Swiss Theatre Yearbook.

I have left until last the two organizations on whose publications I have drawn most heavily, the Arts Council of Great Britain to whom I am particularly grateful: and the Council of Europe, the publications of which have been of constant value, but who, after all, were responsible for initiating the whole venture.

The dress circle and gallery of Buxton Opera House, 1979.

A performance of Gorki's 'The Lower Depths' at the Appel Theatre, Den Haag, 1981.

6

Contents

Introduction

This study was originally commissioned by the Council of Europe on the basis of a resolution passed by the European Ministers with responsibility for cultural affairs meeting at Oslo in June, 1976.

The resolution is in two parts, one dealing with the employment and remuneration of artists, their welfare, unemployment and pension rights, tax provisions and specialist agencies; the other with the accessibility of the arts to society as a whole, especially to people who have had little opportunity for participation. These twin aspects of culture are reflected in the form of the present book although they have been dealt with in reverse order. The first part of the book deals with the administration of the theatre, the second with the artists who work within it. In an ideal society artists and administrators would work closely together, their activities interrelated and interdependant. The latter have established their claim to partnership by coining the phrase 'creative administration', an implication that administrators must help to form the conditions in which creative work can take place (1).

There is a distinction to be made between culture and art. Culture refers to the environment, the quality of life, and human relationships. It is the product or the expression of a community (2). Art is an aspect of culture, and one that some would argue to be of a more individual nature. This book is not basically concerned with the creative process of the artist but with the economic conditions that lie behind, and impinge upon the cultural and artistic life of a nation and a community.

The burden of the Council's resolution is that art and culture have to be encouraged, both among the professionals who practice the arts and the public who responds to them, and they must be democratized. This is the result of evidence that culture is dominated by inherited standards and that these reflect the social attitudes of the bourgeois and the traditional ruling class. Even without setting foot in such political waters it is arguable that inherited culture, traditional and bourgeois though it may be, should be made as widely available as possible for what many consider to be its absolute values. Some art forms, as a result of their standing in society, have accumulated a mass of critical commentary and historical record which has served to underline their élitist nature; while other, usually more 'popular' forms, have only recently become the subject of critical enquiry. A study of the social function of the performing arts as a whole serves to call in question the absolute value of one art over another; and these values vary between one country and another.

No country in Western Europe, for example, attaches such importance to the circus as the USSR.

The debate then turns on the responsibility of government for intervention in cultural matters. To what extent is culture a spontaneous expression of the life of the community in which no government should interfere? Or to what extent should government provide those services which politicians might consider to be for the public good but which through lack of finance or other resources the community cannot provide for itself? Does the planting of trees in the main street improve the culture of a town? Or building a public library? Or opening a Citizens Advice Bureau? Or establishing a civic theatre? Culture is the background to the debate.

This book is confined to the study of one art, the theatre, and one aspect of the theatre, the dramatic. Although the administrative structure of the dramatic is similar in many respects to that of the lyric theatre, and, indeed, in the Federal Republic of Germany drama, opera and ballet are usually housed in the same building, the latter raises problems of finance even more extreme than those of the drama. Operas and ballets are more expensive to stage than plays; while the professional problems of dancers, singers and musicians are different in many respects from those of actors, directors and playwrights.

The book deals with the theatre in those countries whose governments agreed to participate in the original survey, namely Belgium, France, the Federal Republic of Germany, Italy, the Netherlands, Sweden, Switzerland and Great Britain.

Statistics have been kept to a minimum. This has been thought advisable partly through the difficulty of keeping them up-to-date, and partly because of difficulties in comparability. There are very considerable differences in the way that each country, and the funding bodies within those countries, keep their books, define their categories, assume their responsibilities, and intervene in the cultural and artistic life of the people. It is no longer possible to analyze public spending on the arts under the traditional areas of activity. It has been the aim, therefore, to use statistics not for their own sake but to indicate policies. The conditions of work of the artists in the theatre are shaped by the administrative structure of the theatre and the place it occupies in the cultural life of its community, whether by that phrase is meant a locality or a nation. But these structures are the result of a complex variety of cultural behaviour, economic pressures, and historical evolution. That there are more theatres in West Germany per head of population than in any other country in the study is not simply the result of a particular passion on the part of the contemporary German bourgeoisie for theatrical art but of practices and passions that have their root in the eighteenth century and even earlier. It is the purpose of the first part of this book to consider some of these cultural, economic and historic patterns of social behaviour.

No attempt has been made at artistic criticism or an evaluation of quality of work: that must be the subject of further investigation. Indeed we have tried to eschew any kind of criticism, hoping that the analysis of a variety of situations will provide material for future and more detailed studies. Even so we hope that such comments as from time to time we have found it necessary to make will not be taken as supererogation or exceeding the proper limits of the enquiry. It must of course be emphasised that the book is the total responsibility of the author and that neither inaccuracies nor infelicities can be blamed elsewhere.

John Allen,
London, 1981.

Sources

(1) John Pick - *Arts Administration* - E.& F.N. Spon, 1980.
(2) See, for example, Augustin Girard - *Cultural Development: Exper- and Policies* - UNESCO, Paris, 1972.

Part One

The Administration of Subsidy

The interior of the Schauspielhaus, Zurich, 1981.

Street theatre by an amateur company in the Netherlands.

16

1. Who Goes to the Theatre?

Contrary to what is often thought, the theatre-going public is easily identifiable by anyone ready to take the trouble.

The question that forms the title to this chapter is not rhetorical. If we could answer this and the additional 'and why?', or even more pertinently 'why not?', most of the problems discussed in this book could be solved.

But a kind of self-perpetuating mystery shrouds the subject. It is summed up in such expressions as 'There's no accounting for tastes'. Considering the crucial importance of an audience for a successful theatrical performance it is astonishing how little attention has been paid to what industrialists call 'marketing the product'. A most exhaustive survey of theatre audiences was established in 1966 by the French Ministry of Culture (1). The findings were presented to a group of British directors, managers and educationists meeting in Nottingham in 1965. They expressed considerable interest in their importance and proceeded to do nothing similar themselves. A number of local surveys have, however, been carried out in various countries and it is interesting to note that their conclusions have been remarkably similar to those of the French, showing that the pattern of theatre-going is broadly similar throughout Western Europe and that it has not changed significantly over the last twenty years.

The theatre-going public

Figures are inexact but nevertheless show a remarkable consistency between one country and another. Here, then, are the principal findings of the Paris enquiry. It must be emphasised that although they are sixteen years old, subsequent surveys have not suggested any significant change in theatre-going habits.

Of the total population of France 5% go to the theatre at least four times a year; 16% go less than four times a year and then usually in exceptional circumstances or to special or amateur performances; 78% of the population never go to the theatre at all.

The first figure is the most significant. Most enquiries agree that the hard core of the theatre-going public varies between a little under 2% in Britain and a little over 5% in the Federal Republic of Germany, a percentage that increases considerably if children and young people are included. On the other hand there is evidence that between 20% and

30% of the British go to the theatre at least once a year. Such national figures, of course, reflect not only the interest of the population in general for the theatre but the availability of theatres and theatrical performances. More will be said about that in a later chapter.

In Paris 62% of the sample expressed an interest in the theatre; but a distinction should perhaps be made between those who disregard the theatre and those with some kind of academic interest but who for one reason or another rarely go. The distinction is largely defined by level of education, but of that more below (2). Of the hard- or semi-hard-core of theatre-goers, the highest proportion is under 24 years of age. For specialised productions the proportion is even higher. There is some evidence that in recent years support by this group has been wilting but it is an area in which, in view of its importance, research is urgently needed. There is a big decline in theatre-going by those between the ages of about 25 and 35, evidently the result of marriage, financial pressure and young families. (It has been suggested that the best form of subsidy for the theatre would be payment for baby-watchers and child-minders.) In early middle-age there is a modest return to former habits, and a certain levelling-out among the elderly (over 50) except among lower-income groups where regular theatre-going, if it has been practised at all, falls away sharply with age.

Some evidence of the interest of educated young people in the theatre is provided by the information that a system of reduced prices for students, introduced in 1980 by the Society of West-end Theatre, produced 70,000 attendances in the first six months.

There is also evidence that among regular theatre-goers between the ages of 20 and 24 theatre-going comes second only to the cinema within the whole field of provided entertainment. Contrary to popular belief there is no evidence that possession of a television set has any effect on the frequency of theatre-going. The lowest incidence of theatre-going is among factory-workers and agricultural labourers; the highest among the professional and managerial classes. This not unexpected distinction is underlined by the significance of educational background. There is a consistent increase in theatre-going from the poorer educated, of whom 86% never go to the theatre at all, to those with some kind of further or university education of which group some 50% are regular theatre-goers. Level of education is said by the researchers to provide a closer relationship with cultural behaviour than occupational status.

Incidence of interest in theatre also increases with level of income but less consistently than in the case of education. Greatest support for the lyric theatre, however, comes from older age-groups and those with the highest income.

18

In terms of moral judgement - and here we are referring specifically to the Paris Survey - the theatre comes out well above film and television: 35% against 20% believe it offers a 'lasting' experience; but that it demands greater effort, 21% against 10%; though it is less satisfactory as a form of instruction, 45% to 55%.

The findings of the Paris survey are confirmed in another respect by a survey undertaken in Annecy in 1974. Of the sample 10.6% habitually go to the theatre alone (15.3% to the cinema); 29.3% in couples (57.9% to the cinema); 56.9% in groups (30.5% to the cinema, for which one rarely hears of party bookings being made since films can be hired and shown in one's own venue).

The feeling that the theatre is an important cultural element in society is supported by evidence from Germany and Switzerland where audiences visiting the subsidised theatre expect a majority of the plays they see to be of 'cultural significance', the result of a long and significant tradition. This view is held increasingly as the level of education rises. It appears that among this section of regular theatre-goers the theatre appeals more to certain intellectual and aesthetic faculties than to the desire for relaxation or entertainment. Less regular theatre-goers in these two countries prefer musicals and light comedies. There will be a number of passages in this book where the significance of such attitudes will be evident.

Surveys of theatre-going habits were carried out in two British towns, Bristol in 1974 (3) and Birmingham (4) between 1973 and 1976. In Bristol the questions were posed rather differently from Paris but it was still clear that among regular theatre-goers upper- and middle-income groups predominated, with the 16-24 age-group predominating over the older. Of the Bristol sample 11% thought of the theatre as providing a normal evening out, while 9% of the Birmingham sample agreed, although the question was phrased slightly differently. This 9% was heavily biassed in terms of social class, 13% of the higher income groups going regularly against 2% of the lowest. In both towns it was established that regular theatre-goers are not deterred by the distance of their home from the theatre. They were clearly prepared to travel and did so almost wholly by car.

In neither city did a significant number of those questioned see the theatre as being exclusively for the better-off although it was agreed that theatre seats are more expensive than those for the cinema and most sports. They considered the theatre to be generally preferable to or more interesting than television. In neither city were they critical of standards of production, nor did they express any difficulty about buying tickets or finding out what was on.

Yet in both cities there was a kind of apathy about theatre-going. Many more people admitted to being interested in the theatre and to knowing what was 'on' than had recently made a visit. The reasons people in Bristol gave for not having visited the theatre were nebulous - 'tied to the children', 'only to certain productions', 'nothing of particular interest' were the kind of answers that predominated, and to a similar question in Paris - distance, fatigue, late hours, high prices and general inconvenience.

In Bristol a further survey on the same lines as the first was carried out some eighteen months later after a period of vigorous marketing. Theatre-going had increased among people living in Bristol and almost wholly among the higher income groups. It had declined among people living outside Bristol and those of the lower income groups. But it was a period of rapid inflation and the results no doubt reflect a general rise in prices, especially of transport.

A similar demographic and statistical pattern of theatre-going emerges elsewhere. In Belgium, the regular theatre-going public is put at about 5% of the population but a detailed analysis is not available. A generally high level of theatre-going in the Federal Republic of Germany is explained by there being one theatre for every 280,000 of the population, an outstandingly high provision. A report from the Netherlands dated 1976 suggests that about 15% of the population go to the theatre once a year but that the frequency of visits of the average theatre-goer is declining (5). In Sweden, there is said to be regular attendance at the theatre by some 40% of the population (6), the result of a most effective policy of decentralisation which will be described in Chapter 8. In Switzerland, considerable efforts have been made to attract to the theatre young people who have been educated elsewhere than in the Grammar Schools (lycées, gymnases etc.). In German-speaking Switzerland, there is a regular theatre-going public of about 5%; at Lausanne, of between 2 and 4%; in the small town of La Chaux-de-Fonds, where there is a lively local theatre, the figure is 8 - 9%.

An enquiry carried out at the Centre Dramatique de Nice in 1971 showed that members of the professions and higher-ranking administrators and managers made up 16.6% of the regular theatre-goers, 2.5% of the total population; while workers, clerks and the retired made up 4.5% of the theatre-goers, 31% of the population. Similar figures come from the Citizens' Theatre, Glasgow: 58% of audiences are between the ages of 15 and 24; 68% middle-class; 24% still in higher education; with the educational level higher than in the population as a whole (7).

A nation-wide enquiry into theatre-going habits in Switzerland produced a remarkably similar picture to that already established:

about 23% of the population had been to the theatre at least once that year; the proportion was highest with young people between 15 and 24 and then fell steadily with advancing age; those in the higher professional classes were in a big majority; some 24% were season ticket holders (see page 25); younger audiences preferred drama and ballet, older audiences opera and operetta; younger audiences were the best supporters of contemporary drama, more so in Suisse Romand (French-speaking Switzerland) than in Suisse Alémanique (German-speaking) and particularly in Geneva and Lausanne; the biggest influence in forming an interest in the theatre was school; and in reply to a variety of questions it became apparent that television is a far more serious rival to the theatre than the cinema; that distance from a theatre is a more serious barrier than cost of a seat, though far more of the French-speaking population complained about the latter than the former (31% to 12%). None of the other usual complaints drew a significant response, baby-sitters, parking, lack of information, difficulty of buying tickets, public transport or discouragement at school (8).

The upshot of this is a clear indication that the theatre has tolerated a number of unwarranted assumptions for far too long. The cinema did not kill the theatre, for example, although it was a very serious rival to more popular forms of entertainment such as the Music Hall; and through its ubiquity and relative cheapness it has attracted the not-wholly-committed theatre-goer. But the only element it has in common with the theatre is its value as a form of entertainment. It provides a different kind of experience, and evidence shows clearly that intelligent people understand the distinction. Similarly with television. "Shall we stay in and watch television or go to the cinema?" may be a commonly asked question. But the decision to go to the theatre is based on the desire for a wholly different kind of experience. The theatre has tended to be its own worst enemy, often failing to respond to changing social conditions.

Why do people go to the theatre?

The question is far too complex to be answered in a book of this kind; but complex or not it constitutes an inescapable challenge to anyone attempting to run a theatre. The evidence that has already been presented establishes very clearly the limited appeal of the theatre at least as it is at present organised and traditionally viewed in most European countries; and in the course of this book we shall note some of the historical reasons for this as well as the policies that are being developed by radical theatre-workers throughout the continent to win the support of a broader section of the population.

Audience surveys show clearly that the habit of theatre-going is engendered by two groups of people, parents and teachers. So far as the latter are concerned we can hope that the increasingly comprehensive nature of European education will produce an egalitarian attitude to art and culture that will do something to minimise its present class structure; about parents one can be less sanguine. They will naturally bring up children in the light of their own social and cultural mores and in general terms a traditional élitism is all that can be expected. Not that this is necessarily disastrous. The educated young person will buy books and read a 'quality' newspaper and pay an occasional visit to the theatre and thus conform to traditional cultural norms.

It is far more profitable to speculate why so many people should not go to the theatre, for some interesting implications emerge from the various surveys. It is generally established that a very small proportion of the population of any country are regular theatre-goers, visiting four or more times a year. These more or less regular theatre-goers are identifiable by age, income and education. Yet among regular theatre-goers attendance has generally been dropping. The illustrious German theatre has lost some three million 'attendances' since the late 1960's though it is now holding its own, and this despite the fact that the proportion of young people in the 15-25 age group reached a peak during the 1970's, and that in most countries the number of them who have had the benefits of higher education continues to increase along with a fairly general rise in expendable income.

The trend has been different in Paris. Between the end of the war and 1968 the private theatres lost half their audiences. But while between 1968 and 1978 the number of performances dropped only from 11,797 to 11,504, the number of spectators rose astonishingly from 2,869,583 to 3,363,343 with another 500,000 accounted for by café-théâtres. In the same period receipts rose from 61,365,000 F. to 186,364,909 F. but this increase is at least partly accounted for by inflation.

The steepest rise in attendances seems to have taken place in the latter part of the period and is accounted for by a sudden growth of interest in the theatre resulting from the celebrated productions of the Royal Shakespeare Company with *Coriolanus* and the three parts of *Henry VI*, Giorgio Strehler with three Goldoni plays, and the full version of Alban Berg's *Lulu*.

The phenomenon suggests the falsity of another commonly held assumption, that the subsidised theatre has proved a fatal rival to the commercial. Not only has this not been the case but evidence suggests that the subsidised theatre has brought a vitality and interest to the theatre at large from which the commercial theatre has benefited. Vitality is catching.

Another detailed study of theatre-going (9) reveals the importance of changes in spending habits. Between 1950 and 1969 the percentage of their budget spent by French families on domestic goods decreased by 20%, on clothes by nearly 5%; but what they spent on leisure increased by 3% and on hotels, cafés, restaurants and the like by 5%. But the theatre and the cinema did not benefit from this increased expenditure on leisure. The enormously increased expenditure on radio, television, and photographic equipment emphasises the point already made, that people now tend to purchase material goods rather than the appurtenances of a cultural environment.

A similar pattern of expenditure is reported from Italy. Between 1951 and 1976 there was an increase in 'real' terms in the portion of income absorbed by expenditure on durable consumer goods such as motor vehicles for private use, scooters, washing-machines, refrigerators, television sets etc., whereas there was a diminution in the portion of income absorbed by non-durable consumer goods, such as for the most part are recreational and cultural goods and services (10). The trend has continued. With a steady increase in expenditure on recreative activities, the theatre's share has fallen from 28% in the late 1950s to 10% in 1979.

The trend confirms that we live in a materialistic age. Yet history suggests that materialism has never had the last laugh. The two outstanding facts to emerge from the various surveys is firstly that the hard-core of regular theatre-goers is composed of young people; and secondly that they have developed their interest in the theatre from their school-teachers. If managers and directors want to make the theatre more directly available to a wider spectrum of the population it is clear that this is the public with which to start.

Yet since this argument is concerned with solid trends of a profound nature, it is necessary to consider the whole question of why people go to the theatre in the widest context. There are plenty of important suggestions that have not yet been fully investigated. The Canadian professor Erwin Goffman has charted the close correspondence that exists between role-playing in real life and role-playing on the stage (11). Jean Duvignaud, in a number of books (12), has analysed the sociological element that is built into the experience of going to the theatre. Indeed, Kipling's line could appropriately be parodied - "What do they know of the theatre who only theatre know?". A far more energetic and imaginative marketing programme is needed by the theatre as a whole, not through inducements and the distribution of ephemera, but based on a thorough understanding of the social sanctions on which the theatre relies; and it is encouraging to know that the London West-End Theatre Managers are facing the challenge.

23

An important section of M. Girard's enquiry deals with television. Evidence suggests that although there are marked divergencies between members of different social classes and occupational groups in terms of their tastes for various kinds of television drama, there are no significant differences between them in their appreciation of what they see. This remarkable and in many respects encouraging conclusion suggests that although the current practice of theatre-going is largely the outcome of a cultural environment, appreciation of the product is not significantly different among people of different social, educational and economic backgrounds.

Similar observations have been advanced by the Audience Research Department of the BBC. There is a close link between interest in the arts and educational background; people choose what they are going to watch or listen to largely as a result of their education; but their opinion of what they have seen or heard is strikingly similar across the whole educational spectrum. In other words, more middle-class people than factory-workers are likely to listen to arts programmes, but their response will not be significantly conditioned by their class or educational background. All of which implies what has already been suggested, that it is the actual experience of going to the theatre that is alien to the worker rather than the nature of the performance itself.

It is a problem that has increasingly challenged theatre-workers in recent years. Jean Vilar, for whom the problem of interesting the factory-worker in the great classics of the theatre was almost an obsession, said towards the end of his life that he had not succeeded in penetrating below the level of the lower middle-class.

Democrats may find cause for complaint in the limited social support for the theatre; but the theatre is declining only in the light of a past which no one particularly wants to emulate. The contemporary European theatre is more or less preserved within the cultural ethos and habits of a small, bourgeois, well-educated and well-to-do section of the population, sustained by public subsidy which in most countries is well below 0.5% of the Gross National Product. The tradition of theatre-going is largely perpetuated by two groups of people intimately concerned with the education of children and the formation of their tastes - their parents and their teachers. This is far too vulnerable a structure on which to build a theatre of any substance. The demand by the Council of European Ministers for a general democratising of the theatre had been widely accepted by many people long before the relevant resolution was passed at Oslo in 1976. There is hardly a country in Europe in which vigorous steps have not been taken to enlarge the basis of the theatre. What are the immediate and most relevant policies to be taken in pursuance of this aim?

24

Marketing

This is an aspect of theatre practice to which considerable attention has been given in recent years. The best analysis that has come our way is the *C.O.R.T.* (Council of Regional Theatres) *Marketing Manual* (13) which includes essays, analysis, and a heap of practical suggestions under such headings as: theatre marketing - the need for a clearly defined policy in terms of commercial, artistic, social and educational objectives; copywrighting, which includes the wording of advertisements and the design of posters; design of all publicity material; print-productions and buying, informative leaflets, brochures, programmes, seating plans, souvenir booklets and ephemera (including play-synopses in foreign languages); press relations and publicity; mailing lists, showing how they need not become a tedious and ineffective chore; season ticket schemes and party bookings; how to control the marketing budget; pricing the house and various concessionary schemes; audience research; theatre programmes - what kind of and how much information should they contain, i.e. more information?; theatre supporters clubs; promotion of theatre-going among young people; use of advertising agencies and voucher schemes.

Season ticket schemes

Various kinds of season-ticket schemes are almost universally practiced in Western Europe. The logic is unassailable. To sell a significant proportion of the tickets available before a season begins guarantees a certain proportion of income and frees the director and finance officer from the fear of empty houses for a less popular play. If the seats are empty, some of them will have at least been paid for. But the public has no love of paying for seats they are not going to occupy and therein lies the limitations of the practice. The director must make a balanced selection of plays appealing to a wide range of tastes; and if the procedure cushions a manager from disaster, it prevents him exploiting a success. The practice involves a strong commitment by the theatre-goer who decides the dates of his visits several months in advance and cannot change except by private arrangement.

Small and community theatres, unable to operate such schemes, are obliged to spend proportionately more on publicity but claim they are able to offer a more varied programme and appeal to a far wider potential range of audiences.

In the Federal Republic of Germany about 28% of the tickets sold by the subsidised theatres are under season-ticket schemes and another 27% are taken up by various theatre-going organisations such as the celebrated Volksbühne which has some 300,000 members in 88 towns.

The Bund der Theatergemeinden, the other large theatre-going organisation with a Christian background, had 135,000 members and 20 offices (in 1974). These two organisations alone dispose of some four to five million theatre tickets a year, about 30% of the total tickets sold. Intendants, dramaturgs and directors have this potential audience very much in mind when composing their repertory for the following season, although they do not allow the bigger organisations to advise on choice of play, strongly though they are pressed to do so. Nevertheless the history of the Volksbühne shows that in the past the organisation has had a considerable effect upon the development of the German theatre (14).

It is interesting to note in this connection that in Germany the retired and elderly tend to visit the theatre on Sunday afternoons when special performances are sponsored under the initiative of various social service organisations.

In Italy the regional theatres make considerable use of season-ticket schemes. The practice is also common in the Netherlands where Senior Citizens have a permanent pass that entitles them to reductions in theatres. Season-ticket schemes are also widely operated in Sweden where state and municipal theatres offer a discount of between a half and a third for senior citizens.

Season ticket schemes are offered in Great Britain only by the larger and more progressive regional theatres who want to build a regular audience. Regional Arts Associations sometimes offer vouchers which provide a discount on the price of a ticket, but these apply only to single productions. A practice of offering two seats for the price of one is sometimes operated by regional theatres to fill the house earlier in the week. The bigger subsidised companies and many of the regional theatres have supporters clubs but these usually provide little more than advance booking facilities. Most non-commercial theatres offer seats at matinées for senior citizens at very reduced prices.

Theatres and their audiences
The answer to the vital question - are theatres holding their audiences? is - barely. A few examples will indicate the general trend: Between 1975-76 and 1976-77 attendances at the Belgian National·Theatre fell from 72.8% to 65.4%.

Between 1965 and 1975 in France audiences fell in the five national theatres by 40%, in the subsidised by 20%, and in the private, between 1961 and 1974, by 14%, although there has been a remarkable improvement in recent years. It is interesting to note that between 1960 and 1975 cinema audiences decreased by 50% while the sale of books increased by 73% and of gramaphone records by 370%. The latter phenomenon was discussed on page 19.

In Great Britain, in 1976-77, there were eight and a half million attendances, 65% of capacity at performances given by touring and subsidised building-based companies. In 1979-80 the Royal Shakespeare Company played to 82% at the Aldwych Theatre and 93% in Stratford-on-Avon. The National in its three theatres played to 78%.

In the Federal Republic of Germany, attendances at the subsidised theatres reached a peak of 20,354,000 in 1964-65, fell to just over seventeen million in 1972-73, and are now gradually picking up. The present figure represents about 75% of capacity. Of tickets sold, (1979-80) about 33.2% are sold at the box-office, 27.3% to season-ticket holders, and 12.8% to audience organisations and party bookings.

The 80 or so private stages have an audience of about five million, representing over 80% capacity, but many private theatres seat less than 200 people. Some of the more illustrious theatres in West Berlin, such as the Theater am Kürfürstendam and the Schaubühne am Halleschen Ufer played in 1975-76 to 92% and 97% capacity respectively.

The pattern of theatre-going in Italy has shown a quite different tendency from that of West Germany. From 1950 until 1962 there was a gradual decline; but since then there has been a steady increase in overall number of performances, attendances and box-office receipts, reaching a peak in 1978-9 of 48,000 performances to a total audience of about ten million. It is a little disturbing, however, that in spite of a vigorous policy of decentralisation the theatre is still far more widely supported in the northern provinces than in the centre and south of the country while increase in attendances has been far greater in the larger than the smaller towns.

In the Netherlands there was a slight decline in audiences during the 1970s. In Geneva, between 1970 and 1980, the total number of available seats declined by a thousand and paid attendances fell from 248,710 to 117,810 (15).

In Sweden there has been a slight increase in attendances, with an average in 1977-78 of 75% capacity in theatres in urban areas and 71% in rural. In Switzerland, during the late 1970s there was a slight overall decline, with most theatres playing in 1980-1 to between 65% (Schauspielhaus, Zürich) and 82% (Stadttheater, St. Gallen) of capacity.

General indications therefore suggest that the European theatres are holding their audiences, but that in spite of considerable efforts which will be described in later chapters there is no significant increase, either socially or quantitively.

There are also clear indications that the private theatre has by no means had its day and that in spite of the destructive effects of inflation audiences are finding money with which to support the diversions of the private sector as well as the cultural values of the public.

A final note. In any one night there are over 70,000 seats available throughout London, including civic venues, 562,000 in a week of eight performances. This provides accommodation for 5% of the population of Greater London to visit the theatre once a week. Professor Harbage calculates that in Shakespeare's day 13% of London's population went to the theatre each week and that there were enough additional seats for the number to be trebled on feast days, holidays and special occasions. The habit of theatre-going has undergone a considerable decline (16).

Sources

(1) Augustin Girard - *Le Théâtre et le Public - Enquêtes réalisées pour le Ministre des Affaires Culturelles* - Paris, 1966
(2) Alphons van Impe - *Le Théâtre et le Pouvoir* - UNESCO, Paris, 1976
(3) A report on the potential for the arts in Bristol - prepared by Mass Observation (UK), London, 1975
(4) The Birmingham Arts Marketing Project, 1975-6 - Peter Cox Associates, London, 1977
(5) Albert van der Bann - Report for the Netherlands Centre of the International Theatre Institute - Amsterdam, 1976 - unpublished
(6) Bertril Hokby - *Cultural policy in Sweden* - Washington, 1976
(7) Report on in-theatre surveys at the Glasgow Citizens Theatre, unpublished
(8) Szene Schweiz/Scène Suisse/Scene Svizzera - No. 3, 1975, Bern
(9) Michèle Vessilier - *La Crise du Théâtre Privé* - Presses Universitaires de France, Paris, 1973
(10) Mary Fraire - *La Dépense pour les spectacles en Italie par Rapport au Revenue et à la Consommation des Ménages depuis 1951 jusqu'à 1976* - Lo Spettacolo, anno XXVIII no. 2 - April - June 1978
(11) Erwin Goffman - *The Presentation of Self in Everyday Life* - Penguin, London, 1972
(12) Jean Duvignaud - *Sociologie du Théâtre* - Presses Universitaires de France, Paris, 1965
(13) Glyn V. Robbins and Peter Verwey (editor) TMA/CORT/APTM - London, 1978 and Keith Diggle - *Marketing the Arts* - Centre for Arts and Related Studies, City University, 1976.
(14) Cecil W. Davies - *A Theatre for the People: the story of the Volksbühne* - Manchester University Press, 1977

(15) *Le Financement de la Culture à Genève* - Geneva, March 1980

(16) Alfred Harbage - *Shakespeare's Audience* - Colombia University Press, 1941.

A scene from the Royal Shakespeare Company's adaptation of Charles Dickens' 'Nicholas Nickleby' at the Aldwych Theatre, London, 1980.

Janet Suzman as Clytemnestra and John Shrapnel as Agamemnon in John Barton's 'The Greeks', Aldwych Theatre, 1980.

2. The Independant, Private or Commercial Theatre

Definition of the term

The word most commonly used for the kind of theatre that will be discussed in this chapter is *privé* (French), *privat* (German), or *privata* (Italian). In English there is an objection to this term since a private theatre is a club or coterie theatre available only to those who have paid a membership fee. The term 'commercial' is commonly used but is disliked by certain managers who prefer the word 'independant'; but although this term leads to confusion with J. T. Grein's important Independant Theatre of 1891, we shall use it in default of a better word, when referring to London theatres. We shall describe those on the continent as private.

Independant or private theatre may be described as a form of theatre that is based on the provision, usually from a variety of sources, of a capital sum of money to stage a play or a season of plays. Henry Irving once said that if the theatre is to succeed as an art it must succeed as a business. A paper describing the French private theatre, one from which we have drawn liberally in this section (1), describes the theatre as being both art and commerce. In this sense the first wholly private or commercial theatre in history was probably the Elizabethan. The company of which Shakespeare was a member was run as a co-operative with each member providing a number of 'shares' and receiving a proportion of the receipts. The leading rival company, associated with the actor Edward Alleyn, was managed by David Henslowe, a capitalist entrepreneur who drew his money from a variety of investments and used some of it for theatrical enterprises.

With the development throughout Europe of a capitalist *laissez-faire* economy, the theatre developed on similar lines and became, by the end of the nineteenth century, an important source of investment, reflecting in its organisation and productions a market economy, by which is meant an economy which responds to and is shaped by public demand.

A recent survey of London theatres and music halls (2) between 1850 and 1950 establishes the existence at one time or another of over 900 theatrical 'venues'. Although a large number of these were in public houses, an interesting sidelight on the existence of a widespread

31

popular and working-class drama, the list includes some 150 theatres and music-halls. The story is the same in Paris from the building of the Théâtre des Variétés in 1779 through to the Vieux Colombier in 1913. In the late nineteenth century there were some 1,500 theatres, music-halls and places of entertainment in the country.

The French paper points out that it was M. Malraux himself who affirmed publicly and forcibly the importance of the survival of the private theatres. 'Only a dictatorship could conceive the suppression of this kind of theatre', he said, 'In so far, however, as the state increases its help to the public sector, so the need to preserve a balance of theatrical activity, which in the last resort involves freedom of thought in the theatre, obliges the state to give the private theatre the means for a parallel expansion and to pursue its own evolution'.

We shall discuss in due course the relationship between the private theatres and the public subsidised sector. But first we must consider certain aspects of the former's organisation; for it is one thing to build a theatre and another to run it. There have emerged, therefore, two groups of managers, those who have built or owned the theatres, the 'bricks and mortar' managements, and the play-producing managements. The latter group emerged in the early years of the present century when circumstances made it no longer possible for the actor-manager to maintain the role that he had played for several centuries. The producing management employed a director, whose functions will be discussed in Chapter 9, and the director chose the actors, and that is the way, by and large, that things are still done in the contemporary independant theatre.

The present 'crisis' in the private theatre
The theatre has always been in a state of crisis. This in fact constitutes the main criticism of a form of art that is almost wholly structured on the basis of the vagaries of public opinion. Traditionally theatre workers have accepted the 'market principle'.

> The drama's laws the drama's patrons give,
> For we that live to please must please to live.

So Doctor Johnson wrote (3) and so actors have always seen themselves as 'servants of the public', accepting that if the public lacks judgement to enjoy the production on which they have lavished a great deal of time and money, that is the way of things. Public taste is unpredictable.

The production of a play in a London theatre is usually undertaken by an established management. There is no reason why a private individual with the necessary capital should not go into management but he will usually do so, for convenience, in collaboration with an existing management, paying a management fee of several hundred pounds a week. The managers themselves say that there is no shortage of potential and willing backers, especially for musicals, which is the category in which big money can be made and lost. The track-record of the large managements suggests that consistent backers will be comfortably in profit. There appears to be no shortage of housewives, literary agents, accountants and retired naval officers ready to put up £250 towards the production of a new play in London. A regular backer is quoted in the London Guardian as saying that 'it is more risky than some other forms of investment but then the potential rewards are greater', though recent inflation has tended to invalidate this claim.

The Golden Age of the independant theatre was probably around the turn of the century. Many of the more astute and efficient actor-managers retired with a very considerable balance in the bank. Since the 1914-18 War it has been less easy to make a fortune from the theatre. Very considerable sums of money have been made on successful productions but the chances of doing so have rapidly decreased. The 1939-45 War put an end to one of the most vigorous and profitable forms of theatrical enterprise which was the big theatrical tour of the popular success. (The present state of touring will be discussed on page 106-116). In the season 1969-70 there were 65 new productions mounted in the West-End of London. Of the 52 of which records are available, 10 were profitable, making an unspecified 'profit' for management and backers; 42 were unprofitable, representing a loss for all concerned. Among the losers were eight musicals. 13 managers went bankrupt or left the country. The figures for Paris are not dissimilar. Out of some 200 annual productions only about 12 are financially successful, although, as noted, 1978 was a far more profitable year.

It is arguable that the present crisis in the theatre is largely the result of inflation which has pushed up the cost of staging a fairly simple production to some £40,000 in London and 500,000 F. in Paris. A few simple figures relating to the year 1978 will reveal to the layman the nature of the odds. Half this capital sum will have been spent before the play opens. The running costs are likely to be in the region of at least £16,000 a week. If the theatre has a capacity of 1,000 and an average price of £3 a seat - most West End theatres in 1981 had a range of between £2 and £8 - capacity audiences for eight performances a week would bring in £24,000, or £18,000 at 75% capacity. This would provide the manager with only £2,000 to cover his initial outlay of £40,000 and the play would have to run to capacity for six months just to break even, a most unusual eventuality.

An example can be taken from a ballet company which habitually plays at a theatre not in the centre of London. The 'get-out' figure for the company is £24,000 a week. The gross box-office takings, at prices which people think are so high as to exclude the young and the impecunious, is £34,000, or in realistic terms, with discounts, about £30,000. This means that in order to break even the theatre must sell at least 1,000 seats at an average of £3 a seat for seven performances a week.

The result of this hazardous situation is that the commercial manager is increasingly obliged to 'play safe', to avoid, so far as possible, taking risks. He will therefore feel increasingly obliged to stage the kind of play for which he judges from past experience that there is a reliable audience, the comedy rather than the problem play, the thriller rather than the tragedy, a 'divertissement' rather than a classic. And he will of course be tempted to choose plays with a small cast and a single set rather than a spectacular, so that he can reduce both production and running costs.

The private theatres of Paris and the commercial theatres of London have a very impressive record of *créations*, the first productions of new plays. The subsidised theatres in both countries have tended to rely to a far greater extent on the classics. Some of the young French directors have considered that regional audiences, unfamiliar with the experience of regular theatre-going, would prefer Molière to anything by a contemporary playwright. In the British regional theatre a new play by a relatively little known author will empty the house. But the record of the independant theatre is impressive.

There are few authors of distinction, British or French, whose plays have not been consistently staged by the independant theatres of London and Paris. If it is argued that they do little experimental work and that they virtually ignore the classics, the independant managers can reply that this is exactly what subsidy is for. The National Theatre and the Royal Shakespeare Company constantly have classics in their repertory and there are alternative theatre companies in plenty, in and around London, offering a stage to new writers, new directors and new actors. The road from the Fringe to Shaftesbury Avenue is short and the variety of stages considerable.

The private theatre in Europe

Paris and London constitute the Mecca of the independant theatre. In Paris there are about 40 theatres *fixes privés* (permanent private theatres) and between 70 and 80 theatrical venues of all kinds including music-halls but excluding café-theatres. Most private theatres are limited liability companies and their owners are subject to various forms of legislation. There is almost invariably a distinction between the owner of the building, who may be an individual or a group of individuals, or a real estate company with no direct interest in the theatre, and the owner of the lease. It is rarely the same person. French law requires that the holder of the lease should be the director responsible for the artistic and financial management of the theatre, but this is not always the case. Sometimes he will associate with another management while maintaining partial responsibility. Sometimes he will rent the theatre to another individual group, though the law tries to prevent this becoming a regular practice. The anti-monopoly laws prohibit any one individual or group owning more than one theatre although the town of Paris owns four - two subsidised, the Théâtre de la Ville and the Gaité Lyrique, and two *privé*, L'Ambassadeur-Cardin and Le Marigny.

In London there are about 40 independant theatres, eleven 'outer ring' theatres, nine used for other purposes than putting on plays, and a variety of pub and genuinely private theatres. Outside London local authorities own some 300 theatres and venues in addition to those formerly independant theatres which they have bought and set up as trusts. But the dividing line between commercial and subsidised enterprise is far less sharp than in France.

Private theatres are by no means unknown in Italy and the Federal Republic of Germany. In Italy in 1976 there were 56 private theatrical companies, 52 dramatic, 4 musical comedy. These private theatres accounted for some 40% to 50% of all theatrical performances in the country, 50% of all theatre attendances and 70% of receipts (4).

In the German Federal Republic there has been a steady increase in the number of private theatres from 57 in 1965-66 to 76 in 1976-77; they are in 28 towns, with 14 in Berlin, 13 in Münich and 10 in Hamburg (5).

There is no great evidence of commercial theatre in Belgium, except for a few revues and cabarets in the larger towns; in the Netherlands there are about 15 independant companies; in Sweden there are a few private theatres in the bigger towns, rather disparagingly referred to in official documents as 'a phenomenon of big business and so the responsibility of the municipalities'. A few town councils do in fact give small subsidies to some private theatres. It is also the practice in Switzerland for certain municipalities to include the private theatre in their overall responsibility for the theatre.

The relationship between the private and subsidised theatre

In Great Britain, where there is no direct subsidy for the independant theatre, there is increasing collaboration between the two sectors. Some 80 productions are usually to be seen in the Greater London area, over half of them being productions by the 'Fringe', or the subsidised theatre or the two in collaboration.

In France the two sectors are kept rigidly separate; but the Ministry of Culture, aware of unfair competition from the highly subsidized public sector, has encouraged and helped the private sector to maintain its artistic independence. As long as it flourished the Ministry preserved an attitude of non-intervention, but in the face of mounting difficulties and in response to constant demands from the directors of those theatres, the Ministry has established a specific policy, the most significant aspect of which was the establishment in 1964 of a maintenance fund (*Fonds de Soutien*), derived from a parafiscal tax on the price of a seat supplemented by subsidy from the central government (3,472,000 F. in 1976-7, the equivalent of about £430,000) and the town of Paris (1,400,000 F., about £160,000). The Ministerial rubric reads:

> The permanent Parisian theatres, numbering about 50 and concentrated in Paris, have provided up until the last war, almost the only provision for new work in the theatre. Their fall in attendances over the past few years, basically the result of changes in society, have placed them in an unstable situation which has led to intervention by the state. During the last eight years the Parisian theatres have thus developed a practice of collaboration which should be extended to all aspects of their activities.

The fund is administered by an Administrative Council on which are represented the relevant ministries in a supervisory capacity, the town of Paris, and the various syndicates of authors, composers, directors, actors, playwrights and technicians. The money is used for co-operation among private theatres; the promotion of new play-wrights and new plays, especially experimental or unusual productions; the renovation of auditoria and equipment; and the development of policies that may lead to bigger audiences, what is generally called 'marketing the product'.

Problems of the private theatre

The independant theatre offers an easy target for criticism. The first and foremost is that the speculative uncertainty of all its activities precludes the stability and continuity that is essential for serious work. Its commercial basis is deeply resented by many theatre workers who claim that for all its achievements one cannot mix industry and art.

Criticism centres on both the creation and exploitation of the product. The selection of a play, its director, its cast and its designer are conditioned by commercial as well as artistic considerations. If the resulting product is a success it is exploited to the full. The economics of production usually require a run of at least six months. While actors appreciate such temporary stability of employment they will admit that artistically a run of more than three months becomes increasingly unacceptable, some say intolerable. What are we to say about a piece of trivia like *The Mousetrap* which has now occupied a London theatre for 29 years (1981) and shows no signs of coming to the end of its run?

The second major criticism concerns the theatres in which commercial productions largely take place. Critics tend to be divided between a sense of gratitude that a number of theatres do still exist, inadequate in many respects though they may be, and disgruntlement at the poverty of their facilities. Many of the main houses were built in the late nineteenth or early twentieth centuries when every stage was designed with a recalcitrant proscenium arch and an actor-audience relationship that prohibits the kind of osmosis that actors now value; and often with two or even three circles stratifying the audience and creating intolerable sight-lines for those in 'the gods'. The design of the auditorium precludes the convenient installation of front-of-house lighting so that it is now common to see rococo decoration on the front of the circle obliterated by a 'spot-bar' and an impressive array of lanterns. Stages often suffer from a serious lack of wing-space, and storage-facilities, and dressing-rooms are frequently antiquarian with negligible washing facilities. The theatres themselves are often situated in busy thoroughfares with no provision for parking. They are valuable pieces of real estate, but they are expensive to run and bring in a poor return on capital investment. Ground landlords get a far better return on a block of offices. In the difficult matter of preserving old theatres, there is a delicate balance between architectural distinction, economic viability and sheer practical convenience.

A defence of the private/commercial theatre

The commercial theatre of Paris and London is by no means despised by all actors. They recognise the amount of employment it offers, the security of a long-run and the publicity resulting from a successful production. Although working conditions are often less comfortable than in the subsidised theatre, they bring to every production a high degree of professional expertise and a familiarity with working in a certain manner.

The problem of inadequate theatre buildings is one that has to be faced by the subsidized as well as the private theatre. The crux of the discussion is not whether the independant theatre must be blamed or criticised for the inadequacy of the buildings it has inherited, which is neither here nor there, but the extent to which public money should be spent on renovating old theatres and building new ones. This is in fact the heart of the problem of the subsidized theatre. The traditional theatre has in some countries collapsed, in others it is in danger of collapsing. The problem which will be fully discussed in the next chapter is the extent to which the private/commercial theatre should be propped up with public money or replaced by a largely subsidized theatre. The various expedients and arrangements in the different countries will be discussed in the following chapters.

It is not simply a question of either/or. The existence of an independant theatre does not preclude in any way the existence of a subsidized theatre. In fact the two strands reflect the mixed economy that at present exists in most countries of Western Europe. One reverts to the question of how much public money should be given to support a theatre of admittedly limited cultural appeal which is based on traditional conservative belief in the market-test. If the public wants this kind of theatre, let it pay for it. If it is not prepared to pay the market-price necessary for its survival, let it go the way of the horse-and-buggy trade.

Such is the preoccupation of critics with the 'new' drama that very little serious attention has been given to the plays, whether 'divertissements', trivia, or pap, that form the staple diet of the independant theatre. It is therefore worth taking a look at a study of popular drama as a form of mass communication that was undertaken by Mr. J. S. R. Goodlad (6) who analysed 114 popular/successful plays that were staged in London's West End between 1955 and 1965. He suggests that 'popular drama deals with the areas of social living in which members of a community find it most difficult to comply with the moral requirements necessary for the survival of the existing social structure'. His analysis suggests that for Britons in the ten years under consideration these areas were: the institution of monogamy; the judgement of the social power which an individual may be permitted to exercise; money; the control or desire for revenge for real or imaginary wrongs suffered; the control of the use of violence in pursuing private goals.

The popular theatre, he says, . . . enables members of a community to organise their experience of social relations . . . It draws attention to social order by contrasting it with disorder, to morality by contrasting it with immorality. By virtue of its nature as a form of mass communication, popular drama is likely to reinforce prevailing opinion and belief rather than change it . . . People will watch drama in order to organise and confirm their experience of society . . . Popular drama will function as a monitor of morality, particularly those aspects of morality in which there is tension between the instincts of individuals and the requirements of society . . . Popular drama is used . . . deliberately or instinctively . . . to disseminate the moral values upon which prevailing social structure depends. Popular drama, therefore, is likely to function not only as an expressive element of culture but as an instrumental aspect of culture determining the prevailing morality.

Audrey Williamson in her book on Gilbert and Sullivan makes the same point. The operas, or operettas, have the quality of middle-class folk art, celebrating middle-class values in semi-idealistic form. The audience for them is vast and largely uncritical (7). Similarly, Wilson Knight in *The Golden Labyrinth* says "In joyousness or pathos it (Gilbert and Sullivan opera) . . . has become a kind of folk art for twentieth century Britain" (8).

There will be those who argue that this analysis fully confirms their criticisms of the private independant theatre: it reinforces prevailing social and cultural values. To which the obvious answer is - Why not? There will always be those who wish to change a culture and those who wish to preserve it. Democracy ensures that within the laws of the land the battle is to the stronger, that is to the side with the greater intellectual vitality.

The strength and the weakness of the independant theatre is that in a capitalist democracy it is closely related to the economic vitality of that country and its inhabitants. The recent success achieved by the private theatres of Paris is an encouragement to all those who see a valid place for this kind of theatre in contemporary society. But how is this success to be accounted for? Some see it as a result of the stabilizing effect of the *Fonds de Soutien*; others suggest a more fundamental reason. They say that the so-called crisis in the theatre is a crisis not of finance but of repertory. When good enough productions are staged, the public fights for seats and the whole of the theatre receives a kind of enhanced prestige. But a production of such vitality cannot in the very nature of things be one that rests on the reinforcement of established values. The public lethargy already noted is a far more serious barrier to regular theatre-going than a positive dislike or lack of interest in the theatre; but once again, it is not to be overcome by a reinforcement of established values but by that vitality which challenges values, which 'says something new', which suggests to those who have stayed at home a kind of cultural deprivation.

It is extremely difficult to make a reliable estimation of the seriousness of the 'crisis' facing the West-End theatre managers. There is no question of the exorbitantly high cost of production, of the lack of encouragement for would-be 'angels' to invest in production, of the drain on finances from VAT, and the shortage of managements regularly producing plays. But the independant theatre, though down perhaps, is by no means out; and it is encouraging to note the vigour with which it is facing many of the issues raised in this book: the need to investigate its audiences and for more energetic marketing, the encouragement of tourists and young people; relationships with the subsidized sector; pressure on the government for financial help both direct and in a number of indirect ways; and the basic question of repertory - what plays to stage? and how? and where?

Sources

(1) Syndicat des Directeurs de Théâtre de Paris et de la Région Parisienne.
(2) Diana Howard - *London Theatres and Music-halls* - The Library Association, London, 1970.
(3) Prologue spoken by David Garrick at the opening of the theatre in Drury Lane, 1747.
(4) Rilevazione Statistiche sulla Stagione Teatrale di Prosa, 1975-76 - AGIS, Rome, 1977.
(5) Theaterstatistik 1976-7 - Deutscher Bühnenverein/Bündesverband Deutscher Theater, Cologne, 1977.
    Joachim W. Preuss - *Fostering the Performing Arts in the Federal Republic of Germany* - Council for Cultural Cooperation, Strasbourg, 1980.
(6) J.S.R. Goodland - *A Sociology of Popular Drama* - Heinemann Educational Books, 1977.
(7) Audrey Williamson - *Gilbert and Sullivan Opera* - Rockliff, 1953.
(8) G. Wilson Knight - *The Golden Labyrinth* - Phoenix House, 1962.

3. The Case For A Subsidized Theatre

The problem of the national heritage

Since the present distribution of subsidy has given rise to intense disagreement among artists on the division of the money available between the maintenance of the traditional arts, which are often disparagingly referred to as 'high culture', and the creation of a living or 'popular' culture, it is important to establish certain historical facts about the former. It was a common practice among monarchs and rulers of the Renaissance to use art and artists for political purposes. The Tudors, the Valois, the Habsburgs employed the finest artists of the day to project the royal, national or imperial image. Their motives were anything but disinterested. However great their personal love of art, it was the projection of their taste, their resources, their authority, their cultural vitality that motivated them to spend large sums on a vast range of artistic products (1). This was patronage at its most compelling and the results have adorned the cities of Europe with architectural masterpieces and filled the galleries and museums with the simulacra of a society that held very different values from our own. It is the sheer aesthetic quality of these products as well as their considerable historic interest that has led to considerable sums of money being spent to preserve them.

The dependence of the artist on the patron, however, was basically demeaning and summed up in Dr. Johnson's celebrated definition of a patron: 'One who countenances, supports or protects. Commonly a wretch who supports with insolence and is paid with flattery'.

The history of governmental support for artistic and cultural institutions created to preserve these works of art begins in the late eighteenth and early nineteenth centuries when Renaissance values had little but historical interest. The author of an admirable book on the subject (2) makes the point that the growth of governmental support for the arts is an aspect of the growth of government itself; it is an aspect of the extension of governmental authority into the field of culture and the social life of the people. And once a government accepts responsibility for expenditure in any one field, the Minister responsible will seek to expand or at least maintain his share. No departmental head is unaffected by some form of avidity.

The reasons for this governmental involvement in culture are important. The rapid industrialisation of Western Europe in the nineteenth century led to growing concern for the quality of life. A man did not have to be a dedicated philanthropist to react with horror at some of the more vile excrescences of the industrial society, the poet William Blake's 'satanic mills'; while the spread of radical ideas, exported by revolutionary France, led many people to reconsider the role and responsibility of government towards education, and by extension, towards many other aspects of national culture.

It was a conservative belief, common throughout the nineteenth century, that the arts are properly a manifestation of middle - and upper-middle-class society. A more liberal view has been the result of social-democratic attitudes which have been both the cause and result of a basic redistribution of wealth by means of taxation, a policy that has been pursued by every European government in the present century, with the result that most governments are now responsible for the distribution of some 50% of a country's wealth.

There is a growing belief among those interested in such matters that the arts themselves do not contribute significantly to the quality of life but only in relationship to national cultural patterns of which they form a crucial part. Culture has been defined as 'a state of mind, an awareness and grasp of the social context, an ability to communicate and express, a response to and readiness to contribute to the environment in all its forms' (3). In this sense it is possible for there to be culture without art, though by the nature of the latter, this is unlikely. The reverse is impossible: the arts are themselves a manifestation of culture. Culture without art, or involving a poor level of art, would provide a very limited environment for people to live in. The philosophy of nineteenth-century industrial England was a simple one - 'Where there's muck there's brass'; but it was also industrial England that saw the need for a high level of industrial design and created the formidable Victoria and Albert Museum as a step in this development. Many industrialists now accept that although an attractive environment cannot be proved to have a direct bearing on industrial output, it can play a part in human relations. (We shall note in due course the efforts being made by the Arts Council of Great Britain to persuade local authorities to improve the facilities of the theatres they are now purchasing).

European society has inherited a 'high' culture manifest in many forms of art. This traditional culture is often referred to as the 'heritage'. But it is expensive to maintain and limited in appeal; and it is rejected by a growing number of young people as they have rejected so much contemporary culture for its so-called élitism and its remoteness from what they consider to be the cultural needs of most people. Governments, faced with a threat to the survival of this culture, have increasingly assumed the role of patron and established a precedent for preserving the cultural inheritance by means of subsidy. They have been motivated by the assumption that with free entry to museums and picture galleries, reduced price of seats at the opera, and a general widening of the facilities for the enjoyment of the arts, more people would come to accept and take pleasure in their cultural inheritance. It is a disturbing fact that this has not occurred. Attendance at the castles of the Loire and the Stately Homes of England on Sunday afternoons may have taken an upward turn, but consistent interest in the cultural inheritance is still the prerogative of the middle-classes.

Cultural democracy and the Democratization of Culture

Attempts to 'democratize' culture have run into difficulties. This is partly a matter of definition; for what is usually meant by the democratization of culture is the hope that a greater number of people, that is the workers, shall come to enjoy or even participate in traditional artistic activities. In his chairman's introduction to the Annual Report of the Arts Council of Great Britain for 1975-6 Lord Gibson wrote the following paragraph:

> There is, however, a new creed emerging, to which we are wholly opposed. This is the belief that because standards have been set by the traditional arts and because those arts are little enjoyed by the broad mass of the people, the concept of quality is 'irrelevant'. The term cultural democracy has been invoked by those who think in this way, to describe a policy that rejects discrimination between good and bad and cherishes the romantic notion that there is a 'cultural dynamism' in the people which will emerge only if they can be liberated from what one European 'cultural expert' has recently called 'the cultural colonialism of the middle class'.

One is not in a position to question Lord Gibson about his sources, but it is certainly true that there are those who resent the so-called imposition of middle-class values on the workers, thereby, by implication, denying them the right to enjoy Shakespeare.

But is is hard to believe that there is anyone who would accept a debasement of standards in the process of the democratization of art. The assumption behind the suggestion is that the arts are intrinsically élitist and that it would be impossible to 'democratize' them without debasing them. In the process of democratization standards tend to become irrelevant, since for many people it is participation that is

43

considered to be important, not consumption; hence the present emphasis on *animations*.

The heresy is amply redressed by the Secretary-General of the Arts Council of Great Britain in his introduction to the annual report of the following year when he writes that 'the key to enjoyment of the 'high' arts by a wider public is 'a better education in the arts at all age-levels from primary school to adult education' and goes on to explain the Council's interest in Community Arts as a step towards establishing closer relationships between the arts and education. He goes on to say:

At its worst democratic cultural policy assumes that the 'masses' will never be capable of enjoying the best in the arts, and so must be provided with second best, or worse. Surprisingly, Matthew Arnold dedected this trend over a century ago when he wrote that: 'Plenty of people will try to give the masses, as they call them, an intellectual food prepared and adjusted in the way they think proper for the actual condition of the masses'. This is sometimes called 'giving the public what it wants', but it really means 'giving the public what it can most easily be persuaded to accept'.

It is an attitude that is summed up in the remark 'no one ever went broke underestimating the taste of the American people'; but such cynicism is offset by a recent Mayor of the Paris suburb of Gennevilliers who said in an interview that he resented strongly the suggestion that the working-class citizens of his community were not able to meet the challenge of the local theatre which refused to feed its audiences on 'divertissements'.

Although Lord Gibson does not name his 'European expert' the phrase 'cultural democracy' is now in common use. It needs careful consideration, for it is used politically by those who fear that increased government subsidy for the arts may result in an imposition of alien cultural values on sections of the population who enjoy a separate or sub-culture. While there is a good deal of nonsense talked about working-class sub-cultures, it is still reasonable to argue that every community should be encouraged to create its own culture in the sense in which we have already defined the term. But there is plenty of room for manoeuvre between the total cultural isolation of a community and its cultural obliteration by subsidized tours, visits, and every other kind of artistic manifestation emanating from the capital. Middle-class culture need not be additionally provided for, since, by the very nature of things, the middle-classes in contemporary Europe have their culture. But the policy of taking middle-class culture to working-class communities is obviously open to misinterpretation. What kind of theatre does one offer in a working-class suburb? Are Molière and Shakespeare and

44

all the great classics to be excluded because they are bourgeois? M. Vilar had an answer to that. If traditional culture and so-called contemporary middle-class culture are to be wholly excluded from peasant or industrial communities, there is very little left - except the plays of Signor Dario Fo (4).

It is interesting to note that in the Anglo-Soviet Journal (January 1978) the point is strongly made that at the time of the Soviet Revolution the decision to preserve the best elements in traditional Russian culture was taken by the high-priest of Marxist critics, Anatoly Lunacharsky himself, the first Soviet Commissar of Education, in the face of criticism from such revolutionary enthusiasts as Meyerhold but with the full support of Lenin who in 1925 wrote a booklet explaining why the régime thought it proper to preserve the Bolshoi opera and ballet.

It is not the job of any government to insist that the Sicilian worker in Zürich or the Greek worker in Cologne or the Pakistani worker in London should be compelled to see the works of the masters. But it would seem to be wholly acceptable cultural policy that spends public money in making available to such workers at prices they can afford the works of Shakespeare, Mozart, Berio and Beckett. We cannot really endure a situation in which the bourgeois radical screams 'Hands off the working-class!' while the bourgeois conservative grumbles 'Don't waste money on the working-class!' It is not a question of blanketing anybody with anything but of making available to as many people as possible an opportunity to enjoy historical as well as contemporary culture. That it is not easy to do so is one of the reasons for this book. No cultural policy should intrude uninvited into a person's private life; but most people have a key to their front door and a switch to their television set.

The economic theory of subsidy

The theatre, for reasons that were developed in the previous chapter, finds it increasingly difficult to pay its way if it is to provide the range and variety of productions which educationally and culturally are demanded of it. Many new plays, whatever their artistic worth, are not widely supported, the classics have a limited appeal, and plays with big casts are expensive to stage. Opera houses charging the equivalent of £20 for their best seats are dependant on a subsidy of 80% of their gross costs to remain open and preserve their standards.

The historical factors already referred to are important. The state has taken over institutions that were formerly supported by royal patronage. Palaces, monuments, parks, museums and picture galleries, once an aspect of the projection of royal authority, are now almost universally

The Royal Dramatic Theatre (Dramaten), Stockholm, 1981.

The Schauspielhaus, Zurich, 1981.

46

administered by the state. Any vitality they still possess lies in their aesthetic dynamic. While we admire the beauty of the Parthenon we do not think much about Pericles or Phidias or the nature of the culture that produced such masterpieces.

Those theatres which first became the responsibility of the state were usually those most clearly associated with royal patronage and designated 'national' theatres. Outstanding examples are to be found in France, Sweden and West Germany.

The state has an equally strong but less clearly definable responsibility to 'preserve cultural values'. This responsibility is likely to be more readily accepted in a country like France which has experienced a high level of centralized culture over many centuries from that in a small, new or developing country whose government will be obliged to evolve a cultural policy without historical tradition or precedent. Such a policy will involve three major decisions:

1   What aspects of culture are wholly the responsibility of central government (the public sector)?
2   What aspects of culture should be left entirely to the private sector?
3   What activities in the private sector should be assisted by the government and to what extent?

It needs no close scrutiny of the policy of certain governments to note the inconsistent and happy-go-lucky manner in which these decisions have been made. Often, in fact, no decision has been made: there has been nothing but an ad hoc response to precedence and pressure.

Let us consider the first question first. Anyone who has given thought to the question will have his own answer. To provide, therefore, a less subjective basis, let us consider what the economists have had to say.

The first of a number of books that have been written in recent years on the economics of the arts was the work of two American professors, William Baumol and William Bowen. Their book *Performing Arts* (5) stands in danger of being quoted by people who have never read it and becoming the source of 'laws' which the authors never framed. For indeed it is a well-written, erudite and sophisticated study of the subject, unhappily out-of-date, but still providing invaluable guidelines for similar studies.

The American professors, having posed the question why the arts should be exempt from the market-test, single out three arguments in support of public intervention: the issue of income distribution, which has already been discussed; the education of young people (since appreciation of the arts is closely related to educational practice); and the fact that the arts partake of some of the characteristics of public goods.

The distinction between private and public goods has been explained in another useful book on the subject, Professor Mark Blaug's *The Economics of the Arts*, (6). Professor Blaug explains that public goods are those which cannot be provided to one customer without providing them to all customers (such as a public park, for example). Furthermore, public goods, unlike private goods, may be consumed by one individual without in any way reducing the amounts available to other customers. The trouble with the theatre is that it has elements of both public as well as private goods.

This is not to become pedantically involved in economic minutiae, but to establish the democratic concept that certain amenities such as a public park, which on account of its geographical situation, or for some other reason, may be available to only a limited number of people, those living in its vicinity, for example, may still be a charge on the whole community. In this sense it might well be argued that a national theatre, about which we shall have a good deal more to say on page 99, or a municipal theatre, can be considered a 'public good'.

That it should also be the responsibility of government, whether central, regional or municipal, to provide total support for the national heritage is now becoming widely accepted. There would be little room for argument were it not that a certain amount of the national heritage, at least in Great Britain, is still in the hands of private owners. But this is not a subject which comes within the terms of the present survey.

The second question concerns what aspects of culture should be left entirely to the private sector. The answer to this, in terms of the theatre, was discussed in the previous chapter. But the answer cannot be clear-cut. There is a strong argument in favour of leaving the industry of entertainment to the market-test which proposes that people should pay for such aspects of art and culture as they want. The state must intervene when its own control of the distribution of money lessens the amount of money people have to spend as they like, on their own preferences. The state cannot have it both ways, and a practical policy must be based on a relationship between taxes and expendable income. That is why the present practice of interaction between the subsidized and independant theatre seems to be a proper reflection of government policies in a mixed economy.

Furthermore, it is possible that market forces to which the private sector is extremely vulnerable may operate against the popular and minority arts. Because the circus, for example, with all the individual skills on which it relies, is an outstanding example of a popular art, it must not be taken for granted that it will survive inevitable economic pressures. This is another area in which government must declare its policy. The arts that are categorized as 'popular' must not be allowed to vanish on the assumption that popular is to be equated with financial success.

In practical terms the third question is the most relevant to the present state of the theatre. What activities in the private sector should be assisted by the government and to what extent?

The answer is clearly, when those activities which can be seen to contribute to the public good for their educational, social or cultural value, are faltering or ailing.

Government has therefore to decide, across the whole field of cultural and economic activity, when a faltering industry justifies public subsidy. It may do so to preserve jobs; to maintain a product which it considers to be socially important; or to nurse an organization until there is revived demand for its product at an economic price. When government is faced with a faltering theatre it has to decide first upon the social value of its product which is largely a value judgement, and secondly, whether the economic climate or public taste is likely to change in the forseeable future to the extent of enabling it to establish economic viability and independance. It was, for example, only when Britain was at war and civilian morale was of national concern that the government made careful arrangements through the Council for the Encouragement of Music and the Arts to subsidize and ensure the distribution of artistic activities.

A faltering industry or a faltering theatre can be defined as one where there is an income gap between the cost of the product, the total expenditure required to produce it, and the income derived from its purchase in the open market. It is the gap between what it costs to stage and run a play and the total amount that is taken at the box-office. The market-test, therefore, asks the question why those who want a certain service or commodity should not pay for it. 'Insolvency', say Messrs Baumol and Bowen 'does not per se constitute adequate ground for public assistance'.

Various answers have been provided by economists quoted in Professor Blaug's important collection of papers and also by W. S. Howe in *The Economics of Public Subsidy for the Performed Arts*, a paper written for the 1974 conference of the Association of Polytechnic Teachers of Economics. One of the most commonly cited arguments for subsidy, fully discussed by both Professor Blaug and Mr. Howe, and first proposed by Messrs Baumol and Bowen, is that the performing arts are labour-intensive, with limited means of increasing output through the installation of machinery or other devices; with the result that in a period of inflation wages will rise without gains in productivity which will remain virtually stagnant. In the theatre, labour is both input and output; any increase in salaries in times of inflation will result in a growing gap between receipts and expenditure if seat prices cannot be raised proportionately.

The theory is acceptable so far as it goes, but it has been criticized for not going very far. It is true enough that an actor cannot be expected to give more than, say, eight performances a week and that no improvement in the machinery of the theatre will enable him to do so. But there is no absolute value that can be set upon his performance. It is quite proper to apply in the first instance the market-test: how much is the public prepared to pay to see his performance. But again, his performance may not be an absolute. It must be related to his salary; to the size of the theatre and the price of seats; to the economic levels and cultural values pertaining in the country at the time of his performance; to the nature and quality of the play in which he is performing; to the relationship between that play and the public for whom it is intended. These relationships are by no means all susceptible to manoeuvres that would increase his 'productivity'; but a comparative study of technical, economic, and cultural values of the commercial theatre of London or Paris in the 1980s with those pertaining in the 1880s would demonstrate clearly the danger of attaching the economic status of the theatre to a doctrinaire economic law.

But whatever the cultural and economic pressures operating against the theatre, it is arguable that subsidy, whatever its political justification, is intended to bridge the gap between what the product costs and what the public is prepared to pay for it. This in the subsidized theatres of the countries under scrutiny tends to be in the region of 50% or more of gross costs.

Professor Blaug points out that 'varying levels of subsidy between one country and another may simply reflect custom and historical tradition'. The Federal Republic of Germany, as we shall see in a subsequent chapter, provides a very good example of this. 'But', Professor Blaug continues, 'persistent patterns in public support for a particular set of human activities may be the result of certain economic characteristics of those activities'. Agreed; and sometimes political as well. A very interesting example of this was provided by the 'boom' that was enjoyed by the London theatres in the mid-1970s when the debilitated condition of the pound encouraged large numbers of visitors from countries enjoying a more buoyant economy to visit the capital and sample its entertainment. With a 'strong' pound, tourism has faltered.

The American economist Dick Netzer, in an important book on the subject (7), gives arguments in favour of subsidizing the arts, and there are others to be added without exhausting the possibilities. For example, preserving the cultural heritage, which includes the preservation of works of art in museums and galleries, of ancient monuments and architectural rarities, as well as masterpieces of the theatre, is in itself valuable. The debate is particularly tendentious where the lyric theatre is concerned, for opera and classical ballet are notoriously costly and it is arguable that it is hardly worth staging *The Magic Flute* or *Giselle* if they cannot be at least adequately performed. Such lyric masterpieces simply do not lend themselves to the kind of simplified staging which has sometimes proved remarkably successful with the plays of Shakespeare, for example. Even so, the arguments advanced in the chapter on national theatres are of particular relevance in this context.

Mr. Netzer argues that the interdependance of various forms of art is such that if one aspect of the theatrical industry is flourishing it may well bring opportunities and advantages to others. He also includes the importance of providing opportunities for experiment and failure if the arts are to preserve their vitality. This is a matter to which we shall revert.

There is yet another advantage of a vigorous culture. While in these hard times one may wonder to what extent a performance of Molière by the Comédie Francaise can be of help to trade relations, it is no accident, perhaps, that France and West Germany carry out a vigorous policy of cultural diplomacy. It was the Hohenzollerns, the Habsburgs and the Valois who first established the practice of projecting a national image through artistic media. Trade is said to follow the flag. But the flag is a useless symbol unless it stands for a certain intellectual vitality, cultural distinction, or political adroitness.

There remains, however, one important distinction still to be made. It is between the concept of the theatre as a social or educational service and as a developing form of art, a distinction that confuses some of the arguments already discussed. If the former concept predominates, the involvement of the state is not likely to be questioned. Every country is profoundly involved in the education of its citizens. Moreover in an over-productive society in which the purchase of commodities is seen as more desirable than the enjoyment of leisure, the state sees the theatre increasingly as a potential leisure activity by no means divorced from its educational responsibilities and subsidizes it accordingly. A municipal theatre is neither more nor less of a public service than a golf-course, park or swimming-pool. It is to be hoped that the assumption of responsibility for the arts by the Department of Education and Science through the Office of Arts and Libraries is the result of a conviction in the social and educational importance of art, and not an act of convenience.

The crux of the argument lies of course in an elision of the two concepts, that the theatre should be seen as an art which in turn is accepted

The new Barbican Centre for Arts and Conferences, which will be the new London home for the Royal Shakespeare Company, and is likely to open in 1982.

The National Theatre on the South bank of the Thames, London, 1976.

as a public service. Such a point of view is widely held throughout Europe and it helps to account for the fact that although the theatre has a history reaching back to 500 B.C. it is now engaged in re-establishing a sanction from society it has not enjoyed since ancient times.

Subsidy to the theatre can therefore be justified by a number of arguments of which the most powerful is that it can be seen in part as a public service, and secondly, that through the operation of various economic forces, it is a faltering industry. Subsidy is therefore provided to bridge the gap between a theatre's gross expenditure and the maximum receipts it can hope to take at the box-office. But the running of a theatre is a very much deeper question than simply putting on plays and aiming at capacity audiences. It has to attract audiences, find those to which it policy appeals, extend its franchise. It must encourage activity in all its forms and animate the practical involvement of many people both as theatre workers and members of the audience.

A responsibility around which considerable uncertainty exists is the question of standards and quality of work. Contrary to what was suggested above, high standards and wide diffusion are in no way contradictory. There is no argument for confining our leading actors to the National Theatre and sending third-rate tours to predominantly working-class areas, although this may be what tends to happen. The polarity is caused almost entirely by money, by the continued operation of market-forces. A performance of *Hamlet* at the National Theatre costs a great deal of money both from the theatre's grant-in-aid and public's purchase of seats at the box-office. But while the economists have agreed that subsidy may be justified under certain social and economic conditions, they have not included the maintenance of standards among them; and since standards are not immediately involved in a policy of diffusion or the encouragement of activity, the theatre-goer must argue that they are part of a theatre's necessary expenditure. It therefore becomes apparent how delicately the problem of standards has to be weighted against other pressures. It is not a matter of either/or but of a fine balance.

One of the few reports in which such matters have been fully discussed is a recent Australian publication on assistance to the performing arts (8). Here the authors argue, with a good deal of the vigour that is to be expected of an openly democratic society, that a nation is justified in assisting the performing arts in so far as they are expressive of that nation's way of life and contributing to its education and its culture.

We would suggest at this stage of the discussion that the words 'quality' and 'standards' are of dangerous application in a political context. They are not absolutes. They cannot be measured by technical skill nor by any other yardstick of universal application. It would therefore seem proper to suggest that the ideal of democratic culture should be not only to encourage the greatest number of people to 'mess about' self-indulgently in vicarious artistic activities (*animations*), to make it possible for a few gifted artists to receive inflated salaries for performances that are attended by a small and privileged élite, but to establish a policy based on an understanding of the nature of the creative process and the many and diverse levels on which that process, in a complex industrial society, finds expression.

Methods of subsidizing the theatre

A government, having made the political decision to subsidize the theatre, (along with the other arts, no doubt), will do so according to the methods of taxation or raising money it habitually employs. Thus in countries with a federal constitution, such as Switzerland and the Federal Republic of Germany, main support for the theatre comes in the form of direct subsidy from the municipalities who are the principal agents for the raising of income and other forms of taxation. In Britain and Sweden both central and local government are involved in raising money, though by different means - centrally-raised income-tax and a municipal rate on property in Great Britain and both centrally-and municipally-raised income-tax in Sweden; and both make direct subsidy to the theatre.

A government then, has a range of choices within its fiscal or financial system for providing subsidy by tax relief, direct cash grants, guarantees and support in kind. In the case of the arts the options are limited because the organizations concerned are usually non-profit-making. This, as has been emphasized, is particularly true in the case of the theatre. Generally-speaking, and in the countries being considered, the main form of subsidy, or assistance to the theatre, is by means of direct cash grant, a very much more flexible arrangement than tax relief which raises a variety of problems of particular concern to the tax authorities.

There is in addition a good deal of 'support in kind' in the form of the provision of a theatre building at negligible or concessionary rent usually by the municipality, secretarial and marketing services, free equipment, or free car-parking space.

The Arts Council of Great Britain provides a certain amount of assistance to various artistic enterprises in the form of guarantees against loss, for example; project grants, subsidies for transport or catering, and capital assistance. These forms of subsidy can be calculated to match the needs of the situation more accurately and more flexibly than forms of tax relief, though they are difficult to relate to box-office and other receipts.

In Great Britain particularly, and in other countries to a lesser extent, there are various financial advantages accruing from charitable status. It is also in Britain that we find limited but none the less positive support for the theatre from industry on roughly American lines. Both will be referred to later in the chapter.

A final point to be made in this section concerns various forms of indirect taxation, such as Value Added Tax or entertainments duty. The first and greatest problem is to define the area of relief, for at one end of the spectrum there are the more responsible aspects of drama and cinema, religious meetings and sporting events, while at the other there are strip shows and 'blue' films. Wherever the administrator or politician draws the line he is in danger of threatening a whole area of public service or the basis of taxation.

Value Added Tax is the result of the sixth directive of the E.E.C. Inconsistency in its application to theatre between the different countries results from the fact that it standardized procedures at the time the directive was issued. This is why the British Theatre pays the abnormally high rate of 15% and the wealthy German theatre none. The standardization of V.A.T. is one of the future tasks of the E.E.C. It is to be hoped that when the decision is made, the theatre, along with other major cultural and artistic activities and products such as books and pictures, will not be zero-rated but tax-exempt. We hope in addition, since we have emphasized the importance of an ill-defined relationship between the subsidized and private sectors of the theatre, that the former will not be unduly privileged at the expense of the latter.

Level of subsidy: the box-office

One of the most delicate manoeuvres in the whole area of subsidy is establishing the level of subsidy against box-office revenue. If the level is too low it will be ineffectual; if it is too high there will be accusations of extravagance, complacency and self-indulgence. Nevertheless the price for a seat which a manager invites the public to pay represents a subtle gamble with the client's purse. How much can he induce him to pay before he says 'enough is enough'? Even in West Germany, where subsidy is running at a considerably higher rate than in any other country, the theatres are under pressure to price their seats at the highest figure the public is thought to be willing to pay, and so, in common with the independant theatre, to 'maximize' their box-office returns.

But there are two important considerations to be borne in mind. One is that seat prices must reflect the relationship between audience and production. Theatre managers do not always analyse with sufficient care the type of audience that supports a certain type of play and modify their publicity and seat prices accordingly. (See Chapter One).

The second point is that lower seat prices do not attract a socially more diversified audience. The point was established by Messrs Baumol and Bowen. Lower seat prices, generally speaking, simply encourage regular theatre-goers to come more often. The policy of the Citizens' Theatre, Glasgow, in charging 90p. for every seat (1981) has not resulted in a more diversified audience than in theatres that charge three or four times more; but it has encouraged regular attendances.

Considerations on which level of subsidy is based

Central and local government will both decide upon the total sum that can be made available for subsidy. It will then be for the responsible officer(s), with or without a consultative committee, to apportion the sum available among the different claimants in terms of various forms that subsidy can take, or objectives for which it can be given. Here are some possible forms of subsidy as well as considerations that have to be borne in mind in granting subsidy.

Guarantee against loss: a common form of subsidy. It can be applied to a single production or a season of plays.

Special or project subsidies: to cover unusually expensive productions, experimental productions, the production of a new play and similar eventualities.

Demographic considerations: in pursuance of the policy of cultural democracy, theatre directors will be encouraged to establish theatres or to take tours to less thickly populated areas where audiences may inevitably be small - an obvious justification for subsidy.

The nature of theatre buildings: it may be agreed to establish a regional theatre in a certain town where the only available theatre is too small, or too large, or poorly equipped, or in some respect or other inconvenient. Subsidy can be made available to cover or compensate for these or similar limitations.

The lyric theatre: opera and ballet tend to be more expensive to stage than plays. There are many reasons for this, such as the fees that usually have to be paid to opera singers and the expense of an orchestra. An authority might consider it proper that the theatre should be made available for performances of opera and ballet and provide subsidy accordingly.

'Big and Little' directed by Peter Stein, at the Schaubuhne am Halleschen Ufer, West Berlin, 1979.

Italian street Theatre in Pontedera, 1977.

The Palace Theatre, Manchester, shortly before re-opening in 1981.

The repertoire: a particularly adventurous or experimental repertoire of classic or of new plays might merit subsidy. Shakespeare, for example, usually needs a large cast. Racine uses a small cast but would tend to appeal to a small and specialized audience. New plays by new writers (*créations*) often fail to draw large audiences. Many more similar examples could be given.

Price of seats: it is a general principle that the price of seats at a theatre should be kept as high as the public, which it is hoped will visit the theatre, can reasonably be expected to pay; this is particularly true of the commercial theatre. But there may well be other considerations in favour of keeping the price of seats well below economic level. If this were in keeping with agreed policy, subsidy would be justified.

Variations in artistic policy: artistic policy can be expressed in ways other than choice of repertory and attitude to the public. The theatre may be a proving-ground for young directors or young actors; or it may run a workshop for young playwrights. Any such policy could justify subsidy.

A theatre with a strongly motivated educational policy might spend a considerable amount of time and effort on various kinds of *'animations'*, a term that will be discussed in Chapter 11. These activities could be held both within and outside the theatre with the purpose of developing a living relationship between the cast and the community. In the same way the theatre might be particularly interested in giving performances to children and young people at prices well below those charged for adults. Such performances might also be related to a programme of *'animations'*.

The granting of subsidy represents a kind of negotiated agreement between the policies determined by the authorities in support of their decision to make subsidy available, and the policies of those requiring subsidy in the light of a number of local circumstances. Subsidy is not a 'blanket' operation: ideally it should be a sensitively worked out rapprochment between those providing a service and those paying for it.

Here is a description by the Arts Council of Great Britain's Director of Finance of the considerations that are borne in mind in deciding on level of subsidy.

> . . . in arriving at a decision about the size of a subsidy and the ratio of the guarantee element, one has to consider the size of the Council's subsidy in relation to the estimated deficit, the extent and form of an organization's reserves, the financial acumen of the individual company's board, the trend of the box-office, the type of artistic programme projected, the relationship to, and size and type of,

59

local authority and regional arts association's subsidies, the capacity and size of the audience and the catchment area of population, the degree of accuracy possible in certain estimates of hitherto untested artistic products, and so on . . . (9).

The delicacy of the whole operation becomes apparent when one considers how choice in the nature of subsidy, quite apart from its extent, can be used as a means of controlling policy and even exercising a subtle form of censorship. Companies with a policy unattractive to the authorities can be removed from the list and whole categories of activity can be wholly excluded.

Policies governing subsidy

Another word that should perhaps be used in this connection is accountability. Politicians will want to be assured that the credits they have voted for the arts are being used to the best advantage and they will require administrators and directors of theatres to account for their spending of subsidy. Many authorities employ some kind of inspectorate to maintain a relationship between the authority and the various recipients.

Expressed in more exact, though still simple terms, the economist will take note of the policy that is governing the granting of subsidy. When he turns to the recipients he will take note of:
— the objectives for which this subsidy is being used;
— policies that are being followed for reaching the desired objectives and an assessment of their potential affectiveness;
— an order of preferences or priorities.

Among the objectives for which subsidy is being used the recipient is likely to claim that it is necessary
— to maintain standards of performance;
— to increase his audiences;
— to foster original work.

But as will be apparent from the present study, there are many different ways of both interpreting and attaining these objectives. The debate may be complex since objectives in cultural activities are often interrelated, interdependant, and by no means mutually. exclusive. Cultural policy can take many different forms as the cynics suggest when they claim that decision-makers in the arts do not try to get what they want but learn to want by appraising what they think they can get. So it may very well be that a local authority, ready in principle to support a local theatre, will require of its director what the authors of the Australian report might have described as an educational or social policy. The director, on the other hand, might interpret his social and educational obligations by insisting on the importance of individual creativity and basing his policy on the production of new plays. But it is essential that over such complex issues there should be debate and not a mutual and disgruntled withdrawal.

Let us give an example of the complexities and opportunities for misunderstanding that lie behind the apparently straightforward objectives of subsidy listed above.

Is subsidy to be used to meet or increase demand? It is often very difficult to establish the level of demand for a product until that product has been put into the shop or the play has been put upon the stage. The need to increase demand has been implied in everything that has hitherto been said about cultural democracy.

How much importance is to be attached to standards of performance? Standards are not absolute: they depend upon a qualitative judgement. They are not necessarily related to enjoyment or even appreciation. But standards of performance are expensive to maintain, depending upon highly trained artists, the technical resources of the theatre, and many other considerations, often expensive.

The two policies come into conflict when the former, a policy that is based upon the theory of cultural democracy, requires that performances be taken to theatreless towns, for example. It is often difficult to give a theatrical performance in a local school-hall of as high a standard as in the company's own fully-equipped theatre. But under such circumstances other factors come into play. Many members of the audience may not be regular theatre-goers. Objective standards of performance, the size of stage, the quality of the lighting, the adaption of the scenery and other limitations may result in apparently poor standard of performance judged by irrelevant criteria. But most performing artists will have had experience of acting, singing, or dancing under such conditions and often transcending them. If members of theatrically unsophisticated audiences are content, how are we to judge standards?

If the kind of audience at which the performance is being directed constitutes one of the foundation stones for any theatrical policy, the other is the status of the creative artist in the ensemble. That is why it is necessary to emphasise that cultural policy can advance apparently conflicting objectives which may in fact be inter-dependant. Thus it is impossible to consider the audience without the performer, the playwright without the community. The problem with the theatre is that the individual artist must function as a member of an ensemble; the individual spectator enjoys the performance as a member of the audience. It is a problem that will be discussed in the second part of this book.

Support for the arts by industry

The concept of industrial support for the arts is American in origin. This is understandable in a country which has attached such importance to private enterprise that the modest amount of state intervention into private theatrical activities as practiced in Europe has had until recently the appearance of an extreme form of doctrinaire socialism. The European attitude, on the other hand, is that for the state to allow the survival of the arts to be dependant on industrial patronage is to abrogate one of its major social and educational responsibilities.

Since the inception of federal taxation of income in 1913 there has been substantial indirect governmental support for the arts as a result of contributions to non-profit distributing cultural organizations being tax deductible. This has released in current figures more than $400 million annually for the arts.

Since the early 1960s the Federal government has followed the European pattern and made direct subsidy to the arts through the National Endowment for the Arts and Humanities. Its annual appropriation for the Arts programme has been increased from $2,534,000 in 1966 to $82 million in 1976 and $155 million in 1981. President Reagan has proposed a cut of $60 million in 1982.

The Americans tend to argue in more realistic terms than the Europeans. Art is good for society, therefore society must pay for art; and since society is composed of individuals it is for the individual to decide how much of his money he is going to give to art; and he is allowed freedom from taxation accordingly. The same argument applies to industry; and since the more expensive forms of art such as opera and sculpture face the greatest financial problems, they receive the greater help from industry. The Federal government becomes involved only when the sums required are beyond the capacity of private benefaction or industry to raise. The result of a rapid growth in the provision of both public and private money for the arts is that between 1967 and 1977 the number of opera companies rose from 27 to 65 and of professional theatre companies from 7 to 157. The intensely market-oriented attitude of the average American towards the arts is not without its advantages.

The situation is wholly different in Europe where up to 80% of the costs of running subsidized theatres is provided by funds from central or local government. In such circumstances there is little call on industry for help. It is therefore understandable that in Britain, where public subsidy for the theatre is running at a lower level than in most other countries, there should be claims on industry for help.

Britain appears to be the only European country which is following in any way American practice. It is doing so through The Association of

Business Sponsorship for the Arts, an organisation which was formed in 1976 by a number of leading British companies with the initial help of a government grant. The objects of the Association are:

1 to encourage business organizations to become involved in arts sponsorship in the United Kingdom;
2 to advise business on sponsorship opportunities and procedures;
3 to produce informative publications;
4 to develop an awareness within the arts world of the requirements which industry seeks from its sponsorship and to advise on how to improve the presentation of their case to industry.

This is of course a kind of snobbery that resents the association of Imperial Tobacco with *The Magic Flute* or the National Westminster Bank with *King Lear*; but theatre and ballet organisations see the Association as a vital way of launching new productions or tours at a time when inflation and the limits of governmental aid are squeezing them badly. Big business sees it as a way of showing a sense of community responsibility with maximum publicity. 'The great change has been the move from patronage, which is a one-way relationship, to sponsorship which is a two way affair', declares the secretary of the Association.

In 1981 the 60 or so members of the Association spent some £5¼ million on the arts, and some £28 million on sport. Companies are highly selective in what they choose to sponsor since their contribution is made from their budget for advertising. The danger for the theatre as a whole is that companies tend to select for support the most socially prestigious productions which may not be the work of organisations most deservedly in need of help. Nevertheless they help take the strain off public sector funds which can be devoted to more marginal cases.

It has been established then that a government uses taxation for the purpose of influencing the pattern of social and economic activity in the redistribution of wealth. One of the purposes of taxation is to provide money with which to support activities that are held to be for the 'public good' and which cannot support themselves. The theatre, arguably, comes into this category. Government can therefore award subsidy from its own funds, or make possible the provision of funds from private sources for the same purposes by its control of profit. It can do so, following the policy of the British government in 1979-80, by granting tax exemption to private moneys devoted to acceptable causes or by establishing or supporting organisations which channel private moneys to faltering organisations.

Trusts, Charities and Foundations (10)
Most European countries have made legislative provision for charitable

institutions to be set up by private initiative, and these reflect, particularly in Belgium and the Netherlands, the countries' strong traditions of individualism. In France there are many Foundations and Associations set up for artistic purposes, but they are subject to wide interpretation and many controlling factors. In Germany the Foundations do not play a significant role in the artistic life of the country. Regulations vary under the different states and are sometimes in contradiction with tax laws as interpreted by the courts.

British charities are bound by tax laws that had their origin in the concept of a charitable foundation in the time of Queen Elizabeth I. A charitable institution must have as its objective the relief of poverty; the advancement of education; the advancement of religion; or some other charitable purpose beneficial to the community.

In the United Kingdom there are more than 2,000 Trusts, Charities and Foundations which altogether have disposable funds of some £140 million of which about £40 million goes to the arts and a small proportion of this to the theatre. Official comment says that they are extremely secretive in their activities and tend to be unadventurous.

This is not true, however, of the Gulbenkian Foundation which over recent years has spent some £1.25 million on the arts, in addition to its social and educational commitments. A high proportion of this sum has been given to the promotion of enquiries into education in and training for the arts and the economic status of the artist, with profound and far-reaching consequences. A summary of its investigations can be found in *Going on the stage* (1975), *Training Musicians* (1978) and *Dance Education and Training in Britain* (1980). The Foundation also sponsored Lord Redcliffe-Maud's important *Support for the Arts in England and Wales* (1976) and Su Braden's provocative *Artists and People* (1978).

The important Swiss Foundation, Pro Helvetia, will be described on page 95.

A charity, however, does not exist for its own sake but to disburse its income on causes and to organisations that fulfill the requirements of charitable status. Theatres of non-profit distributing rank which have convinced the Charity Commissions of their educational ideals have been constant beneficiaries of grants that have been of enormous value in getting projects 'off the ground' and so enabling public sector funds to be spread more widely.

Summary

In the following pages, in which methods of granting subsidy and the activities for which it is used are discussed in some detail, it has not been possible to relate the two in any specific way. The procedures in each country have been shaped by complex historical, fiscal and demographic considerations. The principles of subsidy that have been analyzed in this chapter are of more or less general application, but it will be seen that each country has developed its own particular procedures in the light of its political structure and the nature of its theatre. It is these various procedures and mechanisms which will now be discussed.

Sources

(1) Hugh Trevor-Roper - *Princes and Artists: Patronage and Ideology at Four Habsburg Courts 1517 - 1633* - Thames and Hudson, 1976.

(2) Janet Minihan - *The Nationalisation of Culture* - Hamish Hamilton, London, 1976.

(3) Finn Jor - *The Demystification of Culture* - C.C.C. Strasbourg, 1976.

(4) For an interesting discussion on the subject see Lanfranco Binni - *Dario Fo* - Florence, 1977.

(5) William J. Baumol and William G. Bowen - *Performing Arts: the Economic Dilemma* - The M.I.T. press, Massachusetts, 1966.

(6) Mark Blaug (editor) - *The Economics of the Arts* - Martin Robertson, London, 1976.

(7) Dick Netzer - *The Subsidised Muse* - Cambridge, 1978.

(8) *Assistance to the Performing Arts* - Industries Assistance Commission Report - Australian Government Publishing Service - Canberra, 1976.

(9) Anthony Field - *Make up My Audit* in *A Tale of Two Cities* - Arts Bulletin, Arts Council of Great Britain - summer, 1971.

(10) See Professor Ignatius Claeys Bonnaert, *Taxation of Cultural Foundations and of Patronage of the Arts in Member States of the European Economic Community*, E.E.C., Brussels, unpublished.

Belt and Braces company with Dario Fo's 'Accidental Death of an Anarchist' at Wyndham's Theatre, London, 1981.

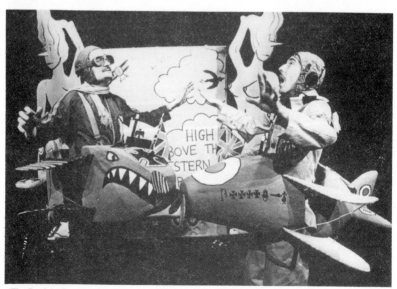
'The Fosdyke Saga' by Bill Tidy and Alan Plater at the Bush Theatre, London, 1981.

4. The Organisation of Subsidy

Ministerial Responsibility

The purpose of this chapter is to describe the administrative machinery that has been created in each country for the distribution of subsidy. It will be clear that the whole process will be self-defeating if artists have cause to repeat the anxiety so movingly expressed by Shakespeare when he spoke of 'art made tongue-tied by authority'.

It is important as a start to bear in mind the demographic limitations of theatre-going discussed in the first chapter as well as the economic justification and artistic objectives of subsidy discussed in chapter three.

It may be assumed, then, that the political decision to subsidize the theatre has been taken and that certain criteria within which subsidy will be available have been laid down. These criteria will establish the total amount of money available for the arts; the proportion of that money to be allocated to the theatre; and the principles on which subsidy to the theatre shall be divided between central, regional and municipal government. The last of these three criteria is particularly important since it reflects the political movement, a lively issue in most countries, towards increasing devolution and decentralization. Professor Blaug's point is relevant that level of subsidy between one country and another may reflect custom and tradition as well as the economic characteristics of the country concerned.

The arts vote is handled:

— in Belgium by the Ministerie van Nederlandse Cultuur and the Ministère de l'Education Nationale et de la Culture Française;
— in France by the Ministère de la Culture et de la Communication;
— in Great Britain by the Office of Arts and Libraries within the Department of Education and Science;
— in Italy by the Ministerio del Turismo e dello Spettacolo;
— in the Netherlands by the Ministerie van Cultuur, Recreatie, en Maatschappelijk Werk (Culture, Recreation and Social Work);
— in Sweden by the Utbildningsdepartementet (Education Department);
— in the Federal Republic of Germany the Bundestag has devolved almost total responsibility for the arts to the states (Länder) and municipal governments (Gemeinden);

— in Switzerland the Federal Department of the Interior has delegated total responsibility to the Cantons and Comunes (municipalities).

Decentralization and regional responsibility

Democracy lays increasing importance on the responsibility of local government. People who pay local taxes want a voice in how their money is spent, although the turn-out at polls in local elections does not always confirm this supposed passion for democratic participation.

There are two kinds of regional administration, elective and administrative. If the elective body has legislative powers, the process is referred to as 'devolution', which suggests autonomy and territorial differentiation; whereas decentralization is an administrative arrangement by which elected administrations are granted certain local powers by the central government (1). The relationship between central and local government is conditioned by a variety of national characteristics. Central governments tend to keep control of those aspects of national life that are not responsive to local variation - the judiciary, the armed forces, the police and postal services, and sometimes, and under some conditions, education. Effective decentralization of the theatre largely depends, therefore, on political devolution.

The legislative power of a local authority is largely governed by two factors, its ability to raise money and its authority to initiate and carry out its own policies.

If, therefore, a municipal council has the authority to carry out its own cultural policies and the money with which to do so, all that it needs is an efficient administration. Stephen Mennell suggests (2) that 'perhaps the most serious administrative obstacles to cultural policy-making are those which stem from old fashioned methods of budgeting for removing those methods involved a fundamental change in the entire municipal administration, not just in cultural policy alone. The Swiss cantons and the German states have considerable freedom from central government control, but in other countries local councils have limited freedom of action with statutory obligations, as is the case in Britain, to provide certain services. Annecy (France), Apeldoorn (Netherlands), Bologna (Italy), and Tampere (Finland) have a deputy mayor responsible for cultural affairs; Esbjerg (Denmark), Exeter (Great Britain, Orebro (Sweden), Stavanger (Norway) and Tournhout (Belgium), have a cultural affairs committee. The 1980 edition of *Leisure and Recreation Statistics* published by The Chartered Institute of Public Finance and Accountancy states that 'Leisure as a unified programme is still a relatively new concept in local government terms and its development as a unified service is due to a great extent to the impact of local government reorganisation. . . . In counties leisure is an area of relatively minor importance . . . (but) In the metropolitan districts there is a tendancy to distinguish between artistic and cultural activities and those which may broadly be called recreational pursuits'. But the report emphasises that so great is the diversity of activities and methods of provision that any tidy or comparative form of statistics is almost impossible.

If the processes of devolution and decentralization are to continue, local government must continue the process of organizing itself in order that it can properly carry out the responsibilities it has inherited and which central government is widely foisting upon it. It is a subject to which particular and individual attention must be given. It is far more difficult to organize a policy for the arts than for sport. Athletes want facilities of a definable kind, whereas artists have a relationship to the community that is in a state of constant flux. They are suspicious of bureaucracy. Cultural, perhaps more than any other activities, are, or should be, responsive to local needs and variations. It is reasonable to suppose that the elected government of the region of Sicily is better informed as to the kind of theatre its citizens enjoy, or the way in which it should spend money on the theatre, than a politician in the Italian Parliament or a civil servant in his office in Rome. Or are we underrating the importance of certain absolute values?

But a result of uncertainties on the part of local authorities is that a number of theatre artists who have had experience of negotiating with their local council would prefer to do business with, and derive all their subsidy from the central government. They find greater professionalism in the Ministère de la Culture or the Arts Council of Great Britain than in the local town hall. In the capital they know the door on which to knock. In their own town the doors are not clearly marked and the various committees have ill-defined responsibilities. It was reported in *The Stage* (London, 1.12.77) that members of the Council of Regional Theatres had rejected proposals that the Regional Arts Associations should be the proper funding organisations for regional theatres and urged the Arts Council of Great Britain to reconsider these devolutionary policies. Their criticism of local authorities was based on the claim that the latter's support of the theatre is inconsistent and not sufficiently founded on a reasoned cultural policy, while their spending has not increased adequately either to keep pace with inflation or to meet their developing responsibilities.

There is little to be surprised at in these doubts. We are dealing with a wholly new area of cultural policy. There have been plenty of examples in the course of European history of kings and their ministers having taken responsibility for various aspects of culture and of having been enthusiastic patrons of the arts; rarely of democratically elected governments assuming such responsibilities; never until the present of local authorities. Never before has it been the case that more than half the country's wealth is spent by its government. The surprise is not that things in this field are inadequate but that so much is going as well as it is.

Of course it is disappointing to hear of the intransigence of politicians who, though liberal in their policies tend to be conservative in their tastes, and dislike plays that are critical of society. Politicians feel very tender about society, especially if they consider they have had a hand in shaping it. They are tenacious for the dignity of their theatre, especially if they have had a hand in financing it; and they are understandably resentful when that helping hand is bitten. It is a splendid precedent that so many young people should go to the theatre in school parties but it is understandable that teachers should be alarmed if sex and politics rear their ubiquitous heads: their training rarely prepares them to deal with such visceral subjects. But we cannot both demand that the theatre should deal seriously with serious matters and then complain when it does so. It is, nevertheless, a serious matter when political interference curtails the work of a company or leads to the resignation of its artistic director. It would be possible to quote examples of this from many countries. It is therefore all the more satisfactory to be able to record that some Swedish towns, for example, have appointed a cultural secretary with the responsibility of establishing a relationship between politicians and workers in the theatre.

Sweden and Germany are not among the most indigent of countries; yet politicians from both have expressed a certain dismay at the cost of theatrical subsidy. But no director of any theatre in any country we have visited has complained of the difficulty of banging on the door of the appropriate minister or official in Ministry or Town Hall: cultural doors are usually open to all and we hope it will remain like that.

It is virtually impossible to give anything but the most rough-and-ready figures for local government subsidy to the theatre. Stephen Mennell in his fascinating *Cultural Policy in Towns* says that 'to compare cultural expenditure in widely differing towns borders almost on the impossible'. There are different accounting methods, a variety of 'hidden' subsidies, and 'exchange rates that probably bear little relationship to the purchasing power of the various currencies in the cultural field. It has not even been possible to demarcate the cultural field in the same way in every town while the organization of cultural life and the extent of municipal responsibilities vary considerably from town to town and country to country.'

Nevertheless available figures suggest that the intervention of regional and municipal governments in supporting the arts depends on the fiscal and economic structure of the country. The former tend to play a far less significant role than the latter. In Belgium, local authorities are empowered to grant subsidies at the level of central government subsidy two years previously. In France there is no consistent pattern. In Britain the local authorities tend to spend on the theatre a total sum that is rather less than that contributed by the Arts Council; but while they often grant a paltry sum in comparison with Arts Council subsidy to their local theatre, they own and run a large number of civic venues and entertainment programmes. Figures on page 143 will show the considerable extent of support for the theatre by Swedish local authorities as a result of tax laws that were mentioned on page 91. In countries with a federal constitution such as West Germany and Switzerland, central government plays a very small part in subsidising the arts - a grant of a million or two pounds in the case of the former for special projects usually in West Berlin, and nothing in the case of the latter. Details of the immense contribution by the West German states and municipalities will be given on page 120 (3). In Switzerland municipal subsidy to the country's eleven permanent theatres is ten times higher than that of the cantons.

Administrative structures (4)

Belgium
The outstanding cultural feature of Belgium is the division of the country into two fairly distinct areas with a line of demarcation that runs roughly from Lille in the west to Aachen in the east. In the north of the country Flemish is the predominant culture, in the south, French, the former having such close affinities to Dutch culture that the words 'Dutch' and 'Flemish' are almost interchangeable and the two languages virtually indistinguishable. Flanked to east and west by the older and still powerful cultures of the Netherlands and France, the country faces problems in establishing its cultural individuality.

The towns of Antwerp (244,000) Gent (158,000) and Brugge (52,000) are predominantly Flemish-speaking; Liège (155,000), Namur (33,000), Tournai (33,000), Mons (27,000) and Charleroi (25,000) are predominantly French speaking. In Brussels rather more French is spoken than Flemish although geographically the town is in Flanders.

The population of just under 10,000,000 (59% Flemish, 39% French/Walloon) is the densest in Western Europe.

The Flemish are therefore still in the position of creating a culture, and in this respect the theatre, with its powerful socio-linguistic elements, can play a crucial part. It can help to create a language, a process that is likened to the contribution made by the Habima Theatre to the creation of the state of Israel. The Flemish language is still developing; there is no standard Flemish. Actors are said to be more at ease, and to play better, when using a dialect than when attempting standard speech. If such a thing exists it is close to Dutch, with similarities even more marked in the written than the spoken language. It is understandable that Flemish culture, threatened with domination by the powerful culture of France, turns for support to Amsterdam rather than to Paris.

The development of French language theatre in Belgium has closely followed the expansion of Brussels as a capital city. At the end of the 1939-45 War the Belgian National Theatre was established in Brussels and a vigorous policy of decentralization led to the extension of theatrical activity in the French-speaking provinces, especially in Liège where the Théâtre Royal du Gymnase had been in existence for a century (5).

A similar policy of decentralization was mounted in Flemish-speaking Belgium where a close relationship between artistic activities and education has been established (see Chapter 11). One of the most interesting of these developments has been the creation of no less than 32 cultural centres with another 37 under construction, designed for cultural activities of all kinds.

The Belgians, however, are critical of the French Maisons de la Culture which they consider lack flexibility. They have therefore adopted a policy towards their own centres of varying the design according to the nature of the centre and the size of the town in which it is situated, the larger centres having a theatre and the smaller a multi-purpose hall. Not even those with theatres have a permanent company and it is not necessary for the director of a centre to have had theatrical experience. But the Belgians themselves assert that the whole policy is still in its infancy and that they await with interest to see what kind of relationship develops between centrally provided and regionally generated culture (6).

In the course of a detailed discussion on the Cultural Centre at Tournhout, 'De Warande', the authors conclude that although many services are provided, there is criticism both of cost and of a predominance of professional programmes. Many people still 'do not find that a cultural centre fits ideally into their pattern of living'. De Warende has reached many people but its participating public tends to be composed largely of students and employees, the young and the better educated.

France

'There is no pre-established scheme for the theatre', says one of the documents issued by the Ministry of Culture, but in the framework of

72

general culture activity there is being constantly developed 'an open, empiric and pragmatic policy to be realized with the collaboration of professional theatre workers'.

The leaders of the main political parties have all expressed their support for the theatre (7) and although as time goes by their political fortunes have waxed and waned, their views are typical of the kind of attitudes politicians adopt towards the theatre. Monsieur Chirac talks about *'création, diffusion, formation'* and praises the generosity of the town of Paris, of which he was the mayor, towards the arts. Monsieur Mauroy, secretary of the Socialist party, speaks eloquently about the importance of regional culture and of *'animations'* as a means of explaining art to the workers. Monsieur Jacques Ralite, a leading Communist, argues how poorly the municipalities are treated by the state in the matter of subsidy, especially when the mayor is a Communist; and Monsieur Jean-Pierre Soisson, Chairman of the Republican party, and subsequently Minister of Sport and Leisure, assumes an optimism, worthy of Candide, about everything.

The cultural budget is the responsibility of the Minister of Culture who has to fight for his department in the cabinet and win the support of the Minister of Finance. The allotment of the budget is then handled by senior civil servants and their staff, in the case of the theatre by the Direction du Théâtre et des Maisons de la Culture in the Rue Saint Dominique.

M. Alain Peyrefitte tells the story of a conversation with General de Gaulle on the subject of developing the regions. 'The regions?' he quotes the General as saying, 'there are only three or four of which we hear too much; the others don't exist. They are quite artificial. As for the departments they have a history. People are used to living in them. But these autonomous regions, they're a brain-child of the Parisian technocrats' (8). In another passage in the same book M. Peyrefitte ascribes the traditional centralization of the country and the direct involvement of the state in many aspects of national life to the necessity for an assertion of authority following the Wars of Religion to ensure the success of the counter-Reformation. This may be the historical reason for the French civil service having acquired responsibility for the management of a variety of services, many of a specialist or technical nature. Its members are trained to a high degree of expertise and to lead, if necessary, technical operations in the field (9).

Increasing responsibility of the municipalities following upon the policy of decentralization has resulted in the financing of local government becoming a controversial issue. It is the same situation elsewhere. The balance between central and local government funding of regional activities will reflect political issues as much in matters to do with the theatre as in any other area of work.

The controlling Council (Conseil Municipal) of the Commune (or municipality) consists of elected deputies with permanent officials to carry out the day-to-day administration. The deputies will be assigned to various specialist committees one of which may include the theatre within its responsibilities. There is, however, no legal obligation for a municipal council to subsidize theatrical activities. Subsidy can be approved or blocked by the attitude of the mayor or even the prefect by whom all municipal budgets have to be approved.

A policy of decentralization is most clearly articulated in France and a cynic would be justified in saying that this was because they were greatly in need of it. It is therefore important to consider how effectively it is working.

Theatrical decentralization (10)

The story of French decentralization begins with the creation in 1895 of Le Théâtre du Peuple in Bussang, a small town in the Vosges, by Maurice Pottecher, a local journalist and playwright. His ideas were supported over the years by a number of others and taken up in 1911 by Firmin Gémier who began to tour France with his Théâtre National Ambulant, stage, auditorium, dressing-rooms and administrative office all packed into a train of waggons drawn by eight British-made steam traction engines of such weight that they destroyed the houses with which they came into contact and the bridges over which they were obliged to pass. After the 1914-18 War the irrepressible M. Gémier created the Théâtre National Populaire and stamped it with all the panache of a great Republican spectacle.

The subsequent history of decentralization involves the names, the work and the writings of such men as Jacques Copeau with his creation of Les Copiaus in Burgundy (1924) and Charles Dullin. The movement was closely associated with attempts, dating from the Paris Commune of 1871, to establish a popular theatre, a concept which many writers have passionately described but which no one has been able to define in any very precise, realistic, or generally acceptable terms (11).

Throughout the last hundred years there have been sporadic attempts by the French government to establish a precedent of subsidy for the theatre but a consistent policy only emerged in the spirit of idealism that pervaded Europe in the years following the 1939-45 War. This policy was largely the creation of Mademoiselle Jeanne Laurent, a graduate of L'Ecole des Chartes and at the time an under-secretary at the Bureau de la Musique, des Spectacles, et de la Radiodiffusion in the office of the Direction Générale des Beaux Arts. Her responsibilities were considerable, her staff negligible, her budget derisory. But she had the five years of war in which to contemplate the potentialities and needs of the French theatre; and the first thing she noted was that a good deal of money was being spent on subsidized tours with very little benefit to the public.

Slender though her resources may have been she showed remarkable tenacity in winning further credits from the Treasury in pursuance of her policy which was one that led to the virtual transformation of the French theatre. This policy was based on the establishment of regional centres with a permanent theatrical company. Mlle Laurent, with extraordinary flair and perceptiveness, chose both the centres and the directors who were to run them - Louis Ducreux at Colmar, the company that eventually became the Théâtre National de Strasbourg under André Clavé (established in 1946); Jean Dasté at St Etienne, having failed to gain the support of the town council of Grenoble; Maurice Sarrazin who turned a company of amateurs into the Grenier de Toulouse; Hubert Gignoux who created the Centre Dramatique de l'Ouest at Rennes; and Gaston Baty who spent the last year of his life, 1952, establishing the Comédie de Provence at Aix.

An important element in the policy of these centres, strongly encouraged by Mlle Laurent and the Direction Générale des Beaux Arts, was that productions staged in the regional centres should be taken on tours of towns and villages in the area. Subsidy was dependant on such a policy.

At this stage two other notable figures come into the scene. Roger Planchon, a young man of working-class origin, was nineteen when in 1950 he established his tiny theatre in the Rue des Marronniers in Lyon and advanced a new theory about decentralization. Conventional tours of towns and villages, he said, could create only a superficial relationship between players and audience; what was wanted were regular performances in each community so that deep and lasting relationships could be established.

The other figure of note was Jean Vilar who picked up the residual traditions of Gémier's Théâtre National Populaire and established in 1947 the Avignon Festival, less because he believed in decentralization than because he disliked working in Paris and thought of the theatre in terms of festivals and a rich 'communion' with the public. He was deeply influenced by his master, Charles Dullin, and André Antoine.

In 1952 the authorities were possessed of an unhappy aberration and Jeanne Laurent was dismissed. The movement towards theatrical decentralization hung fire until the appointment by General de Gaulle in 1959 of M. André Malraux as Minister of Culture. One of Monsieur

The New Schaubühne am Lehninerplatz, West Berlin which opened on September 13th, 1981.

Two scenes from a nine hour version of 'The Oresteia' directed by Peter Stein at the old Schaubühne, West Berlin, 1981.

Malraux's first moves was the creation of the Maisons de la Culture, a dream which he had inherited from the pre-war days of the Front Populaire, and a number of Centres Dramatiques Nationaux (regional theatres) of which there are now nineteen.

The newly created Ministry defined its task as being, 'To make accessible the outstanding achievements of humanity...to the greatest possible number of French and to open to them our cultural heritage...and to help the creation of works of art...' That is an encouragement of diffusion and creativity.

Centres Dramatique Nationaux

The five original Centres Dramatiques were permanent regional companies; the newly created centres took a variety of forms although ministerial rubrics still identify them as regional theatres with permanent companies. The reality, however, is often less than the ideal. A reduction of state subsidy in real terms has not improved the situation: directors are reducing both the size of their permanent company as well as the number of *créations*, and depending increasingly on visiting companies for which they are described as functioning *en garage*.

Maisons de la Culture

In creating the Maisons de la Culture in a Decree of 24 July, 1959, André Malraux specified their three main areas of activity as:

1 to make available the masterpieces of mankind;
2 to ensure the widest possible appreciation of the national patrimony (inheritance);
3 to encourage the creation of works of art and of the human spirit.

Conceived for the pursuit and development of *'animation culturelle'* in a spirit of partnership between town and state, the Maisons de la Culture provide a most interesting contrast to parallel developments in other countries.

The purpose of a Maison de la Culture is to establish a cultural centre on the highest level providing 'a permanent dialogue between creators, artists and the public'. They are intended to provide facilities for a museum and gallery, theatre, library and a meeting-place for a variety of high-level cultural activities. They are built and subsidised in equal shares by central and municipal government.

The first to be opened was in 1963 at Bourges in an existing building modified by the Architect M. Pierre Sonrel. Its list of activities is still comprehensive and impressive. Amiens was next, (1966) and Firminy in the same year. A Maison at Grenoble was opened in 1968 and brings together over twelve organisations. It includes among its staff of 81, seven full-time *animateurs*, one of them an *animateur littéraire*, two part-time *animateurs* in 'exact science and social science' seconded from the university. There are now fourteen Maisons de la Culture and another six under consideration.

It was the original intention that each Maison should function as a major regional centre for creative activity whether in the field of theatre, music or dance, providing a network of *'animations'* and activities, drawing its audiences from the region and taking its own activities into the community, a feature of the plan being that central and local government should share equally both capital and running costs (12).

That Malraux's vision has been considerably modified is not to suggest an element of failure; but understandably enough the Maisons have developed a kind of life of their own, individually rather than collectively, shaped by the interests and personality of their director, their relationship with the local community and the nature of the associations and organizations with which they collaborate.

Collaboration between the Maisons and the Centres takes place when conditions are propitious. Jean Dasté has a good deal to say in his autobiography (13) about the relationship of his company with the Maison in St Etienne. Guy Retoré, for example, wished to establish a theatre in the 20th (working-class) arrondissement of Paris and asked M. Malraux to buy him a cinema which was then up for sale. M. Malraux agreed if the establishment were a Maison as well as a theatre. So for a time the Théâtre de l'Est Parisien combined both functions.

It is understandable that many aspects of their organzation and policy should now be in question: for example, how they should be subsidized, what is the best relationship between the creative and the collective (Seine-Saint-Denis and see page 188/9); what kind of a person should ideally be in charge, a question raised by Roger Planchon (15); confusion between élitism and professional standards which arose in the Maison de la Culture of Nevers.

All this may be no bad thing. A cultural centre is not a museum for the exhibition of stereotypes and artefacts. A living centre must respond to a living culture and a culture is not alive if it does not change. The administrators of the centres are therefore faced with the problem of creating a stable establishment with a flexible and changing content.

In towns not large enough to justify a Maison de la Culture there is often a Centre d'Action Culturelle. There are at present 23, organised, like the Maisons, jointly by central and local government. Their purpose is innovation and co-ordination with less emphasis on *création* than in a Maison but more on *animations*. The centre organizes activities in many other venues with the object of arousing by various means in the public of all ages and social categories 'a sensibility towards artistic phenomena and the possibilities of expression and communication which they make available to man'.

And at that stage we move from the orbit of the Ministry of Culture to the Ministry of Education and all the other ministries which in one way or another are involved in the delicate and complex process of educating the citizens of our democracies. More will be said on this subject in Chapter 11.

But before leaving France we should draw attention to a particularly interesting organisation, L'Association Technique pour l'Action Culturelle, (ATAC). It was formed in 1966, with a subsidy from the Ministry of Culture, for the purpose of providing a forum for directors of all cultural activities and those aspects of decentralization subsidized by the Ministry, and for *animateurs* who though not subsidized might be 'working in the same spirit'. ATAC has developed a variety of responsibilities for information and co-ordination - a play bureau which will be described on page 248, the training of *animateurs*, technical assistance, and so on. Its monthly journal *ATAC Informations* is an invaluable source of information on the decentralized and subsidized theatre.

The anxieties of the directors of the Centres Dramatiques are largely channelled through ATAC and they are of a kind with which readers of this book will become increasingly familiar: the danger that subsidy will prevent death but discourage growth; anxieties attendant on the shifting of responsibility for regional theatrical activity from central to local government; the preponderance of directors who inspite of financial inducements will make no real effort to stage new plays.

None of these problems is unique to France. But it is by ATAC that they have been most clearly articulated, and in connection with the government's method of appointing directors to its national centres that they have been most sharply criticized.

Federal Republic of Germany (14)
The Federal structure of the country consists of 11 Länder or States. Central government, the Bundesregierung in Bonn, is responsible for national services such as the post, the armed forces and international relations, but federal law has invested considerable executive power in the Länder. The constitution of each is slightly different, the variations being the result of historical precedents and the conditions under which each Land was created in the years following the 1939-45 War. The only federal institution in the field of culture is the Parliamentary Conference of the Land Ministers of Culture.

There is further decentralization from the States to the municipalities. There are 57 towns with a population over 100,000 enjoying a considerable degree of executive authority and many smaller towns with a vigorous civic life, many of which have their own theatre.

The professional civil service was created in the 18th century, at first in the highly organised state of Prussia, not merely for the maintenance of law and order but also for the management of important aspects of social and economic life. The professional element is strong. Every officer must be qualified for the job in which he is engaged. In this respect the German civil service is similar to the French rather than to the British.

In the government of each Land (Landesregerung) there is a Ministerium für Unterricht und Kultur (Education and Culture) where requests for subsidy are first received. The precise procedure varies slightly between the different states but in general terms the proposal is considered by the Minister of Finance who sends it with appropriate recommendations to the cabinet where it is discussed by a special parliamentary sub-committee in the light of the total allocation of funds available to the theatre. Recommendations are then forwarded to the Ministerialdirigent who deals directly with the intendant or finance officer of the theatre (15).

With municipal subsidy the procedure is similar. The responsible officer assesses applications, prepares the documents and forwards them with recommendations to the appropriate committee, the members of which will have already discussed with the Director of Finance a total allocation available to the theatre.

Every German theatre in the subsidized sector will depend for the bulk of its subsidy on state or municipality according to various historical precedents; but in Germany, as elsewhere, frontiers of responsibility are often far from clear. Every municipal council gives some subsidy to the theatres within its territory; but with increasing use of the car the greater urban areas, which administratively may lie outside the town boundaries, rely increasingly on town services. Thus the municipal rate-payers are liable to be obliged to support services to which suburban rate-payers do not contribute.

The structure of the contemporay German theatre was largely created during the Weimar Republic. Until the November Revolution of 1918 all German theatres had been run on a commercial basis except for 32 court theatres and 10 municipal theatres. 42 is not an unimpressive number; but following the free trade act of 1869 some 600 private/commercial theatres had come into existence; but since the end of the century they had been in a condition of permanent economic crisis. Attempts were made to analyse the economic and speculative structure of these theatres and in 1911 there were attempts at reorganisation although there was no question of regarding them as anything but a business. But with pressures of war and the economic deterioration of the country during the 1920s the concept of theatre as business began to be questioned and was seen to be inimical to theatre as art.

People then remembered that a century previously certain municipal councils such as Mannheim had foreseen the inevitable bankruptcy of the commercial theatre and begun to restructure the theatre on a communal basis. Many other councils followed suit and began to grant subsidies to the leaseholders of the theatres within their town.

From the turn of the century there was increasing support for the so-called cultural theatre movement from the right-wing bourgeoisie as much as the social-democrats. Both groups rejected the over-materialistic nature of the theatre and sought for a revival of the national theatre movement of the eighteenth and nineteenth centuries which saw theatre as a communal benefit along with schools and museums. This led, from the foundation of the Empire in 1870, to the establishing of a large number of private theatres which still were subject to a certain amount of state control. The achievement of the Weimar Republic, in the decade following the 1914-18 War, was to maintain the federal system, at least where education and culture were concerned, independant of the central government in Berlin. With the creation of the Federal Republic after the 1939-45 War, the federal system was extended and a clause establishing the freedom of art was written into the federal constitution, repeated in the constitution of the Länder, and repeated again in the basic programmes of the political parties. At present there is a vigorous debate, not on the principle of subsidy, but on the relative financial responsibility of the three parties concerned - federal government, states and municipalities (16).

The basic fact of the West German theatre is that there are 85 theatres with 225 stages in 74 towns and cities.

Great Britain

Great Britain consists of England with a population of about 43,000,000, Scotland with 5,000,000, and Wales with 2,500,000. (The United Kingdom includes Northern Ireland which is excluded from the present survey.) It enjoys a constitution based largely on precedent derived from parliamentary and judicial decisions dating back to Magna Carta (1215) and even earlier. Executive power lies with the Prime Minister and the cabinet working through a civil service which was given its present structure in the nineteenth century when the prevailing belief was in private enterprise and local self-government. British civil servants are therefore trained to be 'enablers', not specialist leaders in the field.

In recent years Scottish and Welsh nationalism has emerged as a powerful element in British politics with total devolution from Westminster among the aims of certain nationalists. There was virtually no tradition of public expenditure on the theatre before 1939. Section 132 of the Local Government Act of 1948 empowered, but did not require local authorities to spend a sum not exceeding a 6d rate on cultural and leisure time arts and entertainment facilities. No authority took advantage of the provision and the results were negligible. Penury was generally claimed to be the reason for this.

As a result of wide-ranging reforms, some of which had been proposed by the Royal Commission on Local Government in England chaired by Lord Redcliffe-Maud, which were put into effect by the Local Government Act of 1972, England was divided into fewer and larger districts. Under Section 145 of the Act these boroughs were given authority to provide entertainment of any kind; facilities for dancing; to provide theatres, concert halls or other premises suitable for entertainment or dancing; to maintain a band or orchestra and to provide for the development and improvement of the knowledge, understanding, and practice of the arts. This in fact gave local authorities the power to do just about anything they might ever want to do within limits of the money available. Local authorities in England now receive very roughly 60% of their income from central government under what is known as the Rate Support Grant and make up the rest from household rates. This procedure represents a major element in governmental economic policy.

Reference has already been made to Stephen Mennell's Report on local government in which he suggests that municipal authorities throughout Europe are guilty of failing to establish a clear policy towards the arts or to create a committee structure with the authority to handle the responsibilities which are now theirs through the decentralizing policies of central government. But the various levels of regional and local government are still very complex.

The history of theatrical decentralization in Britain follows a wholly different pattern from that of its European neighbours. During the eighteenth and nineteenth centuries well over 300 theatres were built over the country and a vigorous system of touring was established. The basis of this touring was commercial: there was no movement towards a cultural theatre until the latter part of the nineteenth century and then it was confined almost wholly to London.

The Repertory Theatre movement

The British Repertory theatre movement, comparable to the French policy of decentralization, emerged in the first decade of this century, although the concept of community theatres had been foreshadowed by that remarkable Victorian, Matthew Arnold, in the 1870s. One of the great benefactresses of the movement was the redoubtable Miss Annie Horniman, a tea heiress, who in 1903 gave money to W. B. Yeats to found the Abbey Theatre, Dublin, and who in 1907 bought, and in 1908 opened, the Gaiety Theatre, Manchester, thus giving rise to one of the first schools of regional playwrights. In 1921 the Gaiety Theatre closed in an atmosphere of defeatism and the belief that the theatre could only be sustained in a city with the size, wealth, and sophistication of London (17).

Another great patron of the theatre, Sir Barry Jackson, opened the Birmingham Repertory Theatre in 1913 and proved by persistence that a provincial city could indeed support a theatre and make a significant contribution to the country's culture through the plays it stages and the actors it employs to interpret them.

By the 1930s there were, in addition to the many hundreds of touring theatres, well over a hundred Repertory theatres. They were not in fact proper repertory theatres for they staged plays sequentially and with a few exceptions ran each production for only a certain period, usually a week. Even the Old Vic staged a new Shakespeare production every three weeks, 'end-on', never sustaining several plays in repertory.

The Arts Council of Great Britain (18)

The post-war theatre in Britain has been transformed by the creation of the Arts Council of Great Britain, the result of a decision in 1942 to give permanent form to the Council for Encouragement of Music and the Arts (CEMA), an organization which had been established at the outbreak of the 1939-45 war to bring music and drama to the armed forces and the people of an embattled island. The Council was established by Royal Charter on 10 August, 1946.

The Arts Council of Great Britain is a QUANGO (Quasi-Autonomous-Non-Governmental Organization), funded directly by the Treasury. The total grant is negotiated by a Minister whose political seniority and departmental 'back-up' has been subject, in recent years, to political change. (It is a matter for debate whether the Minister with responsibility for the arts should hold cabinet rank or be a Junior Minister, as the present incumbent, within the Department of Education and Science). The Office of Arts and Libraries now handles a total budget of some £180 million of which the theatre receives a small proportion (about £17 million) within

84

the total Arts Council's budget of about £80 million (figures for 1981-82). But the so-called 'arms length principle', by which the Minister for the Arts plays no part in Arts Council decisions on how the grant should be spent, has been respected throughout the Council's existence.

The members of the Council, its chairman and the secretary-general, though appointed by the minister are not political appointments and hold office entirely independent of the government in power.

The Council consists of not more than 18 members appointed for not more than five years. They are unpaid. The constitution requires the appointment of committees to be called the Scottish Arts Council and the Welsh Arts Council

The chief executive officer is the Secretary-General who may appoint 'such other persons' as the Council may require for the administration of the organization.

Although the executive work of the Council is the responsibility of the Secretary-General and his staff working to the Council itself, considerable advice is provided by a number of panels consisting of an unspecified number of 'experts' who sift through the requests for grant and discuss any other matters of Council policy on which their advice may be sought. The main panels are those for drama, music, visual arts and literature; the extending interests and responsibilities of the Council were reflected in the creation of an increasing number of panels, but recently, in the interests of efficiency and economics, there has been a simplification of the whole administration. The recent emergence of 'Fringe' companies in drama and dance and the increasing prevalence of productions using 'mixed or multi-media' forms are examples of national trends to which the panel structure of the Council tries to respond.

The Arts Council's main source of income is in the form of grant-in-aid from the Treasury. A proposal that such grants should be made on a triennial basis giving both the Council and its clients an opportunity to plan three years ahead was an unhappy victim of the country's economic difficulties.

Figures for grant-in-aid over the last 30 years show a steady if erratic increase from £235,000 in 1945-46 to £81 million in 1980-81. The Scottish allocation has remained at about 12% of the total and the Welsh at about 7%, figures that are roughly related to the populations of the two countries.

The Council's original charter of 1946 did not spell out the objectives for which the Council had been created; but in that year Lord Keynes, one of its founders and its first chairman, described its function in these words:

The purpose of the Arts Council of Great Britain is to create an environment, to breed a spirit, to cultivate an opinion, to offer a stimulus to such purpose that the artist and the public can each sustain and live on the other in that union which occasionally existed in the past or the great ages of communal civilized life.

In the Annual Report for 1948-49 the then acting chairman, Sir Ernest Pooley, suggested that 'We want to support, encourage, advise', objectives that became apparent when the Council's aims were more clearly described in its charter of 1965:

1 to develop and improve the knowledge, understanding and practice of the arts (clearly an educational objective);
2 to increase the accessibility of the arts to the public throughout Great Britain (the diffusion of the arts);
3 to advise and co-operate with the Department of our government, local authorities, and other bodies on any matter concerned either directly or indirectly with the foregoing objectives.

In fact these objectives still remain extremely vague. With reference to the first it might be asked whose knowledge, understanding and practice are to be developed and improved? Knowledge and understanding might be held to apply largely to the general public; practice is something different and involves practicing artists. Yet the Council has been discouraged from involving itself in education or training. Recent change of policy with the appointment of education officers is one of the most productive of recent developments.

The accessibility of the arts has been achieved with reasonable success by support for all kinds of theatres, producing managements, drama and dance companies and parallel activities in the other arts. There is absolutely no doubt that by the simple act of subsidizing a great range and variety of theatrical activity the theatrical life of the country has been transformed.

The third of the Council's objectives, its responsibility to encourage and cooperate with various forms of regional activity was first discussed in the report for 1953-54 in connection with proposals for a Civic Arts Trust, a project which has now been superceded by the Regional Arts Associations which will be considered in the next chapter.

The authority of the Council derives from two sources: its ability to buy its way into an advisory role by means of the conditions it lays down governing subsidy, and the professional expertise of the members of its advisory panels. This is a point at which the critics make a sharp thrust, claiming that the Council's methods of choosing its panels by invitation is undemocratic.

Critics of the Council also harp on vagueness of objectives. The then Secretary-General writing in the Annual Report for 1952-53 rashly stated that 'public patronage, whatever form it takes, must select its roles and objectives with precision.' The Council has perhaps been wise in just not doing this; for precision leads to inflexibility and the Council in a quite remarkable manner has been able to adapt its policies to rapidly changing conditions without ever appearing to change its basic attitudes.

The Council has been the victim of its own success. As a small organization it could clearly choose how to spend its money. But with increasingly varied demands it has been both under the necessity of defining its objectives and yet increasingly less able to do so.

At the same time policy must be distinguished from objectives. The latter are reasonably clear: they provide for a diffusion of the arts while maintaining the highest possible standards of performance. Its policy is the means by which these objectives are to be achieved. It is here that difficulties arise. For while it is democratically proper that the Council should be advised by panels of experts representing many different points of view, it is exceedingly unlikely, through the very composition of these panels, that these many differing points of view can be reconciled into a clearly defined policy. This, as we have suggested, may be advantageous. It would be a wholly different matter in a theatre where the views of director, company, and other members of the ensemble synthesise in a unified production. But the Arts Council must reflect and respond to an almost infinite variety of attitudes and demands.

The aim of creating new audiences is an example of uncertainty in an important field. In his Annual Report for 1962-63 the Secretary-General wrote that 'In the long debate between 'Raise or Spread?' the decision has been adopted to put standards first . . . High values in the arts can only be maintained on a restricted scale'. Diffusion, he continues, inevitably involves the debasement of standards. Enough has already been said on this subject to emphasize its questionable implications.

That standards are absolute, measurable and definable, is an assumption profoundly open to question. It is, we would venture to say, exceedingly dangerous, in a changing and developing culture, to take as a platform for artistic expediency the imposition or preservation of 'standards' that have survived from other cultural periods. No one will ever admit in public that standards do not matter, but it is arguable that in terms of public expenditure they must be seen in relation to, not dissociated from other objectives.

There is a further responsibility to be faced by any funding organisation. It was first raised by the Secretary-General in his Annual Report for 1955-56.

There is another function which the Arts Council is seeking to develop: that of encouraging the production of new work in music, drama, poetry and painting. Just as scholarship depends upon experiment and research, so do the arts need replenishment by contemporary innovation.

And this is really the crux of the matter. It is not very difficult to sustain an organization by granting it subsidy or furthering its demise by withholding it. What is difficult to estimate is whether the present system of subsidizing companies is the most effective way of encouraging creative work in the theatre. Critics point out that in the Council's budget for 1979-80, which amounted to some £63 million, the overall allocation for awards and bursaries to artists, including training schemes, was in the region of £770,000, or about 1% of gross, a higher proportion than in previous years. What has to be decided is whether the artist is best helped by an individual grant or a grant to the organization by which his work is made public, the orchestra that will perform his music, the publisher that will print his book, the gallery that will display his pictures, or the theatrical company that will stage his plays. That is why the present analysis of the institutions that grant subsidy and the establishments that receive it is important.

It is arguable that in political terms the most serious problem facing the Arts Council in the 1980s, and any other central organization responsible for funding the arts, is the decentralization of responsibility and the democratization of the process. This is a subject to be discussed more fully below.

Italy (19)

The Republic of Italy is divided into 20 regions each with its own elected government and certain legislative powers. Five of these regions are autonomous - Sicily, Sardinia, Aosta, Trentino-Alto Adige (South Tyrol), and Friuli-Venezia Giulia (with Trieste as its capital). Reorganization of the remaining regions has not yet been completed. They receive a high proportion of their financial needs from central government and possess certain fund-raising powers of their own.

The country's basic problem of disparity between a fully industrialized north and somewhat impoverished south is emphasized by the fact the 50% of the country's theatrical activity takes place in the north, 12% in the south.

The provinces are decentralized administrative areas, largely concerned with health and education, within the regions.

The Communes (municipalities) are the smallest administrative units. Rome is the biggest with a population of over 2.5 million. There are 37 towns (communi) with a population of over 100,000.

There is no legal requirement for a municipal council to make an allocation in its budget for cultural activities, but some of them do so. When this is the case it is for a committee of the council, chaired by the mayor, to make detailed recommendations. These must be signed by the town clerk who is an employee of the state. It is interesting to note that the Italian town clerk, rather like the French *Prefet*, is the person through whom central government exercises a certain control over local authority spending. The town clerk forwards the application to the appropriate department at the head of which there is an *Assessore* who will examine the documentation and give instructions for payment to the executive officer concerned.

Italy became a unified state only in 1870; its subsequent history led to the planning of a new constitution in 1946 but a number of internal difficulties have delayed its full implementation. The basic problem facing subsequent governments has been the need to preserve political unification while respecting traditional loyalty to the regions, a situation that suggests the country might develop a federal structure like Germany or Switzerland rather than a centralized one like France. It so happens, however, that the country's links with France have for long been close and there has been a tendency for the Italians to copy French centralized procedures even to the appointment of regional prefects (*Prefetta*).

The political and economic instability of the country has delayed full implementation of the 1948 constitution, particularly so far as it affects local authorities; who, as a result of recent modification of local fiscal laws, are relatively poorer than they were ten years ago, with little authority to raise their own taxes and dependant on disbursements by central government. Although local government is potentially democratic in structure, finances are so centralized that only about 3-4% of the gross national revenue goes to local authorities in the form of grant.

Although the Italian government is not ungenerous in its theatrical subsidies, there are only eleven permanent regional theatres in a country with 37 towns with a population of over 100,000 compared with 19 in France and about 50 in Great Britain.

The left-wing parties, in order to win control of central government, have concentrated on local government with some success. The Communists in particular tend to favour subsidy for the arts as a means of encouraging local demand and providing local employment. In this aim they enjoy the active support of the unions.

An unusual figure in Italian local government is the officer, known as the *Assessore*. In Milan, for example, there are 18. They carry a variety of portfolios. In Emilia Romagna there is an Assessore who combines Culture, Fine Art, Tourism, and Information; in Milan, Cultural Initiative and Institutions together with Spectacles; in Rome there is an Assessore for Antiquities, Fine Art, Archives, Culture, Exhibitions, Tourism, Spectacles, Youth and Publicity - a truly cultured man.

Under the assessori are a variety of superintendants and inspectors (*sovraintendenzi*), who are officers employed by the council. The chief executive of La Scala Opera House, Milan, is such an officer, answerable to the Assessore of the Commune of Milan who in turn is answerable to the *Sindaco* or Mayor.

The Netherlands (20)

The Netherlands is a constitutional and hereditary monarchy with the central executive power of the state resting with the crown, and the central legislative power vested in the crown and parliament. The constitution of 1917 introduced an electoral system based on universal franchise and proportional representation.

The kingdom is divided into 11 provinces and 957 municipalities. The provincial governments are empowered to issue ordinances concerning the welfare of the province and to raise certain taxes; the municipalities may also issue bye-laws and raise taxes but the latter do not amount to a very significant proportion of their gross expenditure, most of the money for which they receive from the central government. (Taxes are mostly of the direct kind on income and property). Both provincial and municipal governments have to work in close collaboration with central government.

A municipal council is presided over by a major or burgomaster whose authority, like that of the French prefet, may in certain circumstances be considerable.

Municipal councils vary considerable in their policies but they receive grant-in-aid from central government to cover sport, education and culture: they may determine themselves the proportion they give to each.

Local groups can put effective pressure on central government whose administrators, the civil service, have considerable freedom of manoeuvre 'within the meaning of the act'.

The total population of the country is something over 12 million. There are 15 towns with a population in excess of 100,000, Amsterdam and Rotterdam having an 'urban agglomeration' of over one million.

The Directorate General of Cultural Affairs at the Ministry of Culture, Recreation and Social Welfare is divided into the Museums and Archives Directorate and the Arts Directorate. The latter is further divided into a number of divisions, one of which deals with literature and drama.

Each of the 11 provinces has a cultural council which has less to spend and spends less on the arts than similar councils in the towns. (This is a common phenomenon.) They tend to concentrate on servicing the smaller towns and villages. The towns have a department of the municipal council for dealing with such cultural and artistic responsibilities as the town theatre. As was said above, their policies vary considerably. Rotterdam is reputedly generous to the visual arts. Emmen, a town of 74,000 inhabitants has recently built an extensive arts centre. Interesting material on the cultural life of Apeldoorn will be found in *Cultural policy in towns* (op. cit.)

The *Netherlands Arts Council* was established by law in the 1950s. A revision of its policy came into force in late 1979. Its main function is to advise the Minister on policy for the arts. The Council consists of 50 members carefully selected by a small committee to be representative of the 200 or so cultural organizations invited to propose members. They are organized in three interdisciplinary departments with more detailed work being carried out by specialist committees. A recent discussion document, *Raad voor de kunst - uitgangspunten voor een drama en theaterbelied* [*Advice on art - starting-point for a drama and theatre policy*] carefully avoids the former governmental mistake of proposing a policy for theatre without first having involved and consulted those whom the proposed policy is most likely to effect.

Sweden (21)

The kingdom of Sweden is a constitutional monarchy with power vested in the Prime Minister and his cabinet. The Parliament (Riksdag) is a single chamber with 349 members.

Government ministries are staffed by civil servants of wide experience who act as advisers to the ministers and carry out the routine administration of their department. They are permitted a good deal of independence but are under an obligation to cooperate with each other and to submit proposals to the government concerning policy. They have far less administrative authority than French and British ministries.

Local administration in the 23 counties (Landsting) is entrusted to a Prefect who is appointed by the government as in France and Italy. Local councils can raise their own income tax independently of national income-tax but using the same basis for taxation. They also receive grant-in-aid from the government for such purposes as teachers' salaries, school construction, and fire control. There have recently been considerable increases in the local rates.

As in other countries, the Landsting do not carry much responsibility for cultural activities. This is left to the Communes of which there are 277. Only three towns have a population of more than 100,000 - Stockholm (788,000), Goteborg (422,000), and Malmo (250,000). Only 11 other towns have a population of over 50,000.

The Ministry of Education and Cultural Affairs is responsible for all cultural activities, but the government as a whole interests itself to an unusual extent in social and cultural matters. This is evident in the fact that Sweden spends 25% of its national budget on social services which it is able to do as a result of very high per capita industrial output.

Before putting large-scale reforms before Parliament, the government usually has the matter investigated by a commission. When the commission has made its recommendations, the various interested parties are given the opportunity to express their point of view. The matter is then presented before Parliament and becomes law, or is rejected. The whole process is extremely democratic but sometimes rather prolonged.

On 1 January 1969, the government formed the National Council for Cultural Affairs (Kulturradet) to investigate co-ordination among cultural workers; long term aims of state measures in the cultural field; collaboration between governmental, municipal and other agencies.

The aims are remarkably similar to those of the Arts Council of Great Britain which were noted above. The Swedish Council consists of a chairman and fourteen members who include representatives of unions involved with the arts and conducts its work through three major panels, one covering theatre, dance, and music; one for literature and public libraries; one for art, museums and exhibitions. As with its British counter-part, it allocates funds provided by central government, but it differs in one important respect that the secretary-general is a political appointment.

The cultural history of Sweden since 1945 deserves far more detailed consideration than can be given it here. The Social Democrats assumed that a high level of culture would be a natural result of economic prosperity. When it was realized around the year 1960 that in a period of economic expansion many artists were unable to support themselves by their art, the Social Democrats set about launching a vigorous cultural policy, insisting, however, that it should be a genuinely popular culture including amateur artists and cultural workers at every social level. This was the movement that gave rise to the National Council.

One of the first major acts of the Council was the publication in 1973 of a booklet entitled *A New Cultural Policy in Sweden*. It constitutes the most thorough survey of the condition of the arts, and its recommendations have launched widespread discussions from which valuable developments have arisen. Cultural policy is encapsulated in eight basic principles which have been unanimously agreed by Parliament:

1   freedom of speech
2   wide opportunities for creative activities
3   combatting excessive commercialism
4   cultural decentralization
5   needs of the disadvantaged
6   artistic renewal
7   preserving historical continuity
8   promotion of international exchange

It is clear that these objectives are social rather than artistic, generalized rather than particular. But it is significant to find a Swedish sociologist criticizing the proposals under the rather brutal heading, *Seven Mortal Sins in Swedish Cultural Policy* (22). Professor Swedner, who had been a critic of high culture (*finkultur*) in the 1960s, claims that:

- the report shows too much concern in promoting a certain kind of cultural policy;
- it makes too great an assumption that culture is created in the big cities and then portioned out to the rest of the country;
- and too great an assumption that education is sufficient to destroy the existing cultural élite;
- it assumed too readily that the art and culture that are now being produced and distributed are the most significant art that is now being created;
- he claims that self-expression is still far too closely related to and identified with inherited form and traditional structures - plays, concerts, canvases, novels, etc;
- there is too great a concern with standards of perfection established by professional artists and critics;
- the report discusses culture as if it were an embellishment rather than a form of communication.

This is a very clear statement of the issues that have now become fundamental to the development of a cultural policy, and which are raised virtually whenever cultural policy is discussed. They are based on the growing polarity between traditional bourgeois culture, of which the mainstream of Western European art is the most relevant manifestation, and an art which at the moment defies definition. It is not folk art, for this has been largely destroyed in the highly industrialized countries: folk dance and music survive but not as a living meaningful tradition; not is it a popular art as was manifested in the English Music Halls of the nineteenth century. It is a kind of community art, concerned with process rather than product. Its theatrical expression will be the subject of Chapter 7.

The greatest danger lies in the wholesale dismissal of one of these areas of culture by supporters of the other, for in fact there is a constant and vigorous process of cross-fertilization. But the problems facing cultural administrators in apportioning subsidy between two opposing concepts, neither of which is clearly defined, is not easy. It is a recurrent problem.

Switzerland (23)
Switzerland is a Republic of which some 70% is mountains. Of the population of something over six million, 74% speak German (Alémanique); 20% French (Romand), to the west of the country; 4% Italian, almost wholly in the southern canton of Ticino; and 1% Rhaeto-Romansche, a language that is said to have survived from the Christian-Latin court of Charlemagne. In German-speaking Switzerland a number of dialects are spoken which are generally known as Schwyzerdeutsch.

Switzerland has a federal constitution, probably the most democratic in Europe, dating from 1848, the country's perpetual neutrality having been guaranteed in 1815. The central government, constituted on the most democratic lines, is responsible for customs, post, railways, finance and the armed forces. It guarantees the cantonal system which is the basic political structure of the country.

There are 26 cantons, each with its own elected parliament, law courts and exchequer, responsible for all major services including education, and all cultural matters over which they have soveriegnty.

The smallest political unit is the Commune of which there are over 3,000. There are five towns and conurbations with a population of over 100,000—Zürich, Basle, Berne, Geneva and Lausanne; while Winterthür, St. Gallen, Lucerne, and Biel have populations of over 50,000 and the lively town of La Chaux-de-Fonds, 42,000.

One of the most remarkable aspects of Swiss democracy is the system by which any amendment to the constitution or any act of parliament must be submitted to a referendum if a sufficient number of citizens demand one. The system operates even more intensively at cantonal and communal than at national level.

There is no centrally raised income tax in the country. The confederation depends for its funds, with one or two exceptions, on indirect taxation. The contribution of the confederation to art and cultural is almost wholly for the preservation of the country's cultural heritage, for museums and adult education. Contemporary culture is the responsibility of canton and commune.

As we have found in other countries the contribution of the communes to the theatre is far bigger than that of the larger unit, the cantons. It is, however, the responsibility of the cantons to help the smaller and poorer communes, although it is not a legal obligation. But even the cantons have limited resources and the Clottu report on Swiss cultural policy points regretfully to the Ticino where cultural activity is at such low ebb that the area is described as 'being in danger of becoming a corridor between Zürich and Milan'.

The cultural problems of the country are not dissimilar from those of Belgium. Here is the same small overall population speaking in this case three major languages. In spite of the ethnic identity of the Swiss people it is difficult for French-speaking Switzerland which borders on France, not to be influenced by the highly centralized French culture emanating from Paris. Similarly, German-speaking Swiss looked on Germany as their Fatherland until the Third Reich drove them back on their own resources. Since the 1939-45 War the Swiss have been making particular efforts to create their own cultural identity; but the Report makes a number of references to the absence of collaboration not only between the different linguistic areas but between the cantons themselves.

The only centrally-funded organization helping the theatre is the Zürich-based foundation, Pro Helvetia. Its establishment in 1934 is an interesting example of the policy imposed upon a country that has three main linguistic areas all adjacent to major powers. It was a result of this situation which made it impossible for Switzerland to establish cultural agreement or political treaties with the surrounding powers. When in the 1930s ideological pressures from surrounding countries became harmful to the structure of the state, the government set up the Foundation Pro Helvetia, as a non-governmental organization, to uphold Switzerland's cultural heritage and to foster the arts through, not inspite of, the cantons and the different linguistic regions, since direct interference by the state in the cultural life of the country had at all costs to be avoided (24).

The Report describes the interesting situation that arose in Switzerland after the 1939-45 War. Many people were impressed with the speed and efficiency with which the Germans rebuilt the theatres that had been destroyed, making them increasingly 'more perfect and luxurious'. They wished to do the same although their own theatres had not been destroyed, merely grown old; and not wanting to be a target for criticism, certain authorities launched into elaborate and costly projects. But in general the country followed its own typically federalist policies; various kinds of rebuilding took place in most of the large towns while almost everywhere the building of a new theatre became the subject of endless discussion. An individual note points to the fact that the geographic distribution of theatres in Switzerland has a historical origin responding to the interests of the 19th century bourgeoisie. What is now required is not so much a chain of theatres in the smaller towns but of Maisons de la Culture where modest regional theatrical activity can be fostered alongside a general cultural development based on the vitality of the Swiss amateur theatre (see page 285).

The situation is aggravated by the fact that only Zürich and Geneva are large enough to support separate theatres for opera and drama; elsewhere a single theatre has to serve both although the needs of each are becoming increasingly different. While the tendency is for drama theatres to become smaller, operatic performances still require considerable resources of space and equipment. Although this is a problem that faces every country, it is more acute in countries like Switzerland where there are few large centres of population.

The democratization of cultural policy

It is a reason for regret that discussion of cultural policy should not be more widespread: a rare example of a debate on the democratic administration of cultural organizations took place at the Fourth Congress of the French theatrical unions in November 1977. Discussion was based upon the demand that workers in every sector of cultural activity should have a voice in the framing of policy and greater control of their conditions of work. There should be developed a more flexible method of subsidizing the national theatres with a redefinition of their objectives. This should be accompanied by a recognition of the individual requirements of each of the National Drama Centres, the relation of subsidy to the cost-of-living index, and an extension of contracts from three to five years. The recommendations include specific proposals for the establishment of six National Drama Centres for young people, the creation of ten permanent companies and the discontinuation of subsidy for the 100 or so companies *'hors commission'* (see page 131).

It is possible to see these demands as a further example of the widespread need for involvement. Methods of subsidizing the arts indeed require flexibility. Sharp distinctions between central authority and the localities where practical work is being carried out can only produce insensitivity in the former and a sense of isolation in the latter. The arguments that might apply to workers' involvement in industrial management are not necessarily relevant to the theatre. For the theatre is an art, a social art. It is a response to social pressures. And whatever may be the room for manoeuvre of the individual artist in the theatre - and it is a good deal less in the performing than in the more individual arts - in the collective act of presenting a play to a public there is room for a creative contribution from every member of the ensemble. The hierarchy that calls the actor an artist and the scene-shifter a labourer is as inappropriate as the political pressures that have resulted in the technical staff in some theatres in some countries being paid more highly than the performers, or even the artistic director, a situation by no means unknown in Great Britain. (25).

The next point to be considered is how these mechanisms and procedures, reflecting a considerable variety of historical precedent, political
organization and individual initiative have worked out in practice.
Since continual cross-reference would make the book totally unreadable,
it is hoped that the interested reader will be able to make his own
links between the patterns that have been described above and the
practices that are to be described below.

Sources

(1)   J. C. Banks - *Federal Britain* - Harrap, London, 1971
(2)   Stephen Mennell - *Cultural Policy in Towns* - C.C.C. Strasbourg,
      1976 and F.M.M. Lewes and Stephen Mennell - *Leisure, Culture
      and Local Government* - University of Exeter, 1976
(3)   *Theaterstatistik* 1978-79 (for details see note 14 below).
(4)   Facts quoted in this section have been culled from Europa Year-
      book, 1977; each country's London Embassy and home Ministry.
(5)   Teater Jaarboek voor Vlaanderen, 1976-77
(7)   ATAC Information no. 92 March, 1978
(8)   Alain Peyrefitte - *Le Mal Francais* - Plon, 1976
(9)   F. F. Ridley (editor) - *Specialists and Generals*: a comparative
      study of the professional civil servant - Allen and Unwin, London,
      1978
(10) Denis Gontard - *La Décentralisation Théâtral en France 1895 - 1952*
      -SEDES, Paris, 1973; and Mlle Laurent in conversation. See also
      People's Theatre in France - Theatre Quarterly no. 23, 1976
(11) For example, Charles Dullin - *Ce Sont les Dieux qu'il Nous Faut* -
      F.R.F. Gallimard, 1969
(12) John Ardagh - *The New France* - Penguin, 1968; but the French
      Ministry of Culture has been extremely helpful in supplying
      information.
(13) Jean Dasté - *Le Voyage d'un Comédien* - Stock, Paris, 1976
(14) Detailed statistics on all aspects of the West German theatre are
      published in *Theaterstatistik* (referred to above); Die *Ausgaben der
      Länder für Kunst und Kulturpflege*, published by the Sekretariat
      of the Kulturministerkonferenz, Bonn; and the German Centre of
      the International Theatre Institute. More generalized figures but
      presented in a readable form can be found in Werner Schulze-
      Reimpell's *Development and Structure of the Theatre*.

(15) Information supplied by the West German Centre, of the I.T.I., Berlin and the Ministeriel-dirigent for Bavaria.

(16) Manfred Boatzkes - *Weimar Bracht die Wende* - Reminiszenz (origin unknown).

(17) Rex Pogson - *Miss Horniman and the Gaiety Theatre* - Rockliff, 1952.

(18) Eric Walter White - *The Arts Council of Great Britain* - Poynter-Davis, 1976; John S. Harris - *Government Patronage of the Arts in Great Britain* - University of Chicago Press, 1970; and John Elsom - *Post-war British Theatre* - Routledge and Kegan Paul, London, 1976: and John Pick (editor), *The State and The Arts*, John Offord, 1981.

(19) Information supplied by the Italian Institute, London, and *Education Profile - Italy* - British Council, Rome, 1976

(20) Information supplied by Netherlands Centre of I.T.I., Amsterdam.

(21) Information supplied by Swedish Cultural Council and Swedish Institute, Stockholm. See also Nils Gunnar Nilsson, *Swedish Cultural Policy in the 20th Century*, Swedish Institute.

(22) Stephen Mennell (editor) - *Explorations in Cultural Policy and Research* - Council for Cultural Cooperation, Strasbourg, 1978.

(23) A considerable amount of information on Switzerland has been gathered from *Eléments pour une Politique Culturelle en Suisse* - Berne, 1975, one of the few attempts that have been made to establish an overall national cultural policy based on a detailed analysis of the existing situation. Referred to in text as the Clottu Report.

(24) Michael Stettler - *Image of Switzerland: Pro Helvetia's activities abroad* - privately printed.

(25) Anyone interested in pursuing further diverse proposals for cultural policy should read - *The Arts and the People: Labour's policy towards the arts* - London, 1977;
John Elsom - *The Arts: Change or Choice* - London, 1978 (Discussion paper of the Liberal Party)
The Arts: the Way Forward - A Conservative discussion paper - London, 1978;
As You Like It: A report on private support for the arts by the Bow Group - London, 1978
David Alexander - *A Policy for the Arts* - London, 1978.

5. The Structure of the Theatre

The National Theatre
It is no accident that national theatres have usually existed in countries that enjoyed a strong political identity in the period of the great courts of Europe, France and Sweden, for example, but not in countries which found their national indentity when monarchy was in decline, such as Italy, Belgium and the Netherlands. The case of Britain is exceptional and will be discussed below (1).

Theoretically, anything called 'national' must be a product or service which is financed by the state and which is therefore at the disposal of the citizens of that state. This interpretation can apply to a nationalized industry like the railways or the postal service, less happily to a theatre. A theatre-building can be owned and financed by the state; but a single building can hardly be run for the benefit of the people of that state, for a theatre is a place that gives performances and this is of little benefit for those who live at the farther extremities of the country. 'National' is therefore an epithet with wide and not always fortunate connotations.

The first National Theatre in Europe was the Comédie Française, created by Louis XIV in 1681. This was no great visionary act but the result of a request by the King of Molière's widow to combine the two existing Parisian companies. It has remained the recipient of the largest government subsidy of any French theatre; but it has provided a sense of cultural and intensely Gallic continuity, with a company of the greatest distinction and productions that are comparable with those of any other European theatre. Its somewhat hierarchical structure of *sociétaires* and *pensionnaires* and its public status derive from Napoleonic laws of 1804 and the Moscow decree of 1812 (2).

In a number of other European capitals we find that there is a large theatre dating from the seventeenth or eighteenth century, generously subsidized, but which without perhaps being called a national theatre functions in that capacity. There is such a theatre in Stockholm, the Dramaten, or Royal Dramatic Theatre, which was founded in 1788 by the stage-struck King Gustav III with the status of a national theatre; it became the responsibility of the state in 1880.

The Belgium National Theatre was opened in Brussels in 1945 in a building dating from the early nineteenth century. It is an autonomous institution controlled by a private administrative council which appoints its own director. It is required to stage a minimum of 200 performances a year and to include at least one play by a Belgian author. For this it depends largely on the works of Maurice Maeterlink, Herman Closson, Michael Ghelderode, and Fernand Crommelynk. It employs a company of between 80 and 120 players on a variety of contracts. (The company of the British National Theatre numbers over 150).

The oldest theatre in Brussels, the Théâtre de la Monnaie, is now the home of the Belgian National Opera. The Flemish National Theatre, Koninklijke Vlaamse Schouwburg, was opened in 1875 and the Royal Netherlands Theatre, Koninklijke Nederlandse Schouwburg in Antwerp in the same year (3).

In Germany there was a short-lived national theatre in Hamburg in 1767; it was associated with Lessing at the time he was writing the *Hamburg Dramaturgy*; a National Theatre was founded in Mannheim in 1778 and is still referred to as such; in 1797 King Frederick II turned a theatre in Berlin, where the Comédie Française played regularly, into a Royal National Theatre. We have noted above the recent outcome of these moves.

Great Britain has created a National Theatre at a time when the very concept has become something of an anachronism. Its history has been idiosyncratic and closely related to attempts to do honour to Shakespeare who is by way of being accepted as a 'national' dramatist.

The three Swedish national theatres, the Royal Opera, the Royal Dramatic Theatre, and the National Touring Theatre received in 1980-1 a central government subsidy of 234 m. SKr. out of a total of 350 m. SKr. (66.86%, about £30 m.).

The British National Theatre

The idea of a national theatre was born out of a spirit of renascent nationalism that emerged in the nineteenth century and resulted in the building of the British Museum in 1823 and the National Gallery in 1824. The first important statement in favour of a national theatre was made in 1848 by a London publisher, a whig, and an enthusiast for unusual causes, Mr. Effingham Wilson. He was supported by the historical novelist, Sir Edward Bulwer-Lytton, and some years later by that great educationalist, Matthew Arnold, who in 1879 was much excited by a visit of the Comédie Française to London. Sir Henry Irving was an unenthusiastic supporter of the proposal but it was William Archer, a notable dramatic critic who, in collaboration with Harley Granville-Barker, first produced a detailed scheme which included for the first time, so far as we have been able to ascertain, the concept of two auditoria within a single building.

Meanwhile a second pressure group was moving into action, motivated by the conviction that the plays of Shakespeare merited a special theatre and one that, in the view of William Poel, should be as far as possible a replica of the Globe. In 1908 the Shakespeare Memorial Theatre Movement merged with the National Theatre Movement to create the Shakespeare Memorial National Theatre Committee.

Mr. Geoffrey Whitworth describes the aims of the committee as follows (4).

1 to create a worthy memorial to Shakespeare;
2 to create an exemplary theatre that would offer productions of British and foreign classics with the highest standard of performance;
3 to create a central theatre that would spread throughout the country an appreciation of great drama as a major factor in popular education.

Another ideal, less frequently expressed, was to set standards in the payment and treatment of theatrical workers.

Subsequent formulations of policy all tended to develop these three ideals with continuing support for both the Shakespeare Memorial and the National Theatre. The former proposal, however, was more or less satisfied by the establishment of the Shakespeare Memorial Theatre in Stratford-on-Avon as a result of the initiative of a family of Warwickshire brewers, the Flowers. The theatre was granted a Royal Charter in 1925; was destroyed by fire in 1926; reopened in 1932 and has become an establishment of national and international distinction. The National Theatre was a good deal longer in gestation. A company was formed in 1963 under the direction of Sir Laurence Olivier and moved into the present complex on the South Bank under the direction of Sir Peter Hall in 1976. The country therefore has the benefit of virtually two national theatres (5).

The question now to be considered is whether the aims of the British National Theatre are valid in terms of national theatre as a principle.

The only parallel set of aims we have are those for the Belgian National Theatre. We can dispense with the memorial to Shakespeare since this has been satisfied by the creation of the Stratford theatre. Common ideals include proposals:

To create a theatre offering a wide range of national and international plays with a high standard of production. This is agreed by both companies. What must be asked is whether a specifically national theatre is required for this. It should be the aim for any major theatre. Subsidy may be required for its realization but not, one might have thought, national status.

101

CARL A. RUDISILL LIBRARY
LENOIR RHYNE COLLEGE

To play before as wide audiences as possible. The Belgians carry out this aim with an energetic programme of touring and *'animations'*. The British talk more vaguely about the educational value of great drama; the National Theatre, for reasons involving the employment of actors in the three theatres, has no consistent policy or record of touring.

To improve the status and conditions of actors. Sir Peter Hall has been at pains to offer contracts that offer as reasonable conditions of work to the company as circumstances allow; but in a mixed economy, the interests of actors are also mixed.

The Belgians talk about establishing artistic prestige abroad. Reference was made on page 51. A government might well exploit a theatre production for this purpose but such a policy would not have high priority with most directors.

The French have five so-called 'national' theatres, the Comédie Francaise, the Théâtre National Populaire, the Odéon, the Théâtre de l'Est Parisien, and the Théâtre National de Strasbourg. There is a further category of 20 regional theatres described as Centres Dramatiques Nationaux. Both categories are subsidized by central government but those in the latter category receive additional subsidy from their municipalities.

The term 'national' applied to a theatre invokes a high level of subsidy from central government, high standards of presentation, a liberal repertory and good conditions of work for all employees. National theatres, however, are often disparagingly referred to as 'élitist' for reasons that were discussed in an earlier chapter. Their subsidy usually represents a very high proportion of the total subsidy for drama: the Belgian National theatre, 51%; Britain's two national companies, 40%; France's five national theatres, 41%; and the Royal Dramatic Theatre of Sweden, the Dramaten in Stockholm, 15%.

This disproportion is heavily compounded with the addition of the subsidized opera companies which absorb an even higher proportion of the theatrical budget.

The general administrators of the five French national companies are appointed by state 'decree' and given contracts that provide for a minimum number of productions, performances and *'animations'* within their region for a period of three years.

It may be said, therefore, that a national theatre has a responsibility to justify its somewhat privileged position by maintaining standards of performance and defeating the accusations of élitism through a policy of diffusion and energetic marketing at every social level. But it does seem to be the case, as recent experiences in the Paris theatre described in the first chapter testify, that a centralized theatre with a vigorous and stimulating policy can do much to raise the interest of the community in the theatre as a whole. On the other hand it is for the fund-awarding authorities to see a national theatre in the total context of the theatre.

A final point: most subsidized theatres are encouraged to 'maximize' their box-office receipts by increasing the price of seats to the point at which there will be a diminuation of returns when the public refuses to pay more. On the other hand there is a surviving tradition that by lowering the price of seats a manager is encouraging wider support for his theatre. This does not seem to be born out in practice. Lower seat prices do not induce new audiences but enable regular theatre-goers to come more often. The success of the Glyndebourne Opera and performances at the Opera House in the Palace of Versailles show that some people are ready to pay very high prices for seats at genuinely illustrious performances. Further research into ticket-pricing policies is urgently needed (6).

Decentralization

If there is to be in a certain country a theatre or a group of theatres which by virtue of subsidy and prestige can be described as mainstream theatres, they are likely to be found in the bigger towns, conurbations, and centres of population. This, too, is where the independant commercial theatres will be strongest. But there are many people, and the European Ministers of Culture are evidently to be included, who will be far from satisfied by this state of affairs. We have already made clear that a vigorous national theatre should not be élitist, limited socially to a privileged class or geographically to the major conurbations. There are forms of culture such as the theatre which can more readily be organized in the big towns, but few people are going to argue that the small towns should be left without the possibility of a reasonable range of cultural and artistic activities. Political devolution and artistic decentralization, as we have already noted, are the order of the day. 'Die stadt macht frei' says an old German proverb, and the so-called 'culture gap' must be filled.

In administrative terms the process of decentralization has resulted in the assumption of a good deal of responsibility for subsidizing the theatre by the towns, municipalities and communes. This process has fared better in countries such as West Germany with its experience of federal government and Sweden with its considerable social service programme than in the more centralized countries such as France and

Andre Debaar as d'Harpagon in Molière's
'The Miser', Belgium National Theatre, 1981.

The interior of the Belgium National Theatre, Brussels, 1981.

104

Britain where local authorities are not yet organized to assume such new responsibilities.

The contemporary theatre developed in the nineteenth and early twentieth centuries from a dynamic of free enterprise. This seems to be consistent with the nature of art which involves in the first instance a free and unfettered response to the environment on the part of the artist. In a particular kind of society a particular kind of theatre develops. In France the theatrical dynamic in the early years of the century took the form of Gémier's touring caravan; of Copeau's rejection of the Vieux Colombier and retreat into Burgundy; of Dullin's growing conviction that the theatre in Paris would not flourish if the theatre outside Paris did also thrive. In Britain it took the form of a very considerable touring circuit; of the growth of the Repertory theatre movement; and more recently of the emergence of an alternative theatre.

The process of decentralization did not need powerful arguments in Belgium where the division of an already small country between a French and Flemish-speaking population reduced the area that had to be covered to easily manageable proportions. In the Scandinavian countries the force of social-democratic opinion has provided powerful and widely accepted motivations for a decentralized theatre. Germany was wholly decentralized in the eighteenth century with its more than 200 dukedoms and principalities, and when Bismark achieved the unification of the country in 1870 the vestigial remains of that decentralized culture were evident in the many surviving theatres. The history of the Italian theatre is similar, though decentralization is established by means of touring, not by a grid of permanent regional theatres of which in fact there are only eleven. The Netherlands is another country of geographical proportions that ease the problems of decentralization; but its theatre has been going through a phase of uncertainty and reappraisal as central government, local authorities and the profession itself argue the kind of structure most suitable for the nature of the country. Switzerland is similar to Germany in being already politically decentralized.

Yet it becomes all too easy to sneer at the big city as the source of theatrical evils when in practical terms it has much to recommend it. There are large numbers of people within comparatively easy reach of its theatres. It is provided with all the services and resources a theatre needs: restaurants, bookshops and publishers; mass circulation newspapers and their critics; all the supply services; costumiers, wig-makers, carpenters, electricians; furniture-hiring emporia and curtain-hiring firms. This is not to say that one would not find such resources in a provincial town but simply that one would be unlikely to find them in such profusion or in such close proximity. It is a serious thought that the Royal Shakespeare Company with an international reputation and a fine theatre of its own in Stratford-on-Avon, has been obliged to take a London base, the Aldwych Theatre, until its own theatre in the Barbican is completed in 1982, in order to be able to ensure the participation of the country's leading actors and artists in its productions. It may be that London exerts a bigger control on the country than other capitals, though few would deny the dominating position of Paris in terms of French culture; but it is just by reason of this dominance that if decentralization is to work it must be made to work, and be seen to work, and the effort required may be all the more considerable.

Critics of centralization carry their arguments so far as wishing to see London reduced to the status of a provincial city rather than the big provincial cities made into 'little Londons'.

A far more practical issue has been raised by the authors of an important study of theatrical decentralization (7).

> We have proposed that in cultural matters organizations should be decentralized, dynamic, independant, flexible and to a certain extent democratic. No organization can alone meet all these criteria but we have shown in connection with financing of theatres that it is necessary to set up a regional or potential authority between central government and local administration and to give real power.

No country has yet provided such a regional authority standing between central and local government as the authors propose; but it is a question that is widely discussed in Britain in connection with the structure of Regional Arts Associations. It is arguable that such an authority is an essential feature of any genuine decentralization.

Touring

If, therefore, a country's theatre is overcentralized it must be decentralized. There are two ways of achieving this: by touring or by building regional theatres. We will consider touring first.

Actors have gone on tour since earliest times. Even when there have been permanent theatres in the cities they have gone on tour. Shakespeare was probably suffering from many weeks 'on the road' when he wrote,

> Weary with toil I haste me to my bed,
> The dear repose for limbs with travel tired,
> But then begins a journey in my head,
> To work my mind, when body's work's expired.

He must have been familiar with what the industrial worker now calls 'unsociable hours'.

106

Large-scale touring was a product in the late nineteenth century of emergent capitalism. With large amounts of money available for investment, theatres were built in all the larger towns and companies were formed to fill them. Most of them were either metropolitan companies that had completed a successful run and were 'taking to the road', or specially formed touring companies of metropolitan successes. Cheap railways provided transport and wealthy bourgeoisie provided the audiences. It was a world that was destroyed by the 1914-18 War and transformed by new political and social pressures.

Touring, nevertheless, remained a fairly vigorous though dwindling pastime until the 1939-45 War marked the end of a *laissez-faire* society. It was then that a notable change took place in theatrical thinking. Attention was no longer paid to touring: it was apparently considered to be a thing of the past. Annual reports of the Arts Council of Great Britain, a useful indication of what theatrically-speaking is 'in the wind', rarely mention touring. The dynamic lay in the direction of building new theatres. This was not so much because the old ones had been destroyed, although the destruction of theatre-buildings had been widespread in Germany, as because new theatrical ideas were prevalent. And in any case large-scale touring had simply collapsed.

Two reasons have been advanced for this. The whole concept of touring is in a sense imperialistic. The touring manager is taking, in perhaps a slightly adulterated form, productions that have already been seen and approved by metropolitan audiences to audiences in other parts of the country. Charitably, this is no bad thing. If M. Jean-Louis Barrault does a stunning production at the Marigny it is perfectly proper, especially if he is supported with public money, that he should enable audiences in other parts of France to see his work. But there remains a feeling that Parisian achievement is being foisted on the rest of the country. The argument is therefore not so much that touring is a bad thing as an inadequate thing; and the word inadequate brings us up against the second criticism of touring which is based on the question of standards.

It is perfectly possible to tour a distinguished production for a few weeks in carefully selected theatres and preserve standards of performance; but there comes a time when the sheer hazards and discomforts of large-scale touring begin to tell and the best of productions become frayed at the edges. The reasons for this are simple. After the performance on Saturday night the scenery has to be dismantled and packed into a lorry, or the wagon of a goods train, and dispatched to the next theatre where, with luck, it will arrive on Sunday afternoon or evening, when the staff spend a large part of the next 24 hours 'getting-in', 'rigging' and 'setting-up', technical words that are all too familiar to the technical staff who are responsible for organizing the scenery, perhaps in a theatre that is too small to take it, resetting the lights in a theatre that is ill-provided electrically, allocating dressing-rooms, and so on. The cast will similarly spend Sunday travelling, and on arrival at the new town will search for theatrical lodgings and cheap hotels. The picture of theatrical touring in former times that we find in such classics as Scarron's *Le Roman Comique* and Gautier's *Le Capitaine Fracasse* has only been slightly ameliorated by the existence of the motor-car.

A professional lack of enthusiasm for touring has been encouraged by the growing number of regional theatres offering the kind of work which actors prefer to touring; although for management it is more expensive to run a theatre than a tour.

But let's keep to standards for the moment. There is little doubt that the rapid development of television broadcasting since the war has provided provincial audiences with well-written, closely observed plays at negligible expense, and encouraged actors to stay close to a well-paid source of revenue gained with infinitely less effort than by going on tour. Even so the interaction between stage and television drama is considerable. There are few actors and playwrights who do not work for both media when opportunity arises and quality of appreciation can hardly fail to rise. But television does not touch the crucial question of the relationship between the artist and his audiences.

There is no question what the actor thinks about touring. He may be away from his home for weeks or months on end. He lives week after week in theatrical lodgings or cheap hotels. He spends Sunday travelling from one part of the country to another; and on Monday evening he has to accommodate his performance to a different stage, a different auditorium, and probably a different kind of audience. The bigger companies occupy the bigger theatres for as long as three weeks, although the usual visit is for one week; but there is a growing number of small tours committed to 'one-night stands'. The danger of this irregular pattern of work is a break-down of the whole system: a shortage of theatrical 'digs' and even of stage-staff capable of dealing with a complicated 'get-in'.

The former practice of sending out tours of 'boulevard' successes has traditionally been the responsibility of independant managements. But many of the provincial theatres, especially in Britain, are very large. They were built in response to the wholly different social and economic conditions pertaining in the late nineteenth century. The problem is now that the public will only be drawn to these theatres in sufficient numbers to fill them by highly successful productions that include at least two stars of film or television fame, preferably playing the parts in which they have secured their popularity. There is at present a struggle between the theatre-owners who on the whole would like to sell their premises, and the producing managements, who with the Arts Council acting as a spearhead, consider it crucial to keep open as many provincial theatres as possible, or those at least which are strategically placed.

The realities, however, are more complex. Although there exist a number of large provincial theatres, many of them with a seating capacity of well over 1,000, their back-stage facilities are grossly inadequate by contemporary standards. They must house for a certain number of weeks a year the big commercial tours as well as tours by the major subsidized companies; yet it is usual for the orchestra pit to be inadequate for a full-size orchestra, the dressing-rooms insufficient to accommodate the chorus, and the stage equipment insufficient to meet the requirements of a scenically heavy production.

The British Theatre Directory (8), however, lists some 350 theatres and venues in the United Kingdom and Ireland, a majority of them municipally owned. Many will find it easier to accommodate the small-scale tour, yet to be discussed, than the bigger commercial tours.

Arts Council touring

In 1969, the Council formed a department to take over responsibility for organizing tours of the major companies. The department claims that it has made considerable progress. Its overall responsibility covers the general pattern of large-scale touring, ascertaining from each of the major touring companies how many weeks of the year it is prepared to tour and then mapping out areas of major interest and potential circuits to prevent unnecessary overlapping. The Council has also turned its attention to the facilities that are provided, or, in many cases, not provided; for a theatre is virtually a company's home for a week or more, and a home which for those involved is not the scene of domestic bliss but of intensely demanding creative work. The first task therefore is to improve the condition of theatres for the artists performing in them; the second task to fill them with an appreciative capacity audience. 'Our main object it bottoms on the seats', said the officer in charge, '60% of capacity is not good enough'.

But both objectives cost money and it is the aim of the Arts Council to persuade local authorities to buy and renovate their theatres and having done so to create an independant Trust on which the authority should be represented and to a which it makes a guarantee against loss. The principal arguments against municipal ownership are inflexibility of staff, the danger of political interference, and a contradiction between local authority and theatrical union rates of pay and accountancy systems.

The allocation for touring in the Arts Council's budget has increased from £3,700,000 in 1978-79 to £6,078,000 in 1980-81, an increase of 100% in three years.

European touring

Touring presents few problems in Belgium, for the small size of the country enables companies based on the largest towns, Brussels, Antwerp, Liège, and Gent to cover the area without difficulty, and there are not many regional theatres big enough to receive large-scale tours. The Flemish-speaking Ministry has decreed that there shall be only six touring companies. To qualify for grant they must give six productions a year with a maximum of 140 performances a season in theatres with not less than 250 seats. At present there are three such companies, the Reizend Volkstheater (Travelling People's Theatre) and the Mechels-miniature-theater (Little Theatre of Mechelen), and the Westvlaams Teater Antigone based on Courtrai. The first of these is based in Antwerp and tours in Flanders and the Netherlands. It structures its work on the ideals of Jean Vilar and includes mostly classics in its repertory. The Ministry of French culture is generous in support of tours. Any production of interest may be invited to visit one of the many cultural centres in the country (9).

In France there are upwards of 100 managements concerned with touring. Most tours are of Parisian successes, either with the original cast or, more commonly, with a second company. Some tours include visits to French-speaking Belgium and Switzerland as well as Luxembourg. At any one time, except during the summer, there are some 15 companies 'on the road' with a possible circuit of about 50 theatres, mostly owned by the municipalities (10).

There is a certain amount of regional touring by the National Drama Centres especially those not owning their own theatres, and frequent exchanges usually arranged by ATAC. Each company is expected by the Ministry to cover its own region but shortage of theatres often precludes this (11).

The Comédie Française goes on a provincial tour every two years. In the Federal Republic of Germany there are 20 regional touring companies presenting between 80 and 90 productions annually. The subsidized theatres give over 5,500 tours a year of which about 500 are exchange tours. There are 75 towns which support at least one permanent company and these between them provide regular theatrical performances in some 350 other towns (12).

In the Netherlands there is extensive touring. This is because with a vigorous tradition of democratic local government, the Dutch municipalities were quick to take possession of theatres within their locality. Actors and companies can base themselves on Amsterdam, visit almost any town in the country, and return the same night. In granting subsidy the government lays emphasis on regional assignments often at the expense of other important work.

In Italy there is a very considerable amount of touring by every kind of company. About 25% of all productions in the Italian theatre go on tour. It is difficult to establish the reason for this; but it may well be that the demands made on the theatrical budget by the existence of 13 opera houses leaves little cash for the alternative policy, far more expensive than touring, of establishing more regional theatres. Another reason may be the traditional regionalism of the country and the absence of big industrial conurbations except in the north.

The national touring organization is the Ente Teatrale Italiano (ETI) which was founded in 1942 with the task of promoting theatrical activity and public interest in the theatre by means of acquiring, constructing, adapting and restoring theatre buildings, and developing a variety of theatrical organizations. It now operates a number of touring circuits in different parts of the country with 42 theatres available to its companies. In 1975-6 it was responsible for 1,863 performances in 83 venues to audiences totalling 1,616,000 (13).

The Stabili (permanent regional theatres), of which there are eleven, have tended to withdraw from touring in order to establish fully their own theatre, though this is less true of Bolzano and L'Aquila where a relatively small local population on which to draw places greater emphasis on the need for touring. The more internationally celebrated companies such as the Piccolo of Milan frequently organize international tours.

Regional Theatre Councils, a fairly recent growth, are now beginning to organize their own tours. A report from the Teatro Regionale Toscano (13) describes the establishment of a theatrical circuit that involves both the regional theatres and the regional companies. It also speaks of a determination to improve conditions for professional theatre workers and to develop a closer relationship with their audiences. The Report also proposes closer collaboration with the ETI circuits and includes discussion of a Christian-democrat proposal to replace the word 'decentralization' with 'polycentralization' on the grounds that the former term implies the possibility of smaller communities being swamped by alien cultural initiatives. The report had the support of the Communists, Christian democrats, Socialists and Republicans, but not the Social Democrats and the Liberals.

The intensely democratic dynamic existing in Sweden and a geography that concentrates the population in certain limited and often isolated areas has resulted in both a relatively large number of regional theatres and a considerable number of tours. Every town in fact with a population of between 50,000 and 100,000 inhabitants has its own theatre, supported both by county and municipality. There is a major state-supported organization, the Riksteater, or State Theatre, which sends out over 100 tours annually; all the regional theatres as well as the Royal Dramatic Theatre of Stockholm send out tours and the 50 Free theatres (see next chapter) tour almost exclusively. The Royal Swedish Ballet tours and has been known to give *Swan Lake* in a town in the Arctic Circle playing in a school gymnasium to a taped accompaniment in default of a proper theatre.

The Riksteater (State Theatre) is a remarkable organization. It was established in 1933 'to distribute theatre throughout the country'. This policy has continued and it now sets up about 130 productions a year of which some 80-90 are new or specially staged productions. Many are produced in a region. Of the total number of performances some 1,600 are evening performances in theatres, 1,500 are school performances, and 1,000 for special audiences such as hospitals, homes for the aged, the handicapped, the deprived. In order to establish a living relationship between the companies and the communities they visit, the organizers have developed a dialogue between audience organizations and local communities on the one hand, and the Riksteater's administrators and directors on the other. By the 1960s, resulting from the amalgamation of local societies, there were 140 audience organizations, but they have varied considerably in their vitality and the efficiency of the support they have accorded to visiting companies. Similarly variable, as a result, are the length of the companies' visits.

By 1974 the Riksteater appeared to be becoming institutionalized and overcentralized. Intense discussions on its future took place both nationally and within the organization. These discussions were sharpened by a proposal of the Arts Council (Kulturradet) that since regional theatres respond better to the Council's aims than touring, the counties, or a combination of counties, should provide an administrative area for the touring of Riksteater companies, the regional theatre companies and the 'Free theatre' groups, the activities of which will be described in Chapter 6 (14).

The new regionalized pattern of touring is based on the belief that there must be a living relationship between the visiting company and its audiences, and that the decentralization of the theatre does not necessarily involve widespread touring by the national companies. Indeed it is encouraging to note that a willingness to tour is considered in most countries to be a valid reason for additional generosity in establishing level of subsidy. The Swedish Riksteater received in 1976-77 a subsidy of some £5 million to cover its 130 annual productions and the 1,600 performances given by its companies. Special budgets for touring are provided in Belgium and the Netherlands, 23,700,000 B.F. (£400,000) for two companies in the former (1976-77), and 14 million G. (£3 million) for five companies in the latter (1977-78). Special conditions pertain in the Netherlands where all regional theatres are municipally owned and the companies tend to be independant of the theatres. (See page 141).

In Switzerland the fourteen biggest towns, each of which has its own subsidized theatre, leave few parts of the country wholly remote from a theatre, inspite of the unwillingness of the cantons to collaborate with each other; but this is partly the result of difficulties of communication in a mountainous terrain, as well as of vestigal rivalries surviving from the troubles of 1848.

The Clottu Report makes clear, however, that the development of the theatre in German-speaking Switzerland has led to a concentration of companies in the urban conurbations. On the other hand it is pleasant to note that in French-speaking Switzerland the theatre has found the means of diffusion throughout the region. Here the 'centres of gravity' are Geneva, Lausanne, Neuchâtel and La Chaux-de-Fonds. The Centre Dramatique de Lausanne has played in as many as 22 locations and the Théâtre Populaire Romand of La Chaud-de-Fonds in 29. Other companies have created their own circuits.

Small-scale touring

First we will give examples of what two mainstream companies have done and are doing to introduce new audiences to their work.

First, the Blegian National Theatre. Since there are very few theatres outside Brussels to which it can take its main house productions, and it has an obligation to tour, it organizes tours of *'animations'*. In 1976-77, for instance, a group of three or four players gave 876 performances (*'manifestations' or 'animations'*) based on Molière's *Amphitryon* which was being given in the main house, Maurice Maerterlink's *Pelléas and Mélisande* and Ibsen's *Peer Gynt*. 422 performances were given in Brussels, 421 in the provinces, and 24 abroad (16).

The second example is provided by the Royal Shakespeare Company. In recent years (since 1976) the company has conducted a three or four week season of performances in the main theatre of Newcastle-on-Tyne, together with *'animations'* in schools and colleges in the areas. The *'animations'* have taken various forms: a director with a group of actors has explored a text in front of and in collaboration with a group of six performers as if it were an early rehearsal; they have held poetry readings, simulated rehearsals, workshops, recitals and discussions in schools, colleges, and the university. The return for this tremendous effort has been surprising: an extraordinary superiority in the quality of response from the audiences that came to the evening performances over that of the largely tourist audience that fills the Stratford theatre (17).

Two points must be made about an experience that was artistically and educationally an outstanding success. One was that the actors were sustained by an extremely efficient and hard-working technical staff which included publicity and public relations officers, stage-manager, stage-staff, electricians, wig and wardrobe workers. The second point is that, by British standards, it was extremely expensive. The Arts Council put up extra money and this was matched by a grant from the biggest of the local authorities in the area, the result of the enthusiasm and leadership of a local councillor.

It is of course difficult for a major company to organize a visit of this kind within a demanding schedule. But there can be little doubt that without such forays into alien territory the theatre at large and the major subsidized theatres in particular, will increasingly depend on a self-perpetuating and gradually dwindling audience and it will do so in the name of preserving standards. These standards the Royal Shakespeare Company has courageously put at risk by organizing, from time to time, tours of theatreless towns, playing when necessary in corn-exchanges and school halls. Anyone who worries about a debasement of standards must face the crucial point that standards in the performing arts are not absolute: they are the result of a creative confrontation between artists who are anxious to communicate their performances and an audience which is similarly anxious to commit its involvement. The tourist who wishes to be entertained, the so-called tired business man, the 'radical chic', have every right to go to the theatre; but it is not likely that such audiences will provide that explosive involvement on which the real vitality of the theatre depends.

Small-scale touring, however, is properly the province of those companies, to be discussed in the next chapter under the heading of the 'alternative theatre'. It also involves 'animations' which will be described in Chapter 11.

The alternative theatre, or the Fringe, as it is known in Britain, or the Free theatre movement in Sweden, or the Jeunes Théâtres in Belgium, or the Gruppi di Base in Italy, constitutes, at least in intention, an alternative to the mainstream theatre, whether commercial or subsidized. It is a spontaneous European movement the origins of which

114

are to be found largely, though not entirely, in the events of 1968. The more extreme of these groups reject almost every aspect of the mainstream theatre, its artistic methods, its financial structure, and its social status. Their aim is to create a new relationship with a new audience, and that audience is largely working-class; many groups see themselves functioning in a social milieu that is neither bourgeois nor 'establishment'.

This will to proselytize, to play to new audiences, to bring into the theatre a bigger section of the public than the committed 5%, is an ambition of many theatre directors. They are motivated by a sense of needing to 'educate' a new public and they are prepared to leave their base theatre, if they are lucky enough to have one, to go in search of audiences. But ideals and objectives are immensely varied and reflect this new movement in the theatre.

The Little Theatre movement in Switzerland is particularly interesting in this respect. For each company a tour has a different complexion. The Theatre Populaire Romand is interested in 'formation', 'animation', meetings with local amateurs, and in discussions with all manner of enthusiasts. The Centre Dramatique de Lausanne likes to play difficult modern pieces by Brecht and Peter Weiss, for example, or collective creations. A company from Geneva composed of actors, singers, dancers, musicians and artists has tried to contribute to a genuine decentralization of the theatre in all its aspects and to regenerate a public interest in the theatre.

The 'village-hall' tour tends of course to lack quality of presentation. But it is a curious fact that if the acting and the play (or *animation*) is of sufficient quality audiences accept simplicity of staging as readily as they did in the Elizabethen age.

In 1977-8 there were 188 small and middle-scale tours in Britain excluding specific children's theatre companies and puppets. The number was made up as follows: (18)

National non-building based tours	76
Regional non-building based tours	30
Building based companies	21
Commercial managements (approx.)	30
Others (approx.)	31
	188

The following paragraph appeared in The Stage (4.5.78) and shows the extent of the movement:

A chain of 35 out of 53 Scottish districts have now affiliated to the Scottish Civic Entertainment Association...... (which).... covers 100 theatres and halls from the Shetland Isles to Annan......

The Scottish Arts Council supports, among many other companies, the Gaelic Drama Company (Fir Chlis) to play in the Scottish Highlands and the Western Isles, and the Pier Arts Centre, Orkney. Some companies are indeed thrusting down into communities that have never before had experience of the theatre.

The regional theatre
It is not possible to find a term that is applicable to the totality of the theatre in all the eight countries. The terms 'regional' and 'decentralized' imply the existence of a centralized theatre, a concept that is valid enough in France and Britain but wholly without meaning in Italy, Switzerland and the Federal Republic of Germany.

Let us consider, then, for a moment this question of the size of population and the kind of theatre it might sustain.

There is a widespread feeling in the contemporary theatre that big is no longer beautiful. Many directors would settle for a theatre with a seating capacity of about 500, but they will realise the need to maximize the price of seats if any but the cheaper and simpler productions are to pay their way. If the architect raises the capacity of the house to 800 or 1,000 there will be very much greater financial freedom - provided the seats are filled. It may therefore be better to build a small theatre and play to capacity than a bigger theatre and have empty seats.

There is of course a relationship between the size of the auditorium and the size of the stage. It would not do to build a theatre with a seating capacity of 1,000 and so small a stage that only intimate productions could be mounted. On the other hand it would be equally inappropriate to build a stage large enough to take opera and ballet and so small an auditorium that the price of seats would have to be outstandingly high.

The size of a theatre has to be considered not only in terms of its own internal relationships but of the community within which it is built and the possible catchment area of its audience. No Ministry of Culture, to our knowledge, had laid down the minimum population necessary to ensure the viability of a theatre, but let us take 100,000 as a minimum figure. Unless it is a town with an exceptionally vigorous tradition of theatre-going, the director cannot count on a regular attendance from more than about 4% of the population. This will give him 5,000 regular theatre-goers. How often can they be expected to visit the theatre? With reasonable prices, once a month? Let us suppose that his theatre gives seven performances a week, six evenings and one matinée, for three weeks. He will have 3,500 seats a week to fill, or 10,500 over the three week period. No theatre manager budgets to play to 100% capacity so let us assume that he budgets on 70%. He will have rather more than

7,000 seats to fill, or about 300 a performance, a figure that is surprisingly close to the figure that many theatres do play to.

This will leave him with a number of options. He can hope to collect the missing 2,000 from irregular theatre-goers. To ensure that he does so he may decide to stage a series of popular plays; but by doing so he may alienate some of his regular theatre-goers. He can increase the price of his seats but this may have a similar effect and provide no incentive to those who attend regularly. Alternatively he can decrease the price of his seats and hope to play to a higher figure than 70%.

Whilst we can play around with these figures at leisure the theatre director and his management have to make practical decisions based on these kinds of sums. It must be remembered that the director can count on the regular attendance of only 5% or less of his local population, even if his standards are high and he has supported his artistic activities with energetic marketing and publicity. With very successful marketing he may be able to increase his regular attenders above 5% but he cannot take the figure for granted. If the town within which he is working has a catchment area of more than 100,000 he has a bonus; if less, his troubles increase. But let us note, by way of encouragement, that one of the most flourishing regional theatres in England is in the market town of Salisbury which has a population of 36,000. The theatre, which for many years was a converted cinema, built up a regular audience of which only one-third came from the town, about 650 a week, the rest from a radius of some 30 miles. There is now a new theatre seating 525 where plays generally run for three weeks at 75% capacity. But the theatre is still subsidized by the Arts Council to the figure of £112,000 (1980-1).

Of course it is not obligatory for a director to house a permanent company; he has other alternatives:-

- to receive tours, provided tours are available suiting the tastes of his audience and the resources of his theatre; to mount *ad hoc* productions running for a limited time. This tends to be an expensive and time-consuming policy;
- to let his theatre to amateurs; this can only be a part-time expedient and if the amateurs are of poor quality the 'image' of his theatre in the public's eye will suffer;
- to use his theatre for films and concerts as well as plays. He must be careful not to discourage a regular audience for drama if this is what he wants to establish.

But the genuinely regional theatre does not stop at trying to persuade people to come to its home theatre: it goes to the people. The first five subsidized regional threatres in France thought little of travelling up to 250 kilometres and playing in villages with a total population of little more than 2,000. But this kind of touring is very tiring on the actors. It is also extremely expensive: for the salaries of the actors and a proportion of production expenses must be accounted to every performance and these remain the same whether the actors are playing to an audience of 100 who have paid a few pence for their seats or a Gala at the Comedie Française; while the maintenance of the base theatre remains a continuing cost whether the company is playing there or not. This is why it is usual for grant-awarding authorities to keep a very close eye on the extent and nature of the touring carried out by its subsidized companies. And it is also a reason for the argument that regional touring should be the financial responsibility of local authorities rather than central government.

It is a curious fact that theatre people of almost every kind talk enthusiastically about collaboration but show the utmost reluctance to do anything about it; a reflection, perhaps, on the individual and demanding nature of theatrical art. The Swiss Report is highly critical of the failure of directors of German-speaking theatres to collaborate, even when it is a question of avoiding, as has been known to happen, the staging of the same play by theatres not far distance from each other in the same season. The government-sponsored Foundation Pro Helvetia has given high importance to exchanges within the main linguistic areas to avoid what would otherwise be certain provincialism (20).

The location of theatres
Theatres will therefore be located in the centres of population, big theatres in the big centre, smaller theatres in the smaller. An interesting situation has arisen in the Netherlands where the conurbations are fairly equally spread throughout the country. Most of the 60 towns with a population of over 30,000 own a small theatre, usually with a capacity of about 600; they are served by tours and are not the home of a permanent company. The Ministry of Culture has made attempts in recent years to subsidize companies that cover certain prescribed areas of the country; but their proposals have been attacked both in Parliament for using subsidy to support conservative cultural values and by the profession for seeking to impose upon the country a theatrical structure not in keeping with the organic development of the theatre.

Criticisms of the proposals by the profession go further and we quote them as we have quoted other criticisms of governmental policy as examples of professional sensibility.

The professional theatre has tended to reject a policy of relating subsidy to decentralization; it has expressed dislike of the government's proposal that bigger 'national' companies should be subsidized by central government and the alternative theatre companies by regional and local government; the Association of Dutch Theatres does not accept the distinction between the two kinds of companies. Further disagreement centres on the government's practice of basing subsidy on the salary of the performers and production costs, while leaving the rest to local government. This would seem to be inevitable in a situation where the companies are not usually theatre-based; but when they are, then the practice seems to turn the actors virtually into civil servants, which is what has happened in the Federal Republic of Germany. And finally companies have complained about the complexity of the methods employed for working out subsidy. Central government subsidy is fairly clear-cut but regional and municipal subsidy is worked out on the basis of number and length of visits. One company may have to negotiate with as many as twenty different authorities and in the end the figure may be affected by the political complexion of the council.

We repeat: a theatre must have a policy. It must know what it is trying to do. Some theatres built up a regular audience with a repertoire of 'boulevard' comedies, although the prevailing attitude in the European theatre is that this practice is the province of the commercial theatre. The 'boulevard' comedy may have its place in the general scheme of things, as we discussed in a previous chapter; but a theatre which enjoys that vitality and that living relationship with the community within which it is situated requires that a variety of plays be shown, classics of the past and present, experimental plays, and productions that exploit new and varied forms of staging. This is to say that a living and effective theatre must establish a policy and either persuade the community of the interest of that policy, or change it. A compromise between a theatre and its public must be established and it is the nature of this compromise that concerns directors more than anyone else in the theatre - a problem to be discussed in Chapter 9.

Local Government expenditure on the theatre
It has been extremely difficult to get even approximate figures. This is not through lack of goodwill on the part of the authorities but the result of even more esoteric and variable accountancy methods than exist in the case of central government.

It is interesting to note that where a country has a two-tier structure of local government, one at regional and one at municipal level, regional government tends to leave responsibility for culture to the communes and municipalities.

Over Europe as a whole cultural expenditure by regional government on culture varies at around 1% of total expenditure, but expenditure by municipalities can be as high as 20% as in the Federal Republic of Germany.

A most useful analysis of the culture of fourteen European towns is to be found in chapter four of Stephen Mennell's *Cultural Policy in Towns:* Apeldoorn (Netherlands), La-Chaux-de-Fonds (Switzerland) and Luneberg (FRG) spend one-fifth of their cultural budget on the theatre; Exeter (England) spends a negligible amount (£27,500 in 1980-81) but a considerable sum on libraries. There is a fine theatre in Exeter but it is generously subsidized by the Arts Council of Great Britain and not by the local authority, (£156,500 in 1980-1).

A useful though out-of-date (1970) comment by the Director-General for Youth and Leisure in the Belgian Ministry of French Culture said that the combined expenditure by state, provinces and local authorities on a big range of leisure and artistic activities was in the proportion (per head of population) of 650BF from the state, 300BF from the communes and 50BP from the provinces.

In Flemish-speaking Belgium, a Royal Decree relates subsidy by local authorities for regional theatres to central government subsidy which itself is based on about one third of operating costs of the theatre concerned.

While it is not possible to give the total subsidy to the theatre from all forms of local government in France, it is thought that the total contribution of the public sector is about 17% of the national expenditure on culture. Of this figure 60% is provided by central government, 3% by the departments, 30% by the communes, and 4% by 'Comités d'Entreprises'.

In the Federal Republic of Germany only a very small proportion of total subsidy for the theatre is provided by the federal government. There is a fairly delicate balance between states and municipalities since a municipal theatre often has a catchment area stretching well beyond its own boundaries and into the state. Practice, however, varies considerably and it has been proposed that a more consistent policy would be desirable.

In the season 1978-79 proportions were as follows:

Bund (central government in Bonn)	2,723,000 DM. (0.42%) (£700,000)
Länder (States)	504,769,000 DM. (44.64%) (£127 million)
Gemeinden (Municipalities)	724,253,000 DM. (63.69%) (£200 million)

The total central, regional and local government subsidy for state, municipal, private theatres, festivals and other subsidies amounted to 1,445,838,000 DM (about £300 million or £5 per head of population, a figure that is sometimes put higher). It must be remembered that these figures include opera and ballet as well as drama (21).

As has been described elsewhere (page 89) the position of the Italian communes is complex. The combination of fiscal and administrative reform together with an unstable political situation has resulted in a varied and uncertain relationship between regions and local authorities and central government, with a considerable degree of control in the hands of the latter.

In Great Britain a detailed analysis of local government spending on drama and theatre has been provided in an admirably detailed survey carried out by the Chartered Institute of Public Finance and Accountancy referred to in Chapter 3 (22).

Estimated total expenditure on leisure and recreation services has risen from £373 million in 1976-7 to an estimated £643 million in 1980-1. The important aspect of these figures is that inspite of having had to contain an increase in VAT from 8% to 15% in 1979, recent increases in local authority expenditure on these services have been in excess of 18%. It must be emphasised, however, that this figure includes a very considerable range of leisure services. Expenditure on theatres, theatrical performances and public entertainment was a little short of £34 million which is comparable with the Arts Council's expenditure on theatre (dramatic and lyric) of around £30 million. (£208 million was spent on parks and open spaces and £81 million on swimming pools).

Although comparisons, as has already been emphasized, are dangerously unreliable some of the evident differences in expenditure are striking. The biggest of the metropolitan authorities, Manchester, with a population of 2½ million spent £340,000 in support of theatrical organizations (0.12p. per head of population); while Sheffield, with a population of half a million spent even less; but the London Borough of Hammersmith and Fulham (population 164,000), with evident regard for the Riverside Studios and the Lyric Theatre, spent over £800,000 (nearly 5p. a head).

Expenditure by the County districts on leisure services works out at £10.36 per head, for the Metropolitan districts £13.27; the theatre will take a small proportion of each, but more in the case of the latter than the former since the provision of theatres is greater.

In the Netherlands and Sweden local authority contribution to the theatre has been in the region of 55% of operating costs against 40% from central government, although figures for expenditure have remained fairly consistant. But even in Sweden local authorities vary considerably in their willingness and their ability to support the theatre.

In Switzerland every mainstream theatre with the exception of the Grand Theatre, Geneva, is supported by its own canton, occasionally supplemented by help from adjacent cantons.

Municipal subsidies are between two and ten times higher than those of the cantons, the latter sometimes intervening to alleviate cost to the former.

The figures for subsidy have been fairly consistent, reflecting the stability of an economy that has not been subject to such violent inflation as has been encountered elsewhere.

As an example of municipal responsibilities, in 1972 the town of Geneva devoted 13% of its total budget to cultural expenditure. It devoted 45% of this sum - the actual figures being too out-of-date to be worth recording - to 'spectacles and concerts', 41% to museums and collections, 12% to libraries and 2% to Beaux Arts. In 1980 7.3% of the municipal budget and 7.1% of the cantonal budget provided subsidy for the city's eight theatres.

The Economist of 20th August 1977, published some comparative figures showing that subsidy for the arts in Britain was provided as follows:

37.3% from the Arts Council (from the Treasury)
31.8% from the Department of Education and Science
27.3% from local authorities
0.9% from business

In Germany:

51% from the municipalities
45% from the states
4% from federal government

In the United States:

59% from business and private sources
29% from state and local government
12% from federal government

The figures are given not only for their intrinsic interest but to emphasize the difference of financial structure in subsidizing the arts and the impossibility of making valid comparisons.

The concept of a Community Theatre

A community theatre, broadly speaking, bases its policies on two assumptions. The first is the need to establish a living relationship with its audience. The commercial manager may consider such an ideal to be a will o' the wisp and to prejudice the very foundations of theatre practice. Be that as it may, the community theatre is not basically concerned with offering entertainment to anyone who will pay for admission: its concern will be for those who generally speaking live in the same area and to whose cultural and artistic life the theatre can contribute. We must modify the general concept of the community geographically speaking because the area of its influence may vary considerably. Miss Horniman's Gaiety Theatre, which established the Manchester school of playwrights, had a distinctly regional flavour; whereas the Abbey Theatre, Dublin, seemed to encapsulate a national aspiration, that of the whole Irish people. The vast amount of discussion that is going on in Italy at the present time is largely devoted to regional theatre organization; although to the Italians the term 'community' might seem to be unacceptably 'cosy', the concept is the same, the need to create a theatre that is meaningful to the community that cherishes it.

The assumption involves the means by which such a relationship is established and the only substantial card in the director's hand is choice of play. Obviously plays that directly concern the community within which they are being staged are likely to be acceptable. The Irish plays associated with the early days of the Abbey Theatre created intense excitement, except when the public thought that their countrymen were being shown up in a poor light as at the first performance of *The Playboy of the Western World*. There was considerable excitement in Australia in the 1950s when in *The Summer of the Seventeenth Doll* audiences heard their own language on the stage. Recent theatrical history is full of similar examples.

Yet the dangers of the policy are evident. A community or strongly regional or sectionalized theatre can become intolerably parochial, just as commercial theatre can become irrelevant. The truth probably lies in the fact that art functions at many different levels of relevance. An astonishing quality of Shakespeare is his relevance for audiences throughout the world, through a reverberation of his poetry at a deep level of human understanding. In the capers of a neurotic Danish prince, or an irritable old king of ancient Britain, or the eroticism of a Queen of Egypt, audiences of almost any race, creed, or kind can find a valid comment on their own human predicament. The French return constantly to Molière. The early regional companies staged his plays in preference to those of any other dramatist, and one notes the outstanding success that M. Antoine Vitez enjoyed at the Avignon Festival of 1978 with no less than four plays by the great dramatist. This is not to say that by other standards Molière is greater than Racine, but that in terms of speaking a language that is of particular relevance to contemporary audiences, he is the more acceptable.

It should not be thought that there is a difference in kind between the community theatre in a small town and the Avignon Festival or the

National Theatre. Mr. Geoffrey Whitworth, perhaps the first Briton to discuss the concept of community theatre, envisaged the National Theatre as 'a community theatre writ large'.

The concept itself is not an irrelevant or theoretical one. Discussions with the director of both a French and a British regional theatre revealed a preoccupation with the problem. The British director went so far as to suggest that the directors of many of the British regional theatres were interested only in standards of production. The geographical situation of their theatre was irrelevant. His own concern was with members of his company who carried out small-scale tours of the towns and the villages in his area. Although on the one hand he had discovered that rural audiences were capable of a far higher standard of appreciation than they were often given credit for, he also was convinced of the validity of creating a drama from that area, of getting plays written expressing the spirit of East Anglia, and of staging them with actors who could use East Anglian dialect with complete conviction. The attitude of the French director was predictably more theoretical than this. He was convinced of the necessity for the closest possible reciprocity between his company and his public, but thought that this should be achieved more on the basis of a socio-political discussion than through plays that simply reflect regional preoccupations and dialect (see pages 214/5).

In fact a remarkable manifestation has taken place over the last ten years in the emergence of a movement that defines itself as an alternative theatre, an appelation which in many respects is justified. The whole of the next chapter will be devoted to this phenomenon. But we must integrate this kind of theatre with the present discussion since the alternative theatre represents an earnest attempt by a very wide spectrum of mostly young people to create a theatre with strong roots in, and close association with, various social groups, sub-cultures, ethnic minorities or groupings of people who are not to be identified with that section of the population for whom they harbour the utmost contempt, the despised bourgeoisie.

The alternative theatre companies, dedicated for the most part to the total decentralization of the theatre, like to perform on the street, in village, church and school-halls, arts and community centres, any venue that is not a conventional theatre. But a venue of one kind or another there must be, and the most drastic shortage in the whole European theatrical scene is that of small, simple stages and auditoria where non-conforming groups can stage their non-conforming performances.

The European theatres

The curious thing about the concept of a grid of decentralized publicly subsidized theatres is not so much its originality as the fact that since the war it has become a basic element in the cultural policy of all the eight countries without its having been clearly enunciated. It crept in. It was suddenly there and every government accepted, to a greater or lesser extent, its responsibilities. Some people will remember early conferences of the International Theatre Institute when discussions began to centre on a new movement in the theatre which, though not yet formulated, clearly had enormous potential. The small but impressive figure of Jeanne Laurent seemed for a time to embody this new movement. We now know what she was about (see page 74/5). We might have taken our example from Germany but the country had been *persona non grata* since the early 1930s and many of its theatres had been destroyed in the war. The 'economic miracle', as remarkable in the theatre as in German industry as a whole, had not yet taken effect.

Belgium
The total central government subsidy to the theatre in 1979-80 was about 360 million BF (£3½ million). There were three leading establishments in the Flemish-speaking area, the Koninlijke Nederlands Schouwburg, (Royal Dutch Theatre), in Antwerp; the Koninklijke Vlaamse Schouwburg (Royal Flemish Theatre) in Brussels; and the Nederlands Toneel (Netherlands Company) in Gent. In 1976-77 they received a central government subsidy of 71.7 million B.F. (£1¼ million) The three touring companies have already been mentioned.

There are seven 'chamber' companies:
Fakkelteater, Antwerp
Teater Arena, Gand
National Eigentijds Teater, Gand
Toneelgezelschap Ivonne Lex, Antwerp
E.W.T. - Randstadteater, Deurne
Jeugd & Teater Werkgroep, Brussels
Kroonteater-Podium, Hasselt

20 companies are categorized as 'experimental'. They receive central government subsidy varying between two million and eleven million B.F. (£30,000 - £172,000) amounting in all to some 80 million B.F. (£1½ million). Subsidy is related to the number of paid personel in each company and their salary levels which are carefully graded.

The present structure of the Flemish-speaking theatre is the result of a Royal Decree of 13.6.75 which made the following (slightly abbreviated) provisions for subsidy:
— a maximum of six regional companies, locally based, required to stage at least eight different productions a year, and give a minimum of 160 performances per season in their own theatre which

GRONINGEN

AMSTERDAM

UTRECHT ARNHEM

Netherlands

DEN HAAG

ROTTERDAM

EINDHOVEN

Germany

ANTWERP

MAASTRICHT

GENT BRUSSELS LIEGE

SERAING

BRUGGE

Belgium

NAMOUR

CHARLEROI

France

Should have not less than 450 seats; a director to be appointed for a minimum of 3 years; every theatre to appoint an advisory committee of 11 members; the state to determine the number of activities to be subsidized and to provide subsidy in the form of salaries to members of the companies; regional and municipal authorities to provide subsidy to theatres operating in their area to a total equal to the government subsidy of two years earlier;

— the government to establish its policy towards theatre on the advice of a National Council for Dutch Dramatic Art which shall appoint a chairman, a vice-chairman, and 11 members appointed for four years with appropriate civil servants as observers.

— level of subsidy to be worked out on consideration of:
   - number of performances given yearly;
   - administrative and artistic costs;
   - size of playing audience;
   - number of actors and actresses and their salaries, with increases for performances more than 15 kms from base theatre;
   - subsidies also to be increased for the production of new Flemish plays.

In French-speaking Belgium there are four Théâtres Agrées ('recognised' companies):

Théâtre Royal du Parc - owned by municipality of Brussels;
Rideau de Bruxelles - operating in the Museum of Fine Art;
Compagnie des Galeries - rather more 'commercial' than above;
Compagnie Claude Volter.

The government rubric states that 'in order to lend full support to regional and more or less experimental companies which by their nature are prevented from meeting the requirements of official recognition, the government has created a special fund to cover the most diverse theatrical experiments'. The 10 theatres referred to in this category are:

Théâtre Ivan Baudouin, Brussels - specializing in texts
Ensemble Théâtre Mobil, Brussels - touring and experimental
Théâtre du Nouveau Gymnase, Liège - of great age
Théâtre de l'Ancre, Charleroi
Théâtre de Quatr' Sous, Brussels - a café-theatre
Théâtre Dramatique Ardennais - regional
Théâtre Arlequin, Liége
Théâtre de l'Equipe, Brussels - experimental
Théâtre du Meridien, Brussels

The contract for subsidy is made between the Ministry of Culture and the Director of the Centre who is appointed by the Minister for a period of three years. During this time he must stage a minimum number of

France

TOURCOING ●
LILLE ●
△ AMIENS
△ LE HAVRE
CAEN ● ●ROUEN
● REIMS
□ ● ●
PARIS (4)
STRASBOURG □
● RENNES
● ANGERS
NANTES △
BOURGES △
DIJON ● BESANCON ●
△
NEVERS
△ LA ROCHELLE
△
CHALON-SUR-SOANE
● LIMOGES
VILLEUR BANNE ●
ST. ETIENNE ● △ CHAMBERY
LYONS
△
FIRMINY
● GRENOBLE
TOULOUSE ●
NICE ●
BEZIERS ●
●
MARSEILLES

□ NATIONAL THEATRES
● NATIONAL DRAMA CENTRES
△ MAISONS DE LA CULTURE

128

productions for a minimum number of performances. The Ministry, through its inspectors, pays attention to quality of production and the policy of *'animations'* pursued by the Centre particularly in relation to young people.

France
The early history of decentralization was given on page 74/5. In 19 of the larger towns there is a Centre Dramatique National, a National Drama Centre, but the pattern is not consistent. There is no Centre in Bordeaux (250,000), although there is a subsidized company in the town, Nantes (240,000), or a number of other towns with a population in excess of 100,000; but there are Centres in Aubervilliers (70,632), Caen (91,336) and Tourcoing (89,258). There are 25 municipal theatres all in towns with a population of over 100,000.

There are 16 Maisons de la Culture, but only four, those in Grenoble, Nanterre, Reims and Rennes have an arrangement with a National Drama Centre; others depend on visits, productions by amateurs and a general policy of *'animations'*.

The reason for the variety of pattern is that the creation of a Centre is the result of local initiative. The Ministry of Culture makes no attempt to establish a Centre where there is no local demand. In the same way the establishment of a Maison de la Culture is the result of collaboration between central and local government.

Central government subsidy for 1980-81 was as follows:
National theatres:
La Comédie Française (59,216,154 F.)
Le Théâtre National de l'Odeon (13,863,555 F.) now run in collaboration with the Comédie Francaise
Le Théâtre National de Chaillot (12,500,000 F.)
Le Théâtre de l'Est Parisien (10,244,074)
Le Théâtre National de Strasbourg (12,937,269 F.)
A total subsidy of 108,761,051 F. (about £12 million)

Centres Dramatiques Nationaux
Angers - Théâtre des Pays de Loire (1,950,000 F.)
Aubervilliers - Théâtre de la Commune (4,050,000 F.)
Besançon - Centre Théâtral de Franche - Comté (1,918,000 F.)
Béziers - Les Tréteaux de Midi (2,272,000 F.)
Caen - Comédie de Caen (3,272,000 F.)
Dijon/Vougeot - Théâtre de Bourgogne (2,750,000 F.) *Centre de Création d'Animation Rurale*
Grenoble - Centre Dramatique des Alpes (3,264,000 F.)

Lille - Théâtre Populaire de Flandres (1,480,000 F.)
Limoges - Centre Théâtral de Limousin (2,120,000 F.)
Lyon - Centre Dramatique National de Lyon (3,710,000 F.)
Marseille - Nouveau Théâtre National de Marseille (6,608,000 F.)
Nanterre - Théâtre des Amandiers (3,180,000 F.)
Nice - Nouveau Théâtre de Nice (3,696,000 F.)
Paris - Les Tréteaux de France (3,000,000 F.)
Rennes - Le Théâtre du Bout du Monde (3,216,000 F.)
Saint-Etienne - Comédie de Saint-Etienne (4,282,000 F.)
Toulouse - Grenier de Toulouse (3,676,000 F.)
Tourcoing - Théâtre de la Salamandre (2,988,000 F.)
Villeurbanne - Théâtre National Populaire (12,688,000 F.)
A total subsidy of 72,754,000 F. (about £8 million, an average of £420,000 each).

There are Maisons de la Culture at:
Chambéry, Ajaccio (Corsica), Le Havre, Nantes, La Rochelle, Bobigny (La Seine-St-Denis), Amiens, Bourges, Chalon sur Saone, Créteil, Firminy, Grenoble, Nanterre, Nevers, Papeete (Tahiti), Reims, Rennes.

The Centres have aroused a good deal of discussion on three counts. First, they do not maintain a permanent company. The directors claim that subsidy is inadequate and that actors will not commit themselves for long periods to the provinces. Others say that it is a loss of nerve and courage on the part of the directors who are more interested in their productions being seen in Paris than in the region in which their theatre is situated. (The directors of certain British regional theatres are subject to similar criticisms) (23).

A second criticism, related to the first, claims that the companies are not properly decentralized; that decisions (unfortunately not specified) are still taken in Paris; and that the relationship between the Centres and the companies has broken down.

The third criticism centres on the procedure by which a director is 'designated' (nommé) by the Minister, not appointed. His contract is for three years. The arrangement is well-intentioned: to provide the Director with a sense of continuity and the greatest possible artistic freedom, while leaving opportunity for new talents to emerge. It is claimed to be a better arrangement than that employed in Britain where contractually the Arts Council càn interfere with a company at any time. The contract also specifies that a director must stage a minimum number of productions for a minimum number of performances.

The Director is free to appoint his own administration but it must receive approval of the Minister before grant is paid. If a retiring

Director has established an efficient administration the Ministry hopes that his successor will not want to change it.

Monsieur Jacques Rigaud who was Directeur de Cabinet du Ministre at the time the Centres were established has described how the system of subsidies, guaranteed over the contractual period (*pluri-annuelles*), was developed in response to the need to give companies a sense of security over several years, and an opportunity to establish a cultural policy and a regular audience. The objections of the Minister of Finance had to be overcome on the political level. It has been the policy of successive governments not to direct the cultural policy of the country but to create conditions in which cultural development can flourish and to establish a partnership between the government and in this case the Centres Dramatiques. In these negotiations the Centres should be given the status of serious partners, not sacrificing their independance to control by state guarantees. The danger of the 'prefectoral' appointment of directors has admittedly not been avoided by all Ministers but on the whole the procedure is thought to be going well and to be applicable to French cultural procedures. On the suggestion of Roger Planchon that a certain Minister 'was acting like Louis XIV', M. Jacques Duhamel replied that if M. Planchon and his colleagues saw themselves in the position of Molière and his company, he had no intention of assuming the role of the King (24).

In addition to the five national companies and the 19 regional centres, subsidy is awarded to some 30 distinguished independant companies, referred to as *'hors commission'* and including such well-known names as Robert Hossein, Jean-Louis Barrault, Peter Brook, Lucien Attoun, Antoine Vitez, Jérome Savary and Catherine Dasté. The total subsidy for this category amounted in 1979-80 to 18,062,00 R. (£2 million) (14). The commission itself, presided over by M. Paul-Louis Mignon, considered in 1979 333 applications from independant companies and distributed 10 million F. among 138 of them.

Federal Republic of Germany

The history of the German theatre, briefly outlined in the previous chapter, while providing something of an explanation of the present prodigal situation, does nothing to reduce astonishment and admiration. The latest tally lists over 80 cities and towns maintaining a permanent subsidized theatre which between them boast over 210 stages (or auditoria), in addition to the 87 private companies already noted. All but 18 state theatres are the responsibility of the municipalities.

A unique feature of the German theatre is that most theatres sustain both lyric and dramatic companies and offer a repertory in which opera,

Federal Republic of Germany

Netherlands

KIEL ○

WILHELMS-HAVEN ○   BREMER HAVEN ○   LÜBECK ○

○ HAMBURG

BOCHUM

GELSENKIRCHEN

OBERHAUSEN

DUISBERG

ESSEN

OLDENBURG ○

LÜNEBERG ○

○ BREMEN

CELLE ○

○ OSNA BRÜCK   ○ HANNOVER

○ BIELFELD   ○

○ MUNSTER   BRAUNSCHWEIG

WEST BERLIN

MOERS ○

KREFELD ○

MÖNCHEN-GLADBACH ○

AACHEN ○

DÜSSELDORF

○ CASTROP-RAUXEL

○ DORTMUND

○ HAGEN

○ WUPPERTAL

○ NEUSS

○ KOLN

○ BONN

○ HILDESHEIM

GÖTTINGEN ○

KASSEL ○

○ MARBURG

**German
Democratic
Republic**

TRIER ○

KOBLENZ ○

WIESBADEN ○

○

MAINZ

○ FRANKFURT/M

○ DARMSTADT   COBURG ○   ○ HOF

WURZBURG ○   ○ BAMBERG

MANNHEIM ○

○ HEIDELBERG

HEILBRON ○   NÜRNBERG ○

SAARBRUCKEN ○

KARLSRUHE ○   PORZHEIM ○

BADEN-BADEN ○   □ STUTTGART   INGOLSTADT   ○ REGENSBURG

TÜBINGEN ○   ○ ESSLIMGEN

○ ULM   ○ AUGSBURG   PASSAU

FREIBURG ○   ○ MUNCHEN

○ MEMINGEN

KONSTANZ

Switzerland

132

ballet and drama are mingled. It is only the largest cities such as Berlin, Münich, Hamburg, Cologne and Düsseldorf that sustain independant opera houses.

Overall figures for subsidy have already been given, but it is interesting to note that there are subsidized theatres in six towns with a population of less than 50,000 - Baden-Baden, Coburg, Kleve, Memmingen, Bruchsaal and Schleswig, with municipal subsidies varying between 46,000 and 4 million DM (£1 million).

The German theatres sell currently between 17 and 18 million seats a year; 25% of these are accounted for by season ticket schemes, that is about 4.5 million or a little over 7% of the population, which supports the view that the hard core of German theatre-goers is well below 10% of the population. And these four million bourgeois theatre-goers pay as many as eight visits a year. The problem facing the German theatres is that the need to satisfy this regular traditional theatre-going public dominates choice of repertory and tends to impose an unadventurous choice of play.

Criticisms of performance, whispered from time to time in the British press, made headline news when in 1976 the President of the Republic opened the annual conference of the national organization of German playwrights, the Dramatiker Union, with a short speech in which he challenged the excessive solemnity of the German theatre, its moral preoccupations, the uninviting pomposity of many new large theatre buildings, and the extent of subsidy, admitting that his own predilections were for operetta and 'divertissements' (25).

There is a certain correlation between the population of a town and the size of its theatre. Towns with a population of more than 500,000 usually have a theatre and/or opera house with a capacity of at least 1,000 and sometimes nearly 2,000 as with the Deutscher Opera in Berlin or the National Theatre in Münich. Towns with 50,000 inhabitants tend to have a main house with a capacity between 500 and 1,000.

It is curious to note that towns with more than 200,000 inhabitants have an average of some 4 seats per 1,000 population, while the smaller towns have 8, 10, 14 and even 23 (Tübingen) seats per 1,000. (At a very rough estimate about 3 seats per 1000 are available in the Greater London area but considerably less in most other cities).

Receipts in 1978-79 were on average 17.2% from box-ofice, 82.8% from subsidy. So much interest is attached to the German theatre that it might be of interest to provide further details of the working of two typical theatres, both in Münich (26).

Münich Residenz Theater - Bayerisches Staatsschaupiel
In the season 1976-77 the theatre received a subsidy from the Free

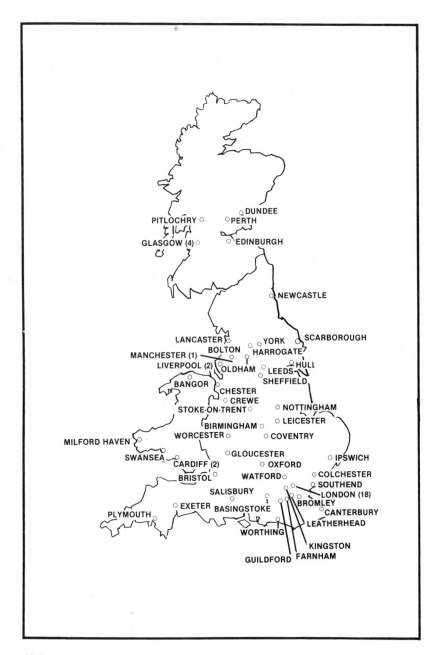

PITLOCHRY ○   ○ DUNDEE
                ○ PERTH
GLASGOW (4) ○   ○ EDINBURGH

○ NEWCASTLE

LANCASTER ○   ○ SCARBOROUGH
      BOLTON   ○ YORK
MANCHESTER (1) ○   HARROGATE
LIVERPOOL (2) ○ OLDHAM ○ HULL
BANGOR ○   ○ LEEDS
       CHESTER   SHEFFIELD
       ○ CREWE
STOKE-ON-TRENT ○   ○ NOTTINGHAM
       BIRMINGHAM ○   ○ LEICESTER
MILFORD HAVEN ○   WORCESTER ○   ○ COVENTRY
SWANSEA ○   ○ GLOUCESTER   ○ IPSWICH
       CARDIFF (2) ○   ○ OXFORD   ○ COLCHESTER
       BRISTOL ○   WATFORD ○   ○ SOUTHEND
              SALISBURY   ○ LONDON (18)
PLYMOUTH ○   EXETER ○   BASINGSTOKE   BROMLEY
                            CANTERBURY
              WORTHING   LEATHERHEAD
                       KINGSTON
              GUILDFORD   FARNHAM

State of Bavaria of 15 million DM. (£4 million) and took 3 million DM. (rather less than £1 million) at the box-office. The theatre usually gives eight productions a year in its main house and one in the delightful Cuvilliés Theatre, for which it is responsible, in co-operation with the Bavarian State Opera. The administrator complains, however, that eight productions are insufficient. Each production has to be played at least 30 times to satisfy the season-ticket holders, and for their benefit it is necessary to plan a seasonal repertory that includes both popular and less popular plays, classics and contemporary. If the repertory fails to attract and audiences drop to 50% the theatre falls short of the 3 million DM. it must take at the box-office. So the theatre stages about 14 productions a year, financing six out of its own resources.

The Ministry insists that the theatre must price its house at the rate of 5,000 DM. (£1,250) per capacity performance. In fact the theatre has increased this figure to the maximum it believes the public will pay, but this is still not enough and the theatre relies increasingly on touring, television and more productions at the Cuvilliés.

Kammerspiel

The theatre received in 1976-77 a subsidy from the municipality of München of 13,700,000 DM. (£3,500,000) and takes 2,200,000 DM. (£550,000) at the box-office. This income just about covers annual running costs of about 15 million DM. (£4 million).

The theatre has a permanent company of about 60 players on one, two and three year contracts. Their combined salaries amount to 5 million DM. a year. The theatre spends 600,000 DM. (£150,000) a year on scenery, a remarkably low figure. There are some 4,000 season-ticket holders.

The theatre is run by an Intendant who is on a five-year contract. Ultimate financial control and legal responsibility is in the hands of a Finance Officer who is contracted for life and who understands the workings of the city hall. His position is therefore said to be impregnable.

The main house holds 730. There is studio theatre seating 299, built as a rehearsal room, with the same floor space as the stage of the main theatre. The theatre also runs a Youth theatre and a theatre in the Elisabeth Platz holding 521.

The theatre employs five dramaturgs, one of whom is also a director and responsible for two productions a year.

The theatre gives eight productions a year in its main house, sometimes nine, one being outside the season-ticket scheme.

Great Britain

The British Theatre presents a complex picture. Though far more poorly subsidized than that of any other country with which we are dealing it is considerable in extent. The 50 or so private/independant theatres in London have already been discussed. There are also 13 London-based subsidized companies and about 50 regional subsidized companies together with another five in Scotland and two more in Wales. There has also been mention of 190 small and middle-scale touring companies, a figure which will include many but not all the Fringe or Alternative Theatre groups.

The regional theatres are extremely active, most of them providing continuous seasons of 40 weeks or more of the year. There is also a very large number of Christmas and holiday entertainments of a seasonal character, many of them run by local authorities.

The Theatrical Managers Association (now Theatrical Management Association) was formed in 1894 by Sir Henry Irving, and merged with the Council of Regional Theatres (subsidized) in 1944 to become TMA/CORT and with the Association of Touring and Provincial Managers in 1978. Membership of the new tripartite organization, now numbering 500, is a complex structure with commercial, subsidized and municipal interests overlapping and intertwined. One of the reasons for the merging of the three organizations was not a spirit of idealism but the increasing amount of government legislation involving management which is better dealt with collaboratively than piecemeal. For example:

Government pay policy
Contracts of Employment Act
Trade Union and Labour Relations Act
Employment Protection Act
Health and Safety at Work Act
Unfair Contract Terms Act
Sex Discrimination Act
Race Discrimination Act

A recent recruit to commercial management has been the Arts Council itself; first through organizing a production, a tour and a West End presentation of *My Fair Lady* and *Oklahoma!*; and secondly through its contribution to the Theatre Investment Trust to which it has made a major contribution. This is a modest capital on which commercial managements can draw on the same basis as other backers. Further proposals for collaboration between the Arts Council and the Society of West End Theatre (managers) are under consideration. The Trust would benefit from more generous capitalization.

Another profitable form of collaboration is that between the independant/private managements and the subsidized theatres. It was estimated that by late 1970s about half the productions in the West End owed their origin or had some relationship with the subsidized sector. A regional theatre near London, one of whose productions was transferred to the West End, gained £25,000 from the transaction.

The following table will show the manner in which the Arts Council allocates its funds between the various categories of theatre. The figures in brackets show the percentage of total grant (27).

	1978-79	1979-80	1980-81
	in £s	in £s	in £s
Nat. Coys.	21,000,000 (26.1)	16,650,000 (26.3)	£12,868,000 (25.7)
Touring	6,078,000 (7.5)	4,915,000 (7.7)	3,700,000 (7.3)
Drama	10,340,000 (12.8)	8,090,500 (12.8)	6,958,000 (13.7)
RAA	7,660,000 (9.5)	5,150,000 (8.1) A	5,501,000 (10.8)
Dance		No Allocation	2,307,000 (2.8) B
Total disposable grant	£50,600,000	£63,125,000	£80,250,000

A - Not a drop but a recategorization
B - Dance is a growing activity in the contemporary British theatre.

An interesting feature of the post-war British theatre has been the number of new theatres that have been built, a phenomenon which suggests a greater willingness of local authorities to put up capital for building than annual subsidy to keep the theatre open. Between 1957 and the mid-1970s 83 new theatres were built together with sixteen conversions of existing buildings and twelve major restorations or improvements.

It is interesting to compare the contract for subsidy offered by the Arts Council of Great Britain with that of the French Ministry. The Arts Council's contract is made not with an individual but with the theatre's Board of Governors or Management Committee and signed by the Chairman. The theatre must show that it is a non-profit distributing organization, that its management committee meets every three months and that various other requirements are met, such as minimum payment of royalties to authors of not less than 7½% exclusive of VAT. The Council also lays down certain regulations covering complimentary tickets, foreign tours, commercial sponsorships and lettings of the theatre to amateur societies.

Italy

This is a country where the theatrical scene is complex. The establishment of the first of the Stabili (permanent theatres) will be described

137

Switzerland

BOLZANO

BRESCIA

MILAN

TURIN

TRIESTE

VENICE

GENOA

BOLOGNA

Italy

L'AQUILA

ROME

SARDINIA

below. There are now eleven. The Ministry rubric requires that the town in which a Stabile is established has a population of at least 300,000. This is true of Catania, Genoa, Milan, Rome, Trieste and Turin; the population of Bolzano and L'Aquila is considerably smaller. On the other hand there is no permanent theatre company in Naples (1,235, 544), Palermo (633,537), Florence (545,050), Venice (363,719) or Bari (335,139).

Subsidies to the eleven permanent regional theatres, the Teatri Stabili, in 1978-9 were as follows:

Centro Teatrale Bresciano	141	m.L.
Emilia Romagna Teatro	377	
Piccolo Teatro di Milano	624	
Teatro di Roma	428	
Teatro Sloveno, Trieste	146	
Teatro Stabile dell' Aquila	296	
Teatro Stabile di Bolzano	251	
Teatro Stabile di Catania	348	
Teatro Stabile del Friuli-Venezia Giulia	324	
Teatro Stabile di Genova	561	
Teatro Stabile di Torino	424	
	3,920	m.L. (£20 m.)

In addition to the Stabili there are over 120 Teatri Cooperativi (Co-operative companies), a striking development of the last few years, and (as was noted on page 35) there were in 1976-77 between 50 and 60 private theatres. There is also in Italy a considerable amount of touring as well as a large number of Teatri di Base (basic or alternative theatres).

To qualify for subsidy the Ministry requires that a theatre or company must be not only established in a town with a population of at least 500,000 (though this does not always seem to be required); but that the theatre is supported by the municipality; that the directors are approved by the Ministry; the auditorium is adequately appointed; that the company plays for at least six months of the year and includes at least 12 actors engaged for the whole season. The contract issued by the Ministry affirms, in addition to the above requirements, the importance of collaboration with local organizations, of decentralization, and the necessity of including educational, didactic and experimental activities in the programme of work. In 1978-79 total government subsidy to the Co-operatives was 4,26 m.L. and to the experimental companies 217 m.L.

139

The Ministry's regulations refer to the particular importance of touring, of decentralization, and of national coordination, as well as insisting on the necessity for vigorous promotional initiative on every level.

Each Stabile has an administrative council on which all aspects of municipal and regional government are represented.

The creation of the Piccolo (Little) theatre of Milan can be taken as an example of what happened elsewhere in Italy and in a number of other European countries.

The Piccolo Theatre was founded in 1947 by two young men of the theatre, Paolo Grassi and Giorgio Strehler. They proposed to do in Italy what had already been done in other countries; this was to create a public or community theatre subsidized by funds from the community (*collectivita*) in the same way that citizens pay taxes to the state and the municipality (*commune*), in proportion to their income, for the support of important institutions like hospitals and schools and for public administration and justice. Grassi and Strehler believed that the theatre should be included in this category of social initiatives as a kind of school for adults, a place where the public can become familiar with the texts of the great dramatic poets, and probe the problems of society, history, morals and thought. They wanted in short, to create an art theatre without having to depend excessively on the box-office and above all where they could offer prices within the range of every social class. They were successful in their objective and the Piccolo Theatre has since been subsidized by the Commune of Milan (28).

The central government grant of 11,000 million Lire to the theatre in the season 1976-77 was made up as follows:

Major theatres	3,000 m.L.
Commercial theatre and youth	3,000 m.L.
Cooperative	2,000 m.L.
Experimental companies	550 m.L.
ETI and touring generally	1,100 m.L.
Drama schools and training	350 m.L.
Touring circuits promoted by regional bodies	1,000 m. L.
	11,000 m. L.

It is interesting to note that the national subsidy for opera, ballet and concerts, of which the 13 opera houses take up the lion's share, was 74,000 m. L. There is also a subsidy of 200 m. L. for circuses.

Netherlands

The organization of the theatre in the Netherlands is distinguished by the administrative separation of companies from theatres. Each has therefore to be considered separately.

There is a theatre in most of the towns with a population in excess of 100,000 and most of them are municipally owned. A typical Stadsschowburg is administered separately from, but generously subsidized by the town council (Utrecht, for example, 80%). Until recently a company visited a theatre for a single performance; now the large companies stay for two or three performances and make return visits. A theatre is therefore negotiating some 500 performances a year with upwards of 100 companies, for the private (free) managements representing about 50% of the total theatrical activity follow the same procedure as the subsidized companies. Bookings in the main auditoria are made between one and two years in advance, frequently before a play has gone into production. The whole procedure is expensive in time and money.

Financial arrangements made between theatre and company vary considerably. Some companies pay a rent for the theatre and take all the receipts; others make various percentage arrangements as is customary in the British theatre. It is usual, however, for local authorities to pay up to 60% of operating costs of the bigger companies, such as Globe, Centrum and Appel. The minister awards subsidy on the recommendation of the Arts Council.

Government policy towards the theatre has tended to emphasize the necessity for companies to be geographically based to cover various areas of the country; but this has been difficult to work out in practice. The Vereiniging van Nederlandse Tonzelgezelschappen (Association of Dutch theatre companies) has resisted governmental interference in their work.

In the Netherlands the whole structure of subsidy has been subject to greater change than in other countries while the government, subject to professional pressure, no longer makes any attempt to categorize the subsidized companies. Thus, in the following list, there are to be found the leading mainstream companies, Haagse Comedie, Publiekstheater and Appel, Proloog and Werktheater, whose work will be discussed in the chapter on the Alternative Theatre, Mickery, a theatre in Amsterdam which functions as a show-case for the alternative theatre companies, and Poëzie Hardop, a company which specializes in various poetic forms. Level of subsidy is based on operating deficits with the responsibility for subsidy between central and local government clearly established in every case.

Amstel Toneel	991,000 G.
Amsterdams Volks Theater	846,000 G.
Appel	1,069,000 G.
Baal	727,000 G.
Centrum	2,155,000 G.
Genesuis	258,000 G.
Globe	1,584,000 G.
Haagse Comedie	2,749,000 G.
Mickery Theater	1,070,000 G.
Nieuwe Komedie	2,018,000 G.
Poëzie Hardop	385,000 G.
Proloog	2,342,000 G.
Publiekstheater	1,840,000 G.
Sater	1,042,000 G.
Theater	2,227,000 G.
Theater Unie	96,000 G.
Toneelraad	2,712,000 G.
Tryater	267,000 G.
Werk in Uitvoering	311,000 G.
Werkteater	1,309,000 G.
Voorziening (Noorden)	1,039,000 G.
	27,087,000 G. (£5 m.)

Level of subsidy is based on operating deficits.

There are also about fifteen commercial companies which receive no subsidy but benefit from playing in municipally-owned theatres where they get better terms than from 'bricks and mortar' managements. They secure the services of leading actors and actresses whom they pay better than do the subsidized companies.

The separation of companies from theatres results in a considerable amount of touring even though most companies have established a fairly close connection with the theatre in the town in which they are based.

Of the more important companies the Haagse Comedie based in The Hague, and *Publiekstheater* of Amsterdam are 'more or less' national companies; they give a large proportion of their performances in the theatres where they are housed, the *Haagse Comedie* gives about a quarter of its performances away from home-base, and the *Publiekstheater* about two-thirds outside Amsterdam. Their repertoire is fairly traditional and aimed at a general public. 40% of their subsidy is provided by central government, the remainder from the municipality where the company is playing, and occasionally the province. The negotiation of subsidy in the Dutch theatre is often a complex process.

142

Sweden

It is surprising to find that until the early 1960's there were only three professional theatres of any significance in the country, the Royal Dramatic Theatre in Stockholm, and theatres in Malmö and Göteborg. The theatre in general was well-subsidized, poorly supported, and of no great cultural significance. Change was brought about in the first instance by the appointment of Ingmar Bergman as artistic director of the Dramaten in 1963. Mr. Bergman, developing the work that had already been initiated by the director Alf Sjoberg, freed the theatre from a dominating Ibsenish realism and emphasised both simplicity of presentation and clarity of text in a well-trained company of actors. This revival was furthered by the emergence of the Free Theatre Groups, the work of which will be described in the next chapter.

In 1980-81 there were 18 regional theatres together with two theatres in Stockholm, the Municipal Theatre and the Dramaten. These were:

	Cen. gov. subsidy 1975-6	Municipal subsidy 1975-6	Landsting subsidy 1975-6	Cen. gov. subsidy 1980-1
Stockholm Stadsteater	8,820,000	15,884,000	-	14,729,000
Göteborg Stadsteatern	5,875,000	9,838,000	-	10,048,000
Malmö Stadsteater	11,100,000	14,291,000	-	18,517,000
Stora Teatern, Göteborg	8,840,000	11,269,000	-	14,279,000
Folkteatern, Göteborg	1,818,000	2,577,000	-	3,367,000
Borås Stadsteater	1,389,000	1,753,000	-	2,683,000
Helsingbors Stadsteater	1,856,000	2,228,000	183,000	3,577,000
Stadsteatern Norrkoping-Linkoping	4,678,000	2,228,000	650,000	8,101,000
Uppsala/Gavle Stadst.	2,552,000	3,660,000	15,000	4,208,000
Norbottensteatern	1,805,000	910,000	880,000	3,051,000
Vasternorrlands region-teater	630,000	-	1,056,000	2,209,000
Länsteatern i Dalarna	478,000	639,000	639,000	947,000
Länsteatern i Jönköping	-	285,000	-	631,000
Länsteatern i Säffle	478,000	-	632,000	698,000
Stockhoms läns - o skär gardsteater	-	-	?	698,000
Västerbottens Talteater	-	-	-	616,000
Västmanlands länsteater	-	-	-	1,601,000
Dramaten	32,031,000	-	-	2,036,000

The above figures are in Swedish Guilders and should be divided by seven to get the English equivalent. In 1980-1 central government allocated 350 million Skr. to the theatre, dramatic and lyric (c. £40 million); of this the 21 regional theatres (3 of them being opera houses)

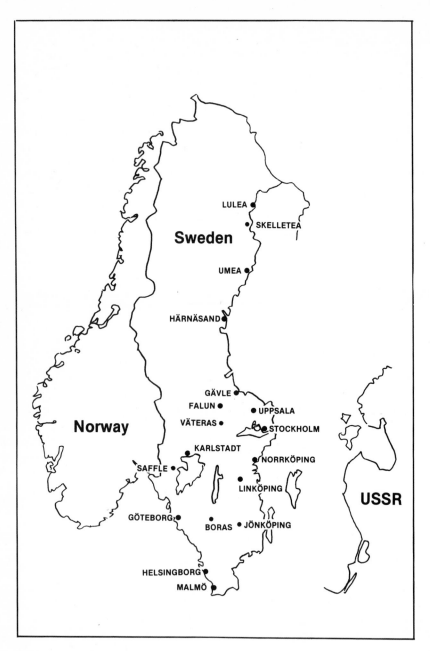

received 98 million Skr. (c. £10 million). Central government grant covers 55% of salaries, the rest being made up by regional and municipal authorities, who provide subsidy considerably in excess of central government. It should be mentioned that of the Gross National Product 12% is consumed by central government and 20% by local government.

Switzerland

Szene Schweiz/Scène Suisse/Scena Svizzera for 1977/8 lists 19 professional theatres, 60 little theatres (Kleintheater/Théâtres de poche/Piccolo Teatri), 32 specialist companies, 7 companies in Italian Switzerland and a variety of, mostly summer, festivals. The edition for 1980-1, following the spreading custom of eschewing categorization, lists 89 companies in Deutschweig, 50 in Suisse Romand and 13 in Svizzera Italiana; but the Swiss Bühnenverband/Union des Théâtres Suisse, includes 17 professional theatres.

There is a tendency for policy to be rather more static in the bigger German-speaking cities such as Zürich than in the French-speaking areas where attention is given to problems of touring and decentralization.

The following list includes all the mainstream theatres with their subsidy (entirely from canton and municipality) for 1980-1 and the percentage of subsidy against total costs.

Basler Theater	21,038,395, SF.	(86.45%)
Centre Dramatique de Lausanne	1,920,000 SF.	(60%)
Grand Théâtre de Genève	15,032,232 SF.	(59.76%)
Schauspielhaus, Zürich	12,654,800 SF.	(72%)
Städtebundtheater Biel/Solothurn (Bienne-Soleure)	1,172,800 SF.	(67%)
Stadttheater, Bern	11,464,200 SF.	(74%)
Stadttheater, Chur (Coire)	230,000 SF.	(c. 35%)
Stadttheater, Luzern (Lucerne)	4,553,755 SF.	(75.25%)
Stadttheater, St. Gallen	6,643,700 SF.	65.4%)
Theater am Neumarkt (Zürich)	1,798,000 SF.	(75%)
Théâtre Municipal de Lausanne	1,600,000 SF.	(50%)
Théâtre Populaire Romand, La Chaux-de-Fonds	545,000 SF.	(60%)
Théâtre de Beaulieu, Lausanne (in a separate category)		

78,570,682 SF. (£20 m.)

The Confederation gives no subsidy to the theatre. Subsidies, however, are variable and depend on many local interests. The towns and

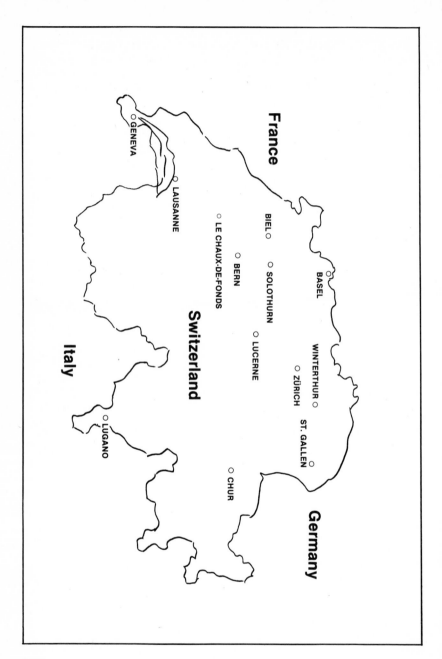

France

Switzerland

Italy

Germany

GENEVA

LAUSANNE

BIEL

LE CHAUX-DE-FONDS

BERN

SOLOTHURN

BASEL

LUCERNE

WINTERTHUR

ZÜRICH

ST. GALLEN

LUGANO

CHUR

146

cantons have one or two representatives on the controlling council of the theatres they subsidize but not in any way to interfere with the artistic freedom of the theatre whose independance of the 'money-givers' (Geldgebers) is assured. Most theatre-workers have a contract for a season that usually runs between September and June.

Reference has already been made to the somewhat equivocal attitude of the Swiss authorities to new theatre building.

Regional Arts Associations

Thus we find considerable variations in the structure and administration of the European theatre. Even in the countries where public subsidy is running at a lower level than in, for example, the Federal Republic of Germany, the amount of money involved is considerable.

But while it is evident that there is a certain consistency of policy between the subsidized theatres of different countries, there are very considerable variations in methods of control and finance. By 'control' we mean the machinery by which level of subsidy is apportioned; and this involves the methods by which this control is exercised. The Strasbourg Report on cultural promotion (see page 106) advances the need for a regional or provincial authority to act as an intermediary between central and local government and the subsidized theatres.

Grave doubts have been expressed by both the French ATAC and the British CORT (Council of Regional Theatres) as to the wisdom of granting too much responsibility for the theatre to local administrations. Both organizations consider central government demonstrates greater professionalism in negotiating and greater resources in finance. The grudging and captious attitude of certain prefets and mayors in France and municipal councils in Britain have served to substantiate these anxieties.

But while it is extremely unlikely that any central government is going to make an exception of the theatre in its decentralizing policies, there is considerable evidence, analyzed in some of the Council of Europe's publications, that local authorities are not always structured in a way to make them satisfactory entrepreneurs or theatrical managers. Thus there has been a movement in Britain to create just that kind of intermediary authority that has been proposed. This has taken the form of the Regional Arts Association, a creation of the last 15 years and one which is still undergoing a process of administrative adaptation.

There are at present 11 such Associations (29). They are autonomous organizations each covering a certain number of local authorities as newly constituted in 1974. They came about in the slightly haphazard way in which such developments tend to happen in Britain but are the stronger for being the outcome of a good deal of discussion and local authority initiative following the closure by the Arts Council of its regional offices. They do not conform to any administrative pattern laid down by the Arts Council or central government; they present no uniformity in their financial structure, but tend to respond to regional, cultural and administrative patterns; and since they provide similar services they have developed certain common features.

These services include grant-aiding, promotion, publicity, advice and research, planning and co-ordination, and generally developing in a variety of way the arts and culture of their region.

They have been subject to a good deal of criticism for being slow in making decisions, for their cumbersome panel-structure and general administrative incapacity. But stream-lined efficiency is hardly to be expected in under-funded organizations still struggling to establish an authoritative identity. The important fact is that they exist and that recent discussions with the Arts Council show an acute and mutual awareness of the problems and the extreme importance of establishing relationships that reflect the realities of regional responsibility. But the basic problem with which they have to contend is their own precarious autonomy. And this means money. At present they are dependant on grants from the Arts Council, from their local authority, and from private and industrial sources, any of which could dry up or be cut off at a moment's notice.

It is a problem as much for the Arts Council as for the Regional Arts Associations themselves; it is as much a problem for every country as it is for Great Britain. The problem, expressed over-simply for the sake of clarity, is this. The executive power of a state in the 1980s is largely shared between central and local government. Between the two there is a responsibility for culture and thereby for subsidizing, paying for, or helping to support various cultural and artistic activities. But central and local government administrators are not entrepreneurs, nor educationists, nor artists. It is their responsibility to establish lines of communication with entrepreneurs and teachers and artists; and they must do so with regard to certain basic principles such as the supreme importance of regional identity and a sense of pride in place; of the necessity of bridging the gap between the artists and the community; of confronting artists with their public which requires acceptance of an increasing degree of local responsibility; of opening the arts from the closed world of the professional to involving the new-fleshed passion of the amateur. If the devolutionary process in the arts is to have real significance it must carry the policy of decision-making right the way down to the level at which the village community has the responsibility and the opportunity to make its own cultural decisions and create its own cultural environment. This is a programme which involves every kind of cultural and theatrical activity, from National Theatres to an amateur performance in the village hall, and includes Regional Arts, Arts Associations, Maisons de la Culture, Centres d'Action Culturelle, Actions Culturelles à Charactère Inter-ministériel, Adult Education Centres, Evening Institutes and Arts Centres of which in Britain there are nearly 200, the Swedish Volkshuset and the Swiss Migros.

Another example of how delicate may be the relationship between central government and the recipient of subsidy can be seen by contrasting the contracts pertaining to subsidy. Ministries are clearly anxious that their money should be well spent, that the recipients should be companies of some substance; that they will put subsidy to adequate use and justify the expenditure of public money in a 'statistical' way. Thus the Belgian and Italian contracts insist on a minimum number of performances and productions. The French throws responsibility on an individual and suggest that the British contract, made with the theatre's Board of Governors, is dangerously imprecise and leaves scope for unwarranted interference. The reply of course is that the French contract provides opportunity for excessive bureaucratic control. It is clearly a problem calling for what the EEC calls a 'measure of harmonization', a term now unhappily treated in Brussels with considerable hilarity.

Summary

In this chapter we have tried to demonstrate the pyramidal structure of the theatre in Europe. The pyramid of course may not always follow an exact geometrical design. Where there are a number of national theatres, or theatres which being in receipt of the highest level of subsidy can be considered as representing the higher standards, a phrase frequently discussed in the foregoing pages, the top of the pyramid will be flattened. Its sides may bulge or contract according to the extent, in quality and quantity, of the regional decentralized theatre. We hope that its basis will be broad and firm, representing a considerable amount of community involvement in the theatre by both amateurs and professionals, in all forms of participation as theatre workers as well as audiences.

But most of all it is to be hoped that there will be a strong structural relationship between all levels of the pyramid. The argument will become clearer if we abandon at this point the metephor of the pyramid, for its connotations of stone and concrete are inappropriate. We are building, in terms of human feeling, the kind of life that people deserve, the ways in which they wish, individually and socially, to express themselves, and the cultural atmosphere in which they want to live.

These aspirations can only be expressed in terms of administrative structures, theatre buildings, playing spaces, figures for subsidy and many other practicalities; but these in turn represent the conditions in which the artist works and forms a relationship with his community. Although this chapter has been written in a manner that presupposes the hierarchial structure of the theatre, moving down from the expensive national theatres to the popular community theatre movement, it is essential to conceive the total organic relationship of the whole structure with offshoots of the mainstream theatre thrusting into the community and the community showing, as occasion offers, an interest in the highest forms of national culture.

Sources

(1) See, for example, A. G. Dickens (editor) - *The Courts of Europe: Politics, Patronage and Royalty 1400-1800* - Thames and Hudson, 1977, and Hugh Trevor-Roper - *Princes and Artists: Patronage and Ideology at Four Hapsburg Courts 1517-1633* - Thames and Hudson, 1976.
(2) Sylvie Chevalley - *La Comédie Française Hier et Aujourd'hui* - Dichier, 1979.
(3) Teater Jaarboek voor Vlanderen 1975-76 - ITI, Brussels.
(4) Geoffrey Whitworth - *The Making of a National Theatre* - Faber, 1951.
(5) Richard Findlater - *The Complete Guide to Britain's National Theatre* - Heinemann Educational Books, 1976; and John Elsom and Nicholas Tomalin - *The History of the National Theatre* - Cape, 1976.
(6) Robert Hutchinson - *Economic Aspects of Arts subsidy* - Unpublished.
(7) J. Goldberg and P. Booth - *Dècentralization de la Promotion* - Council for Cultural Co-operation - Strasbourg, 1976.
(8) Published by John Offord, Eastbourne.
(9) Source of this and all subsequent information on Belgian Theatre - Ministries of French and Dutch Culture, Brussels, and Belgian Centre of the International Theatre Institute. (For details, see Appendix 1).
(10) Association pour le Soutien du Théâtre Privé, Paris.
(11) ATAC (see Appendix 1).
(12) For source of all information in this chapter on the theatre in the Federal Republic of Germany see Appendix 1.

(13) For source of all information on the theatre in Italy in this chapter see Appendix 1.
(14) Personal visit. For sources of other information on Swedish theatre see Appendix 1.
(15) For sources of information on Suiss theatre see Appendix 1.
(16) Source: *Rapport sur L'Activité du Théâtre National de Belgique* by courtesy of the General Administrator.
(17) Source: Royal Shakespeare Company marketing department, by courtesy of the General Manager.
(18) Roger Lancaster - *Moving on* - Arts Council of Great Britain, 1978, unpublished.
(19) *A Tale of Two Cities* - Arts Bulletin No. 5 - Arts Council of Great Britain, June 1971.
(20) Pro Helvétia Annual Report for 1976.
(21) West German Centre of ITI, Berlin, and Teaterstatistik, 1978-79.
(22) *Leisure and Recreation Statistics* 1980-81 - CIPFA, 1980.
(23) Jeanne Laurent - *1946-1976* - ATAC/Informations, March 1976.
(24) Private letter.
(25) Dramatiker - Union Mitteilungen, No. 4 1976.
(26) Information on both theatres from personal interview.
(27) All figures relating to Arts Council of Great Britain from Annual Reports and Information Bulletins.
(28) Programme note on the History of the Piccolo Theatre - *La Storia della Bambola Abbandonata* - 1976.
(29) *Partnership in Practice: the Work of the Regional Arts Association* - standing conference of RAAs, 1975, and in particular for a description of policies etc. Catherin Itzin - *The British Alternative Theatre Directory* - John Offord, 1980; also *Towards a New Relationship* - Arts Council of Great Britain, 1980.

Het Werkteater's 'Hello Fellow' in a marquee at Zuiderhoek, 1981.

Max Stafford-Clark, Artistic Director of the Royal Court Theatre, London.

152

6. The Alternative Theatre

Definition

The 'alternative' theatre describes a movement that has been growing throughout Europe for more than a century. It is a theatre which presents itself as an alternative to what may be called the 'mainstream' theatre; it proposes an alternative in organizational structure, artistic methods and ideology, social attitudes and political content. Although it is a more or less identifiable movement there is no generally accepted definition. The British term 'fringe' is widely used but it is one that does less than justice to a movement that has its own objectives and is more than a mere periphery to the mainstream theatre. The Italian term *teatro di base* does not translate well into other languages and might not always be acceptable as an appropriate description of some of the work it is intended to cover. The Swedish term 'free' theatre is not wholly acceptable in a European context since it is one that was used in 1887 by André Antoine (Théâtre Libre), in 1889 by Otto Brahm (Freie Bühne) and in 1981 by J. T. Grein (Independant Theatre) to describe the new theatrical movement that was identified with the plays of Ibsen and Hauptmann. Terms such as the German *'keller'* theatre, the French *'théâtre engagé'*, and the Belgian *jeunes théâtres* are descriptive rather than generic. So the term 'alternative' is perhaps the most generally acceptable.

Description

The movement has been well described in general, though perhaps exaggerated terms, in an Italian publication, *Il Terzo Teatro* (1). Here is a précis of the article.

The third theatre can be accorded an anonymous position well outside the accepted theatre of official culture, subsidized and protected, concerned with the presentation of accepted and acceptable plays and the industry of entertainment. It is the theatre of the avant-garde, of experiment, of research, iconoclastic, a theatre of the streets, defiant of tradition, open to every new artistic influence in contemporary society.

It exists outside the centre of capital cities, composed of all theatre workers who in skill, training, and the level of wages they receive, hover somewhere between the amateur and the professional theatre. Traditionists consider it to be a phenomenon of greater sociological than artistic interest. It is a movement essentially of young people and it exists in many countries.

In its ability to draw on the basic elements of the theatre, this third theatre has a particular kind of vitality in contemporary society. It is in the position of creating new expressive forms of a viable and humanistic kind through which human aspirations and needs can be transformed into action. Former abstract definitions of 'style', 'line', 'school', no longer apply. What characterises the third theatre is its diverse experiments which in fact are difficult to describe. It is as if the personal needs of many people, difficult to articulate, need to be transformed into action not in terms of contemporary aesthetics, but incorporating the whole of contemporary life. How to function spontaneously but not in isolation, to find the courage to immerse oneself in fiction but not to pretend - those are the problems.

The movement clearly had its origin in certain socio-cultural activities to some of which we referred in the previous chapter. Vilar was clearly one of them. But his aim was rather to broaden existing theatrical culture than to create a new one. His concept was of a theatre for the production of the masterpieces of traditional culture. Culture he saw as a universal heritage, transcending social distinctions and enabling the participants to enlarge the scope of their choice, to enrich their personality and their life. Many young people must have sensed this energizing quality of Vilar's work, for it was at the Avignon Festival that the alternative theatre first began to discover its identity.

The strongest incentive and leadership in the creation of an alternative theatre came from such American companies as La Mamma and Bread and Circuses which began to tour Europe in the early 1960s and which were far more radical in the whole nature of their work than anything that Europe had created.

There were other kinds of development. One was undoubtedly the Théâtre Populaire Romand which came into existence in the early 1960s and became what might almost be described as the municipal theatre of the Swiss (Francophone) town of La Chaux-de-Fonds in 1968 (2).

In return for subsidy the company proposed to develop a policy under four headings:

1 To establish theatre as a real centre of artistic creation;
2 To establish a policy that would bring a new and permanent public to the theatre;
3 To establish close relationships with local schools by presenting plays to older children and creating them with the younger;
4 To carry out a programme of 'animations' involving research and wide variety of discussions, exhibitions and other means of furthering public involvement in the theatre.

154

The 'rationale' of the company is interesting: to help twentieth century man to follow the evolution of ideas and of society and to play a part in its transformation; to demonstrate human relationships and to analyse the actions of man. In this way the theatre opens the mind to the reality of the world, develops a critical sense, excites the conscience, regenerates sensibility, awakens creativity and helps in the birth of a new society. The innocent might well ask whether it is really in the nature of the theatre to be able to tackle such a programme as this; but it is of the kind that is constantly preferred by alternative theatre companies. One wonders how far Roger Planchon, whose views on regional theatre were listed on page 75, would support such a programme.

Anyone who has attended with any regularity performances by alternative theatre groups will have realized that if the performance is not of a more or less identifiable play, he must be prepared for almost anything to happen. That is why an analysis such as has been attempted in the following pages is so difficult. And that is also why the word 'alternative' is only loosely applicable as a description of a type of theatre that may, at one extreme, be almost indistinguishable from the mainstream theatre, while at the other it may be one among a varied and unexpected succession of what can only be called 'theatrical images' or the near amateur activities of community theatre groups - and none the worse for that.

If politics, sociology and various kinds of actor-audience relationship form the basis of many of these performances, there is something even more profound that provides a common link: it is kind of caring about mankind. Programmes are as likely to carry quotations from Nietzsche as from the Bible, from Karl Marx as often as from the writings of Christian saints. It is sometimes difficult to see the relationship between the performance and what are claimed to be its spiritual antecedents; but it is rarely that the commitment of the performers is not evident, however chaotic and confused their presentations. Many performances by alternative theatre groups lack the kind of tension that is usually associated with theatre-going, but in this they may be following the precepts of Brecht. They are offering alternatives to Aristotle as well as to much else in the traditional theatre; but they have extended the conventions of the theatre in a refreshing manner.

Early history of the movement

The catalyst that turned innumerable grumblings and rumblings into theatrical form was the curious sequence of events that took place in 1968, although it is possible to detect the seeds from which the movement sprang in many countries some years earlier. In The Federal Republic of Germany, for example, small theatres were estabished in the cellars of bombed cities immediately after the war; and since they were considerably cheaper than premises at street level the companies stayed there after the cities had been rebuilt. At first they staged the simpler plays of Brecht and other writers who had been banned under the Third Reich, as well as introducing the work of such contemporary playwrights as Slavomir Mrozak and, in due course, Harold Pinter. They were particularly successful in the later 1960s when they were able to identify with the student revolutionary movement and became involved in presenting a great deal of street theatre. This aspect of their work has deteriorated in recent years as a result of public disenchantment with politics (3).

The more ostensibly political groups of West Germany were then replaced by a generation of which there are now thought to be some 30 or 40 over the country. The central theme of their work centres round the family, education and local politics, rather than issues of international importance. But their roots are not strong. They are obliged to cope, as alternative theatre groups throughout the continent are obliged to do, with the conflicting demands of personal survival and the determination to find a satisfactory way of working as artists of the theatre. They tend to refer to themselves as the 'Free Theatre Movement'.

Certain municipalities subsidize the Free groups, but the annual amount of subsidy they receive is smaller than the daily subsidy of the Berlin Opera, for example.

Britain's social revolution, of which the Fringe is a striking example, dates back to at least 1956. Some of the more obvious manifestations of the upheaval were John Osborn's *Look Back in Anger* (1956), and the new group of playwrights associated with George Devine at the Royal Court Theatre from 1955 onwards; Richard Hoggart's *The Uses of Literacy* (1957); Kingsley Amis's *Lucky Jim* (1955), Colin Wilson's *The Outsider* (1957), the first (anti-nuclear bomb) Aldermaston march (1957), Free Cinema, Encore magazine, and the Suez débâcle.

The Scots claim that the creation of the Fringe was the work of the American Jim Haynes who in 1963 became director of the Traverse Theatre, Edinburgh, where during the next few years he mounted 75 productions (4). When a number of other companies, clearly of a non-conformist kind, began to play at the Edinburgh Festival, Ian Hunter, the Festival's artistic director, invented the term Fringe to describe their relationship with the mainstream performances.

Jim Haynes in due course moved to London and opened the Arts Lab in Drury Lane which provided an immediate venue for the many young actors, directors and playwrights who no longer wanted to work in the mainstream theatre. The fact that the Traverse had once been of questionable repute and that the Arts Lab was associated with drugs, gave a rather sinister quality to the whole movement which for a time became known as the 'underground'; but the removal of the censorship of plays in the previous year changed what might have become a subversive movement into part of a new counter-culture, fostered by the events of 1968, the Vietnam war, the Democratic Convention in Chicago, and the Russian invasion of Czechoslovakia, and expressed in cultural terms most vigorously in rock music.

Although the situation in Britain in the 1960s was ready for this kind of development, it was the Americans who showed the way. Jim Haynes had been working at the Traverse; Charles Marowitz and Ed Berman had come to London in the early 1960s; Ellen Stewart's La Mamma troup, Bread and Puppets and Julian Beck's Living Theatre were regular visitors. The events of 1968 gave an impetus, shape and purpose to a movement that had yet to discover its identity.

The alternative theatre in Europe

Let us begin by describing a company whose ideals are almost wholly artistic. The Ensemble Théâtre Mobile of Brussels was formed in 1968 as the Théâtre du Parvis and played in a disused cinema. Its repertoire included Edward Bond's *Saved*, John Arden's *Live Like Pigs*, Strindberg's *The Dance of Death*, and Shakespeare's *Measure for Measure*. The group was composed of dissident actors who were looking for something different from the conditions in which they were obliged to work in the mainstream theatre.

The director of the company puts his aims like this. He would like to stage not more than two productions a year, to rehearse each one for three to four months, and to give not more than 25 or 30 performances of each. He wants time to work, time in which to create an ensemble and he would like a bigger company than his present six or seven. In 1976-77 his repertoire consisted of Marivaux's *La Double Inconstance* - the present popularity of Marivaux must owe something to the example of M. Patrice Chéreau - Balzac's *Les Paysans,* derived from the Théâtre National de Strasbourg, Ibsen's *A Doll's House* and a play by a Belgian author. He engages his actors for a period of eight to nine months though he would prefer to give them contracts for a full year. At the end of their engagement most of them live for three to four months on social security and then return for another season.

A model artistic policy, it would seem. But the Minister, in common with the authorities in certain other countries, has imposed a number of conditions for the granting of subsidy, of which the least acceptable are a minimum number of performances of a minimum number of productions in theatres of a minimum capacity. Here is clearly a basic conflict of interests between the public authorities who want value for money, and the artist who wants money to establish values. (5)

Nevertheless the Belgian Jeunes Théâtres have struck out bravely and it is from within their own country that critics have commented on their violent theoretical declarations, their distrust of the playwright, a deviation that will be discussed in a later chapter, and a tendency to swing from violence to overintellectualism.

So the alternative theatre is a challenge as well as an extension of the mainstream theatre. This was clearly expressed in the well-known episode that took place in Amsterdam in 1968 when, during the performance of Tankred Dorst's *Toller,* members of the audience pelted the actors, who were from the Nederlandse Comedie, with tomatoes. This vegetarian outrage is now interpreted as a popular protest against a form of decentralized theatre that appeared to sustain an élitist culture at the expense of more democratic forms. This is repeatedly the platform on which the alternative theatre has based its claims to offer an alternative and it is therefore not surprising to find a marked element of political radicalism in all the more identifiable groups.

The sociologist Madame Josette Coenen-Huther has analysed the spectrum of political commitment to be found in the alternative theatre. She suggests that the groups fall broadly into three categories. (6) The first comprises companies who take a broad and genial view of life, with aspirations for a better world and determination to create an artistic ensemble. A discussion among a group of young French actors with visions of this kind is described on pages 168/9.

The second category, and perhaps the largest, includes groups with a more positive social commitment; they create their own 'productions' - a case where the French word *'spectacle'* is far more appropriate - on subjects of current social importance such as the place of women, immigrants, racial prejudice, old age, and so on, and do so in a critical and challenging manner.

The third category comprises groups of pronounced political commitment, intensely radical, anti-capitalist, wholly opposed to the so-called 'system' or 'establishment'.

It would be impossible in practice to sustain these distinctions with any clarity; but they serve to delimit some of the areas within which the alternative theatre operates. The first category, for example, should perhaps be extended to include what has been described below as 'mixed media' presentations, a term that can be very well applied to Britain's Moving Being; but applied to the Swiss Theatre Onze the difficulties immediately become apparent. The basis of the latter's work is clearly the training of the actor, but this training seems to have as its aim the need to make theatrical statements about the human condition of a most pretentious kind. *Echomort* seems to be trying to say by non-verbal means what Nietzche and a number of other philosophers failed to say with all the resources of a highly articulate language. This is not to sneer but simply to make the obvious point that however admirable the intentions of such ambitious companies, it would be a pity if esoteric experiment led them into a continually more exclusive élitism and away from the theatre as a socially cohesive form of expression.

The first British group in this category was The People's Show, a company that was not overtly political but based its work on a form of 'performance art' that used the visual as much or more than the verbal: surrealism rather than socialist realism. Welfare State, Steven Berkoff's London Theatre Group, Lumière and Son, and Pip Simmons, well-known on the continent, are also in this category (7).

Some vivid examples of work in the second category come from France. It is curious to find, however, that in a country which in the past has been associated with a vigorous experimental theatre, there is now no clearly identifiable alternative theatre movement. There are many independant groups of this kind, some of whom receive subsidy, and there is considerable discussion about the role and nature of the theatre in the Centres Dramatiques and throughout the other theatres of the country; but the only identifiable grouping is that of the 'Action pour le Jeune Théâtre', members of which can apply for state or municipal subsidy. The companies that constitute the French 'Fringe' tend to emerge suddenly and vanish with equal rapidity. The outstanding groups can be identified but not categorized.

The influence of Brecht on the French theatre has been immensely strong. There are critics who say that this has not been altogether for the best; that the inheritors of Brecht have lost their way; their work is theoretical, their plays and productions grey and teutonic, and rather dull.

An article in *Le Monde* (28.4.77) describes examples of the productions we have in mind. M Ferenzi first discusses the work of Ariane Mnouchkine who is perhaps one of the outstanding directors in the contemporary European theatre. Madame Mnouchkine founded the Théâtre du Soleil as a worker's co-operative in 1964 and achieved success three years later with a production of Wesker's *The Kitchen*. In 1970 she took over a disused cartridge warehouse in the military complex of Vincennes (the Cartoucheries) since when she has become associated with a unique kind of epic staging that found impressive expression on *1789, 1791, David Copperfield, Molière,* and the most recent, *Mephisto.* Paul Kessel in a short description of her work (*Platform,* Winter, 1979) quotes Madame Mnouchkine as being wary of politics. 'One should not mix political with theatrical motives', and, 'Theatre is a subtle political act. In order to create good theatre one needs a distance from the political realities of society'. She sees her work as a bridge between politics and art.

A useful summary of the work of Madame Mnouchkine and of much else in the contemporary French theatre is to be found in Paul-Louis Mignon's *Panorama du Théâtre auxxe Siècle* (N.R.F. Gallimard, 1978).

But perhaps the most constant and consistent element in the work of the alternative theatre groups is the creation of their own productions. M. Ferenzi gives us another example in the work of Jean-Paul Wenzel who directed a play, in collaboration with the Centre Culturel Communal de Bobigny, on the theme of, and entitled *Naissance d'une Ville* (Birth of a Town). For several months the people of the town had been invited to express their views on living in that community, to describe their habits, confess their fears and hopes, and recount how they used both their time and the space at their disposal. Out of this material the cast created a play, a production, a *'spectacle'.*

Other examples. The company of the Théâtre de l'Unité made use of authentic material, based on the frustrations of a group of factory workers, for their production of *Dernier Bal.* La troupe Z, having already staged a piece on the struggles of industrial workers, presented a play entitled *Rutabaga's Blues Topinambour Polka* on the economic problems of factory workers.

Expressed in theoretical terms these groups are trying to become involved in, and so find a way of expressing a new social reality in which, as the Italian writer said, the fiction of the stage is increasingly invested with the reality of life. In political terms their attitude is largely Brechtian - to teach, to elucidate, to prepare the way for action.

'Where are the plays written for today's masses?' asked Jean Vilar in 1960. They have been born from the events of 1968, says M. Ferenzi. The productions of the movement, rejecting classical form, are based on real life circumstances, authentic episodes, transformed by the artistic process only so far as is necessary to give them stage form. The players, like those of Aquarium, want 'to join the workers', or like Le Théâtre de L'Unité 'to create a contemporary dramaturgy based on the preoccupations of a new audience'.

It is the practice of these companies to seek out their material from the areas of society where they wish to express it. The script and the production are the work of the collective, the form of presentation emerge as the company works on the material. Of course each company has its chairman, its *'responsable'*, as the Italian co-operatives do - Jacques Livchine of the Théâtre de l'Unité, Ariane Mnouchkine of Le Théâtre du Soleil.

The danger of such productions is that they represent a mere reflection of reality, a sub-theatre which prefers witness to form, agit-prop to more considered forms of presentation. M. Ferenzi says that the groups are alive to the dangers. Ariane Mnouchkine is acutely aware of the importance of tradition. She has been working recently on Molière. She is deeply interested in Greek tragedy and the Italian improvized comedy. Similarly with Dario Fo in Italy. The four companies we have mentioned are aware of their professional responsibilities. They attempt to pay salaries. Their survival may ultimately depend on the sheer theatrical quality of their work rather than the vigour of their political ideas: at least the two elements are related.

Madame Coenen-Huther includes in her discussion Theatre Werkgroep (Brussels), Het Werkteater and Sater (Amsterdam), Le Théâtre de la Communauté de Seraing (Liège), Le Théâtre de la Claque (Baden, German-speaking Switzerland) and Le Théâtre Populaire Romand (La Chaux-de-Fonds). Had her enquiry been more extensive she could have included examples from many other countries.

In the Netherlands Het Werkteater enjoys a considerable reputation. It owns a well-equipped building in the Kattengat. In the eight years of its existence the company has moved from impressionistic and experimental work to a naturalistic style in which members compose their own plays on a variety of contemporary social and political themes. During a visit to London in the spring of 1978 they deployed two companies both of which gave accomplished improvized performances on the subject of death, speaking in fluent English.

The Théâtre de la Communauté was formed in 1964 by a group of left-wing students from the University of Liège. They were given a theatre by the municipality in the working-class district of Seraing but finding that the workers would not come to the theatre, they decided to go to the workers, basing their plays on a social reality that was evident to their new audiences.

British groups in this category would include Joint Stock, Hull Truck, Foco Novo and Wakefield Tricycle, socially-committed, perhaps broadly radical companies, but without a particular ideological commitment. Women's Theatre Group and Gay Sweatshop are constituency companies aiming at particular audiences, Shared Experience and Clapper-claw at particular methods of presentation; and so on (8).

Madame Coenen-Huther places in her third category De Mannen van den Dam (Antwerp), Proloog (Einhoven), Der Rote Rübe (Münich), and 7:84 (Britain).

7:84 takes its title from the claim that seven percent of the country's population owns 84% of its wealth. 'It aims to stage and tour plays which present a socialist analysis of Britain today, touring particularly in theatre-deprived areas; and to develop a style of theatre which is not avant-garde but popular, using music, songs, comedy' etc.

Of similar intentions are Belt and Braces, 'a roadshow company which produces articulate socialist entertainment from a working-class view-point'; Red Ladder, another Marxist company based on Leeds; North-West Spanner, based on Manchester; East End Abbreviated Soap-Box Theatre (London), the first of its kind, formed in 1965 and still going strong; and many others (9).

An outstanding theatre group in the Federal Republic of Germany, where there is not a strong alternative theatre, is Der Rote Rübe (The Red Beetroot), formed in 1971 by a group of drama school students who wanted to develop the tradition of political theatre initiated by Piscator and Brecht. They live as a commune, give a single production each year, and adapt their method of work to their material. They are so organized that every member of the group can make a major artistic or admin-istrative contribution. Their collective decisions take a long time to reach but carry great force when they are eventually accepted. Their aim is to create an anti-bourgeois theatre and to reach some of the 95% of the population whom they claim never go to the theatre.

Through difficulties in categorizing we will deal with the alternative theatre in Italy as a whole. At a conference that took place in Casciana early in 1977 (10) there were 800 representatives from 300 'Gruppi di Base'. The report of the conference makes formidable claims on behalf of the groups that were present, at the time raising the intellectual temperature with an impressive array of cultural and political abstrac-tions. It is apparent that in the Italian alternative theatre there are marked differences of view on almost every artistic and cultural objective.

The Italian Gruppi di Base consider themselves to be a movement quite as important as anything existing in the mainstream professional theatre. They are controlled by the Associatione Teatro Italiano di Sperimentazione Teatrale (ATISP), but they claim to be related not to geographical territory or even a region but to 'the class struggle in all its organizational forms and to the social structure which should be at the service of a cultural production'. They are not passive observers of this struggle but men and women ready to play their own part and make their own contribution. On that account they must in no way copy bourgeois models. It is interesting to find that in a long report there is no mention as to how these groups intend to achieve their avowed aims; the single reference to a practical issue occurs in a paragraph that is pointing out the dangers of psycho-drama, and methods of acting used in training which, inspite of claiming to be valid in terms of personal liberation, can lead to a general debilitation. The subconscious has no contribution to make to their work. There must be no confusion between the transformation of private images into public forms of expression, which is debarred, and the public exposition of private fantasies, which is acceptable. They propose interregional co-ordination and demand a reallocation of funds even if this means diverting money from the permanent theatre. The political authorities and local organizations, all too often lamentably ignorant of their work, must recognize their existence and accept that their legitimate policies are a true expression of democracy. Hence they demand new cultural and theatrical legislation which shall give expression to the cultural demands of the masses.

They claim that they are neither agit-prop nor avant-garde but that they must be differentiated both from the professional experimental groups, which at present receive a government subsidy, and the co-operatives. The latter they describe in slightly disparaging terms as 'ensembles' with the traditional structure of theatrical companies. The Gruppi di Base are different. Within each group there is a total suppression of individuality in terms of the group's political objectives. The evolution of a group involves the dialectical education of each member of that group in so far as he or she contributes to and is in turn developed by his relationship to the total activity of the group and this results in personal, organic and even physiological development.

Every group must be dedicated to research into the recognition of a new reality in the cause of developing humanity. In this process lies the very heart of their work, They refer repeatedly to the need to create 'uno specifico teatrale nuovo' (a new theatrical model) based on a dialectic involving confrontation with social reality, recovery of material from an expropriated cultural patrimony and new economic-political methods of production. Their work is social before it is artistic and they reject current concepts of decentralization on the grounds that genuine culture is local and endemic and so cannot be decentralized.

In the official Italian statistics of subsidy there is no reference to Gruppi di Base but in the section devoted to professional experimental groups - 44 Complessi (not Gruppi) - we find that many of the Gruppi in fact do receive subsidy as Complessi. The line of demarcation is ill-defined, as indeed it should be.

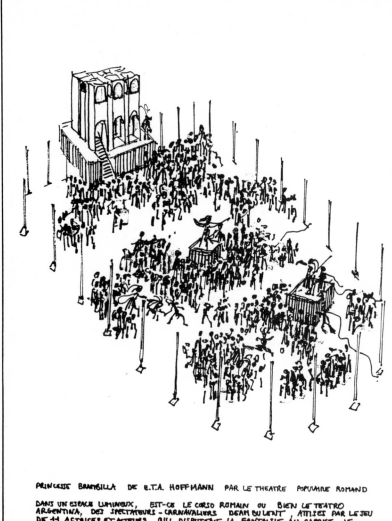

PRINCESSE BRAMBILLA DE E.T.A. HOFFMANN PAR LE THEATRE POPULAIRE ROMAND

DANS UN ESPACE LUMINEUX, EST-CE LE CORSO ROMAIN OU BIEN LE TEATRO
ARGENTINA, DES SPECTATEURS-CARNAVALIERS DEAMBULENT, ATTISES PAR LE JEU
DE 14 ACTRICES ET ACTEURS QUI DISPUTENT LA FANTAISIE AU CAPRICE, LE
FANTASMAGORIQUE AU FANTASTIQUE, SUJETS A TOUS LES VERTIGES.

A rough designer's sketch of the setting for Théâtre Populair Romand's production of E.T.A. Hoffman's 'Princesse Brambilla, La Chux-de-Fonds, 1981.

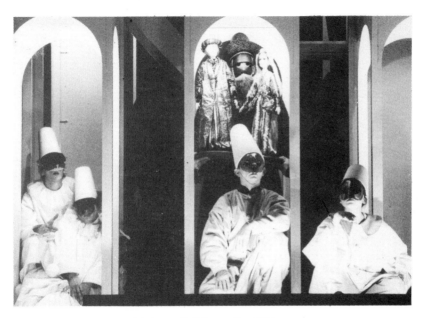

Two scenes from 'Théâtre Populaire Romand's 'Princesse Brambilla'.

If we turn for a moment to the Sperimentali, which may include some of the Gruppi, we find that their activities are predictably more modest than those of the mainstream companies. Their repertoire is almost entirely Italian and they rarely give more than three, or at the most five new productions a year. As elsewhere they follow the practice of taking idiosyncratic names such as - Ouroboros, Il Fantasma di Opera, (The Phantom of the Opera), Odradek, and La Caverna di Plato (Plato's Cave), as well as descriptive titles such as a Teatro Laboratorio (Theatre Laboratory), Teatro Lavoro (Work Theatre), Teatro Mobile (MobileTheatre), and Teatro di Poche (Pocket Theatre).

The emphasis in the work of these groups varies from extreme political content to what they call a 'theatre of gesture and mime', a term that is being used with increasing frequency but whose precise significance is not clear. Many of the groups do not care for the term 'experimental' theatre for it suggests a preoccupation with formal and self-consciously studied methods of production; nor do they care for the term 'popular' theatre. Their main interest, in fact, when they are not being overtly political, is in finding the most effective way of using all the basic materials of the theatre - the work of the playwright, the actor, the director, the place of the text, and of music, and the whole development of the collective.

The 1975-76 season saw the beginnings of closer collaboration between the ATISP companies (the Gruppi) and the main theatrical circuit, ETI. This has been taking place particularly in central and southern Italy where local organizations and regional touring circuits have been making considerable efforts to change their policy with regard to the Sperimentali as well as the Gruppi. The problem is that the official mind is trying to define the groups in recognizable theoretical terms; while the groups are in a sense obscuring their identity in their determination not to be identified with any existing theatrical model.

If we look through the list of groups with descriptions of their work we get a fairly clear picture of their nature and their aims - Il Gruppo Teatro Esperienze, (the Experimental TheatreGroup), Brescia: Collettico Teatrale di Brugherio. Milan (Theatrical Collective); Gruppo Teatro Proposta, Bergamo; Gruppo Teatro Politico di Soresina (Political Theatre Group), Cremona; and so on. 'The group works in a house now turned into a centre'; 'the policy of the group is to develop animations and street theatre based on a suburban area'; 'the group proposes to develop a collective form of living'; 'the group is self-constituted and self-financed and proposes to...' etc.

Now Switzerland. The student revolt in Paris in May 1968 and the appearance in Switzerland of such small foreign groups as Living

Theatre, The Open Theatre, and Grotowski's Laboratory Theatre created an immediate response in French-speaking Switzerland. Alternative groups were formed in Geneva and Lausanne.

The German-speaking theatre had already been influenced by the political plays of Heiner Kipphardt, Peter Weiss, and Tankred Dorst; on top of this came a considerable challenge to the literary theatre in the productions of Peter Brook, Ariane Mnouchkine, and Luca Ronconi. It was from this challenge that the alternative theatre developed. But in this respect the German-speaking theatre has always been less creative than the French, perhaps because the pre-war German influence was destructive while the French had long enjoyed a tradition of experimental theatre which after the war produced such writers as Tardieu, Ionesco, Beckett, Genet, Adamov and Obaldia.

For a time the Petites Théâtres with their idealism and experimental methods attracted considerable interest, especially since the mainstream theatres were going through a period of political uncertainty; but recently the situation has changed, the mainstream theatre has reinvigorated itself and it is the Petits Théâtres that are now in a state of uncertainty. But of their importance there can be little question. They provide a stage for new authors and new actors; they provide a bridge between the mainstream theatre on the one hand and the amateur theatre on the other, while blurring distinction in both directions.

Mixed media and the alternative theatre

It is a curious fact that much of the British theatre, alternative, educational and avant-garde, is preoccupied with mixed- or multi-media presentations. The following description of the work of the dance-drama company Moving Being is typical of the kind of thing that many groups are interested in.

Moving Being's basic tenet is that there exists a body of material, ideas, propositions, that are not accessible to existing separate forms of expression, but are of essential and immediate concern, and the natural place for them to be brought together is the theatre. Performers and audiences participate in an exchange of what should be of mutual concern. In dance, this exchange is at once at its most abstract and its most specific and personal. Specific in the sense that when it really works the combination of dancer and choreographer depicts literally the condition of being moment to moment, as you watch it; a statement of our position and physiology, all the more intense and accurate because it is mute..

Similarly involved in an extension of dance, but with not perhaps so articulate a programme, is the Dutch group Penta, a company that has evolved a curiously individual style for dealing with contemporary themes, in mimetic rather than choreographic style, but distinctly physical and gestural rather than literary, and with a very high visual quality of presentation. There is also Hauser Orkater which was formed from a combination of artists, musicians and actors and whose rather terrifying and socially critical performances project much of the atmosphere of a rock group.

Innovations such as these are at least a partial reply to the French director who said that if the alternative theatre continues to be as grey, as self-consciously solemn and as unentertaining as much of it tends to be, it will alienate old audiences in the very act of trying to win new ones. Forkbeard Fantasy and the Kipper Kids might not be in the same class as Mme. Mnouchkine's company at the Cartoucheries but they probably bring a splash of colour to what is all too often a drab scene. Social reality is not everything. The transformational process of artistic creation must be left free to find its own imaginative environment, however whimsical it may turn out to be. A living theatre will even find occasion for a dionysiac celebration of disorder.

The non-political Fringe

It is in the context of the alternative theatre that it is most convenient to describe the curious phenomenon, for which the French are delightfully responsible, of Café-Théâtre. This was another attempt to create where the mainstream theatre had left a vacuum, though here the emphasis is on employment, on giving actors and actresses a chance to be seen and playwrights an opportunity to be heard, rather than on promoting a political or social message.

The first Café-Théâtre was established in 1966 in the Café Royal, Boulevard Raspail, though its claim to be the first is disputed. In the next few months Caté-Théâtres sprang up throughout France as well as in other European countries. They came and went, of course, but in 1977 there were 28 in Paris giving a great variety of performances (11) and in 1981 they are still part of the theatrical scene.

But they are ephemeral. Actors take a collection and the author is lucky to get any royalties at all. Staging is minimal and records are inexact. Performances cover a range of theatrical styles from Jean Anouilh's *L'Orchestre*, which ran in one café for 500 performances, to anthology programmes of classical authors, cabaret turns and erotica towards midnight. The crucial element is the availability of food and drink.

Ethnic drama

Most European countries include within their population at least one minority ethnic group, a result of either the country's colonial past or more recent industrial expansion. Britain has at least four major ethnic groups and a number of smaller ones. Each group must be enabled and encouraged to find its own voice and its individual cultural forms just like any indigenous social or community group. It is arguable that drama is one of the most potent of these expressive forms since, as has been described in another connection, it enables the audience to hear its own language and enjoy its own related forms of physical expression. There will inevitably be some kind of interaction, sometimes exacerbated by political passion, between the celebration by each ethnic group of its own cultural traditions, and assimilation of and by the dominant culture of the 'host' nation. Evidence suggests that nationals from the more ancient and integrated cultures, such as the Chinese, the Indians, the Poles, and the Ukrainians will wish to preserve their own traditional cultural forms however much they accept the process of assimilation, while people such as the West Indians, whose culture has been torn apart, are ready to reject prevailing cultural forms and make their artistic statements as original creative acts.

The drama of such ethnic minorities falls within the category of alternative theatre since it is an alternative to the dominant artistic forms; and in so far as the alternative theatre provides opportunities for social protest or the exposure of social malaise it is not surprising to find that a number of 'coloured' groups use drama as an opportunity to air the problem of having a black skin in a predominantly white community.

The Swedes seem to be alone in making an annual grant (for 1980-1) to amateur immigrant groups of 100,000 SKr. (£15,000).

The alternative theatre and education
The recent history of the alternative theatre has been particularly interesting in the Netherlands (12). During the 1970s there arose a vigorous debate throughout the Dutch theatre on the policy of presenting the classics to audiences of industrial workers. Alternative theatre and Theatre-in-Education groups pitched in. It was generally agreed that any significant change in cultural behaviour was basically an educational problem, whether the education was that of children, young people, or adults.

Theatre workers on the one hand and teachers on the other found it difficult to make an immediate working arrangement. Though in the broadest terms their aims were similar, their practice was different. Moreover it was found, not unexpectedly, that the perceptions of sixth-formers and those of less able pupils, created two wholly dissimilar sets of problems. The company called Proloog, which pioneered this educational work, found many school children 'creatively crippled'. Hence they became increasingly critical both of the educational system and, by extension, of society itself. It was at this point that the Theatre-in-Education groups developed a sharp political focus, associating themselves with trade unions and their problems, with inner city areas, with people suffering from social deprivation, and with the educational problems of teachers under pressure from the pragmatic policies of big business. It is easy to see why Theatre-in-Education and alternative theatre groups, with a sharp eye on contemporary social reality, cannot find a solution to their problems in the drama of Aeschylus and Racine. But it is also easy to understand how it is that politicians should be hesitant to subsidize companies that bite the hand that feeds them. In an age of terrorism a man must have a secure political philosophy to recognize the essential validity of social criticism in all its forms.

There were in 1978 some 15 fully subsidized companies but the alternative theatre groups are not catgeorized separately from the mainstream companies, and in fact the Ministry of Culture is attempting to view the theatrical life of the country as a whole.

There are now 13 Theatre-in-Education companies independently categorized, while the Mickery Theatre in Amsterdam is also generously subsidized to function as a shop-window and meeting-place for alternative theatre companies from all over the world.

The most firmly established groups in the Netherlands, with total subsidy for 1977-8, percentage of central government subsidy shown in brackets, are:

Baal, Amsterdam - experimental (1,200,000 G.) (40%)

Werktheater, Amsterdam - experimental (1,000,000 G.) (100%)

Sater, Amsterdam - alternative/political (660,000 G.) (100%)

Genesius Theater Company, Groningen - educational/alternative (360,000 G.)

Werkin uitvoering (Work in progress Theatre Group, Groningen - educational/alternative (470,000 G.)

Proloog, Eindhoven - political/alternative (2,000,000 G.)

Toneelraad, Rotterdam (4,900,000 G.) (40%)

Subsidy is also provided to Onafhankelijk Toneel (Independant Theatre Company), the Ro Theatre Company (both experimental) and the Diskus Theatre Company (political).

Subsidies for single projects are also available on basis of operating deficit.

The group Poezie Hardrop which stages poetry in dramatic form is subsidized partly from drama funds (200,000 G.) and partly from the budget for literature.

The experimental groups tend to operate at local or regional level; the educational groups travel rather more widely although still restricting themselves to a certain region.

The Theatre-in-Education movement, TIE as it is usually called, has been especially strong in England as a result of the particular kind of teacher-training in drama that developed in the 1950s and 1960s. The educational aspects of the work will be described in Chapter 14; but the somewhat non-conformist methods of many groups have enabled them to make common cause with the alternative theatre companies, as happened in the Netherlands. In many cases the distinctions are imperceptible: the word 'education' is susceptible to a variety of definitions and applicable to people of all ages. What's educational sauce to the goose is equally so to the gander.

Playwrights and the alternative theatre

One of the achievements of the British Fringe has been to throw up a remarkable number of new playwrights. The alternative theatre companies have offered a stage to young writers who in former times would have been unlikely ever to find an audience. It is perhaps only necessary in the present context to mention some of the names for readers to realize the extent of the creative potential that has been released. Some critics place them in groups but the categories as always are difficult to sustain. There is a group that takes a highly critical and analytical view of British society: it includes David Hare, Snoo Wilson and Howard Brenton. Another group includes more directly political writers such as Trevor Griffiths and David Edgar, who have had successes with the National and Royal Shakespeare theatres respectively, and John McGrath, the director of 7:84. Others not so easy to categorize are Sam Shepherd, John Grillo, Heathcote Williams, Stanley Eveling, David Mercer, John Spurling, Chris Wilkinson, Barry Keefe, Stephen Gooch, Robert Holman, Stephen Poliakoff, and readers will think of many more. E. A. Whitehead and Edward Bond are close to the Fringe in spirit but have had notable success in the mainstream theatre.

The proliferation of playwrights in Britain may be related to the fact that the actors in the alternative theatre groups have shown less enthusiasm than their European counterparts for collective creations. This strange form of theatre, in which actors dispense with the services of the writer and create productions themselves, will be discussed fully in Chapter 10. But although the custom is by no means unknown in Britain, especially among alternative theatre groups, it is less widely practiced than on the continent.

The organization of the alternative theatre

It is probably in Sweden that the alternative theatre is most fully organized though here, as elsewhere, subsidy still falls well behind the
level of the mainstream companies.

The alternative theatre groups in Sweden are known as 'Free' theatre
groups. The first to be formed was Narren in 1965, followed by a group
that broke away from the Royal Dramatic Theatre and called itself
Fickteatern (Pocket Theatre).

A considerable impetus was given to the movement by the events of
1968 and there are now more than 50 such groups. Most of them are affiliated to a central organization known as Teatercentrum which is situated in a disused school on the outskirts of Stockholm, where they can
hire a rehearsal room for the modest sum if they are subsidized, even
less if not. Teatercentrum was founded in 1969 with a subsidy of
280,000 S.K. (£40,000) which enabled the organization to rent its present
premises. An important part of its work is now to carry on negotiations
with the government on behalf of its member groups (13).

The Free theatre is almost wholly subsidized by central government
through the Cultural Council and the Ministry of Employment. There
are no conditions provided that the group has been in existence for at
least two years and can provide adequate documentation of its work.
There is, however, a growing conflict between the adult education
policy of the social democrats and the cultural committees of the local
councils, the argument being that municipal authorities should take full
responsibility for all cultural activities in their area (14).

For the season 1980-81, 46 Free theatre groups and 11 dance and
music groups received a total subsidy of 9 million kroner (£2 million) 9%
of total subsidy.

The relationship between actor and writer, here as elsewhere, is a
changing one and reflects a changing society. But the problems are
enunciated as clearly in Sweden as they are elsewhere: that the theatre
must depict a social reality that has not customarily been seen on the
stage, and it must reach audiences that are socially and culturally less
than privileged.

There was a period of hostility on the part of certain politicians
towards the Free theatre groups on the grounds that they were a disturbing element in the well-balanced and stable society which they had
created so conscientiously. The politicians cherished the ideal of a
people's culture, though what this is no one has been able to define; but
recently there has been a considerable change of heart and both central
and regional government have given a great deal more support to the
movement.

It is greatly to the credit of the British Arts Council that its panels and officers responded rapidly to these new developments and local initiative. In 1969 it distributed £21,675 to Fringe companies, increasing the sum next year to £91,000, distributed among 45 companies, which was 4% of the total theatre budget.

At this point a number of small theatres opened to provide a venue for Fringe productions. Oval House opened in 1966 and for the next decade was largely associated with youth drama. Charles Marowitz opened his Open Space in 1968; the Soho Poly opened in 1970; the King's Head, Islington, in 1971; and the Bush Theatre, Shepherd's Bush, in 1972. The last three were distinctive in being 'pub' theatres and also in offering short plays at lunch-time. In 1971 480 new plays were staged in Great Britain.

In 1972-73 there was the same significant movement we have noted in other countries, away from politics and towards a new social reality. The emphasis became less on converting audiences than finding new ones.

As we read through the list of Fringe companies in the extremely informative *British Alternative Theatre Directory* where 236 groups are listed, we find the same broad categories to which the Belgian sociologist has already drawn attention. First the broadly social: 'A community theatre whose aim is to contribute to the animation of the local population as audiences and participants in theatre projects through collaboration in the creative process' (Common Stock Theatre Company); 'a commitment to new work and to extensive exploratory rehearsals with a particular group of actors' (Joint Stock Theatre Group); and so on.

Then there are the more socially committed: 'Red Ladder Company takes plays into the community. Our work is based around feminist and socialist perspectives. The plays deal with the problems of working people'. And so to the politically committed of which we have already written.

Nevertheless the alternative theatre presents a challenging problem to the politicians and administrators who have problems enough, financial and otherwise, with the mainstream theatres. Then in addition to moral issues that might arise in connection with subsidizing groups that are hostile to the authority by which they are being subsidized, there is the problem of identification. If they can be identified as a genuinely alternative movement to the mainstream theatre as in Sweden, Italy, Britain (after considerable debate), and Germany, where they are virtually swamped by the extent of the subsidized theatre, they will be subject to certain centrally imposed requirements and subsidized accordingly. If they are not clearly identifiable, as in France, Belgium and the Netherlands, or the authorities do not wish to identify them, subsidy will be based on other forms of evaluation.

There are problems on both sides. The authorities want to be assured that they are spending public money wisely. The groups and companies have mixed views about identification. It is impossible to say in any generalized sense whether a group will make its greatest effect by becoming known as a kind of extension of the mainstream theatre, a plausible alternative whose differences are of degree rather than of kind, or by vigorously and clamorously asserting its artistic principles in the form of a challenge to the established theatre.

A particularly interesting situation arose in Belgium where by Royal Decree of 20th June, 1975, considerable encouragement was given to the Jeune Théâtre largely through a quadruple increase in a special subsidy. The Minister defined the Jeune Théâtre as a theatre which researches and puts to the test the most free and original forms of theatrical art. In Article Three the Commission Consultative du Jeune Théâtre is required to help the Minister to encourage original work by young Belgian 'animateurs' and the research of authors who want to break from tradition 'as well as preserving the excitement of originality'.

The report to which we have already drawn attention points out that admirable though these proposals are, they exclude a certain amount of important work. Some companies have moved away from the Jeune Théâtre to investigate other aspects of theatrical art; while the creation of new forms of theatre is by no means necessarily a matter of age. Definition can be inclusive of an identifiable movement; but it can be dangerously exclusive of equally valuable but more individual work.

It is these same anxieties on the part of the authorities that result in the alternative theatre being subsidized at a considerably lower level than the mainstream companies. These anxieties are predictable - standards, subversive material, amateurism. And it is impossible for anyone to suggest what proportion of the work of the alternative theatre is of a distinguished quality. But this is not the point. If the limitations of the mainstream theatre, whether commercial or subsidized, are clear, it must be for an alternative theatre to chart new lines of development. This development can only take place within two areas, the content of the plays and their manner of presentation. But the motivation, reason, justification or excuse for these new developments are such as no serious lover of the theatre can ignore - the absolute necessity of expressing in theatrical terms a new reality and in so doing introduce a new audience to the theatre.

It is the manner in which the artists in the theatre are dealing with this new reality that will form the second section of this book.

The quandary of the administrator with no clear policy to guide him is clear. The Ensemble Theatre Mobil provides an interesting example.

M. Marc Liebens was the first director of a Jeune Théâtre to request subsidy, and because the company had been in existence for some years, to receive it. But there were difficulties. Conditions governing subsidy in Belgium require that the company should give some 150 performances a year. There must be value for money. M. Liebens wanted to give 50 or 60. The Minister proposed, but did not enforce the suggestion that he should give 90. Most companies are required to present at least six new productions a year. M. Liebens wanted to stick at two. The official mind tends to see this as an excuse for the company to enjoy the benefits of subsidy without making the necessary return. Yet we know perfectly well that it is by no means uncommon for companies to rehearse for six or nine months before staging a new production provided that they have the resources. It is no more reprehensible than the custom of the British regional theatres in the 1930s of staging a new production every Monday evening for months on end, a feat of which members of the Moscow Art Theatre on one celebrated occasion showed themselves to be not critical but envious.

Meanwhile in 1980 the Flemish Ministry of Culture awarded grants totalling 93 million B.F. (£1¼ million) to twenty groups which was probably enough to keep them off the bread-line if not to achieve their objectives.

In France alternative theatre companies, which are not categorized as such, receive ad hoc subsidies on the advice of the Consultative Committee *hors commission* (see page 131).

In the Federal Republic of Germany some of the private theatrical companies consider themselves to be examples of alternative theatre. In recent years their independant existence has tended to be undermined by the work of the studios in the state and municipal theatres which attract the more interesting plays, the more enterprising audiences and the better actors and directors.

Entertainment (15) for January 1981 reports that at the 1980 Edinburgh Festival there were 6,000 performances by 391 groups from 48 countries playing to a total audience of 392,000, an increase of 24% over the previous year. Many of the groups could in no way be categorized as belonging to the alternative theatre as the movement has been defined in this chapter, but no matter for that. The significance of the figure lies in the vast number of young people who want to stage a 'performance', whether it be of dance, drama, or some kind of mixed media. The implication appears to be that if the mainstream and largely middle class theatre is barely holding its own, as has been discussed in the earlier chapters of this book, there is nevertheless a profound upsurge of interest in the theatre from a broad social stratum of young people who are not pursuing a vicarious quest for radical entertainment but demonstrating a determination to participate in the creative act whether they have been professionally trained or not. The broader implications of this phenomenon form the subject of the penultimate chapter.

Sources

(1) Eugenio Barba - *Il Terzo Teatro* - Ridotto, Rome, January - February, 1977.

(2) Josette Coenen-Huther - *Huit Ans de Politique du Théâtre à La Chaux-de-Fonds* - unpublished.

(3) Thomas Petz - *The 'New' Theatre in the Federal Republic of Germany* - West German Centre of the I.T.I.

(4) Peter Ansorge - *Disrupting the Spectacle* - Pitman, London, 1975.

(5) Personal Interview with Marc Liebens; see also Mark Quagebheur - *Le Devenir du Jeune Théâtre en Belgique Francophone*, Dossiers de C.A.C.E.F., Brussels, 1975.

(6) Josette Coenen-Huther - *The Theatre as an Instrument of Cultural Innovation* - C.C.C., Strasbourg, 1977.

(7) Catherine Itzin - *Alternative Theatre: a Major Influence on the Establishment* - The Stage, London, 8.3.79.

(8) *The Alternative Theatre Handbook* - TQ Publications,London,1976.

(9) *British Alternative Theatre Directory* (edited by Catherine Itzin) - John Offord Publications, Eastbourne, 1979.

(10) Reported in Scena (Milan) no.1 and 2, February - April, 1977.

(11) Bernard de Costa - *Histoire du Café-théâtre* - Buchet-Castel, 1975.

(12) *The History of Drama-in-Education in the Netherlands* - Netherlands Centre of the I.T.I., Amsterdam.

(13) Stadgar (rules) statistik, Verksamhet-berattelse (activities and records) - Teatercentrum, Stockholm, 1977.

(14) Stephan Johansson - *Free Theatre in Sweden 1976* - Swedish Centre of the I.T.I., Stockholm, 1976.

(15) Nicholas Wood - *The Selling of the Fringe* - Entertainment and Arts Management, Eastbourne, January 1981.

Part Two

The Artists

Bertolt Brecht's 'Saint Joan of the Stockyards' at the Théâtre de l'Est Parisien, 1981.

7. The Artist in Society

This enquiry, as originally conceived by the Council of Europe, was sharply focused on 'créations', the first production of new plays. In order to provide a point of reference for the work of the artist in the theatre it has been necessary to consider the structure of the theatre within which such artistic work is taking place. We must now look at the foreground, the production of new plays and the creation of new productions.

The theatre is notorious for the number of disciplines it involves. Indeed, the theatre has sometimes claimed to enjoy a superior position in the hierarchy of the arts for that very reason. By the same argument the theatre can be disparaged as an art that lacks individual identity and exists only as a compound of the others. But of its all-embracing nature there can be no question: actor, singer, dancer, director, choreographer, composer, designer, instrumentalist and a variety of technicians can all find room for their skill in even the most modest of productions.

The present enquiry will concentrate on those three arts or skills on which the art of the theatre most wholly and unquestionably rests, the art of the actor, the director and the playwright. We shall deal with them in that order. This is in no way to disparage the essential contribution of other artists and technicians but simply to concentrate on those whose work is an essential part of a living theatre.

An artist fulfills a different role in society from the technician or manual worker. He is a creator and he creates not from a blue print, a plan or a model, but from his thoughts, his feelings and his imagination. The material with which the artist gives expression to his inspiration varies immensely; but the material through which the theatre artist creates is the human body, his own in the case of the actor, other people's in that of the director. The author is in a somewhat different situation since his text stands between him and its interpretors or creators.

Since the creation of an artist is the product of his inspiration, it has no obvious social value like the creation of a motor-car or a tooth-brush; yet the widespread practice of public subsidy is based on the assumption that the artist has a valid contribution to make to society. But his contribution cannot be measured quantitively since there are severe limits to the productivity of the human body as an element in the theatrical product (as was discussed on page 47), while its quality is almost wholly a value, and hence personal judgement.

Until recent times the artist has tended to oscillate between a fairly humdrum position of worker-craftsman and an artificially exalted one, in which he has assumed something approaching divinity, and demanded a privileged position in society. Special claims for the artist were advanced by Michelangelo and have been repeated with renewed vigour by romantic artists of the school of Shelley who have tried to place the artist on a different level of existence from the ordinary citizen. It is not just that a certain number of men and women of outstanding talent have lived quixotic and non-conforming lives but that they have come to be accepted, or to accept themselves, as a class apart, touched by the god, unresponsive and unyielding to the laws that affect the rest of us. That is why there is much to be said for the developing policy that can be described as 'the demystification of culture'. No one is against the great creative artists; but many people are anxious that what the artist stands for and achieves should infect and be an influence upon society as a whole. We speak of the marvellous ability of the artist to regenerate society, to reorder experience, to transform the chaos of reality into perceptible form. This process should have nothing to do with class.

One of the most striking developments in recent European culture has been the manner in which the practice of the arts has been absorbed into the curriculum of many schools. Who has not been astonished by the artistic achievements of which children are capable? This is not to claim that every child, or every adult for that matter, is a potential artist, but to hesitate in claiming that the only true artists are those who are capable of living on what they create. The market-test is good enough so far as it goes but it does not go very far. It does not include the proposition that there are some things just as important as the *Pieta* of Michelangelo; the need to cultivate the taste, the creativity, the inventiveness, and the sensibility of feeling that lies in every single one of us, the existence of which is perhaps the greatest educational and artistic discovery of the age. This is to debase all art, it will be said, to reduce everything to the level of the common man. Not at all. It is to argue that the great creative artist is the peak of a pyramid whose base is the creative vitality of the mass of the people. As the great Irish dramatist, J. M. Synge, observed,

> The poetry of exaltation will always be the highest; but when men lose their poetic feeling for ordinary life, and cannot write poetry of ordinary things, their exalted poetry is likely to lose its strength of exaltation, in the way men cease to build beautiful churches when they have lost happiness in building shops' (1).

Many artists have achieved this exceptional position in society by exploiting market-forces and the rarity value of the product. This is not to say that many works of art have not deserved the adulation with which they are treated by society but simply that society has given them a quite artificial economic value which in turn has influenced the social status of the artist.

The particular problems of the theatre artist

The outstanding problem of the theatre, as has already been said, lies in the fact that it is a collective activity. However forcefully and in whatever capacity an individual may exploit his personality, he must be prepared to work collectively with other actors, a designer and a variety of technicians both behind the scenes and in the front-of-house. An actor has little opportunity to exercise his skills outside the ensemble of which he is a part. It is therefore difficutl to imagine how an actor can be assisted as an artist except by keeping him in work in a variety of productions and in companies with an artistic policy. It is arguable that it is more valid to subsidize the company than the actor, the theatre as much as the individual that works within it.

The director functions in a more individual capacity; but he has even less opportunity than the actor to function totally outside the collective. For he must have a company to direct. In one sense he is the parasite of the theatre, creating his visions by imposing his interpretations on and through a company of actors.

If a distinction can be made between the creative and the interpretative artist, and it is one that many people would reject, this is the point at which to do so. If there is a pre-eminently creative artist in the theatre it is the playwright. Things may be different in the future; but at present it is the conceptualizing of the playwright and his ability to transform his concept into words, and words that are dramatically shaped, that is the basis of any theatrical enterprise.

And the problem is how to help him, provided he wants help. You can give a man a million dollars but it will never make him a creative artist. You can buy a book on brick-laying and if you have a modicum of manual skill, you can build a wall. But you cannot buy a book on playwrighting and hope to write a play unless you have that strange and indefinable ability to imagine, to invent, and to conjure words and situations out of experience. Education can help. Patronage can help. But neither can initiate.

It begins to be plain why the administrator will always tend to subsidize the company rather than the individual within the company. We labour the point because critics of grant-awarding bodies such as the

Arts Council of Great Britain or the French Ministry of Culture like to pillory the bureaucracy for granting 1% of the budget to the artist. We must temper a certain indignation. No policy for the arts can ever be plain-sailing.

The legal protection of the artist
The countries of Western Europe have established a variety of regulations for the protection of the artist. Those concerning copyright and performing rights will be mentioned in the chapter on playwrights. For the protection of the performing artist every country has legislation that broadly covers casting agreements and contracts of engagement; the legal protection of performers; industrial relations; work permits; ownerships, duration, transfer and infringement of copyright (see below); licences, terms, and conditions for the production of plays; administration and legislation of theatres; agreements with agents, personal managements etc.

Some of this legislation applies to actors, some to writers, some to theatre-managers and owners. We shall refer to the relevant enactments in their context (3).

If we look at national legislation a little more closely we find that much has been done even if a great deal remains yet to do. The present century has seen the transformation of the position of the artist in society. The right to work was first announced as a basic principle of society by the French Constituent Assembly in March 1791; but it was not again included by any government as a basic tenet of political philosphy until it emerged as Article 427 in the Treaty of Versailles (1919) and then again in the Universal Declaration of the Rights of Man (Article 23, 1948) ratified by most members states of the E.E.C. over the last five years.

The century, however, has seen throughout Europe enormous developments in the provision of social security, and in most countries of sickness benefit, for the unemployed worker of whatever social class he may be. The artist can take advantage of these services like any other worker.

Further social legislation has established a network of employment offices constituting a national means of advertising the availability of work and putting potential employers and employees in touch with each other. Details will be given at the end of the next chapter which deals with the actor. Meanwhile the European Commission has suggested that SEDOC, the European system for the international clearing of vacancies and applications for employment, could be used to supply employers and workers in the cultural sector with exact, regular and objective information on the market with which they are concerned. The Commission goes on to say that initial difficulties are being overcome and that SEDOC is likely to become fully operational. This appears to be an area where international action can appropriately be taken.

The Treaty of Rome

The Treaty of Rome provides the legal basis for the European Economic Community which has its offices in Brussels. The E.E.C., as reference to the treaty itself quickly reveals, is almost wholly concerned with the harmonization of certain political and economic practices among its member states, the treaty spelling out such policies in considerable detail.

Throughout the 200 pages of the English version of the treaty there is no direct reference to culture, or a cultural policy, and it is only the recent publication of the (sadly inadequate) *Community Action in the Cultural Sector* that suggest an awareness of this ommission (4). The process of political and economic 'harmonization', the word that is used by the Commission's officers, nevertheless involves certain areas of legislation of considerable importance to artists. One of these concerns taxation. The application of this to actors, directors and writers has been dealt with under the appropriate sections. The problem of Value Added Tax was dealt with in Chapter 4. The important question of the harmonization of copyright laws will be discussed on page 261.

Another provision in the treaty of considerable concern to artists is the freedom of movement for all workers within the community with full transferability of social security benefits. Workers may enjoy equal treatment in applying for jobs and priority over workers from non-member countries.

The various unions of actors, musicians and visual artists have questioned the desirability of such freedom for cultural workers. For one thing they claim that it would prejudice the development of local cultures which, through being labour-intensive, must be sustained by subsidy. They also emphasize that it is only through a certain protectionism that some countries have been able to build up their national opera and ballet companies, for example. It has been pointed out that virtual free-trade in the lyric theatre has resulted in France, to give one example, being faced with a wholly unacceptable level of unemployment among singers (5).

The same report also criticizes the ineffectiveness of state employment agencies in placing artists in jobs. It suggests that the nine countries of the EEC should each introduce legislation to encourage the development of specialized state employment agencies for the artistic professions. It also suggests that the Community as a whole should expand the Community Job Placement Service so that vacancies not filled in one country can be advertised in another.

While it is no business of a book originally commissioned by the Council of Europe to criticize the policies of a newer but more powerful European union, the European Economic Community, we should emphasize that a number of British organizations which were invited to give evidence on the Commission's document, *Community Action in the Cultural Sector*, almost universally expressed regret that cultural action should be limited to nine countries bound by a political and economic treaty, and expressed the hope that 'harmonization' within the Community should be a prelude to harmonization (of conditions affecting cultural workers) throughout Europe' (6).

British Actor's Equity Association went farther in its evidence and suggested that,

> the views expressed by the European Committee on the International Trade Union Organizations of Artists and Musicians and Technicians....have been so largely ignored or disregarded by the Commission indicates the absolute necessity for the establishment of some effective consultative machinery through which the organizations representative of the overwhelming majority of the workers in entertainment in Europe can play a constructive role in the debates on the formation of the European policy for the cultural sector.

Finally it should be pointed out that the International Labour Organization itself has stated that the income of artists is often well below subsistence level even in the wealthier states of the community. One is hesitant to attribute too many of our present cultural ills to poverty but there is no question of the indigence generally afflicting the cultural life of Europe.

An interesting piece of information commends itself as postscript to this chapter. This is a proposal by the government of Ireland, announced in February 1981, to offer an annual salary of £4,000 to 150 creative artists - interpretative artists are excluded - to form a loose association of 'gifted ones', the Gaelic *Aosdana.* The scheme is intended to bringe a sense of cohesion and confidence to artists at a cost that will amount to only one seventh of the Irish Arts Council's total budget.

The project was the outcome of a report, commissioned by the Arts Council of Ireland, that revealed the appalling insecurity of all artists, and the number of whom, unable to concentrate on their own profession, relied on a variety of jobs to earn a modest living.

Sources

(1) J.M. Synge - Preface to *Poems and Translations* - Everyman, 1941.
(2) *Expert Committee for a Preliminary Study in View of the Elaboration of an Instrument on the Status of the Artists* - UNESCO Paris 1977.
(3) Edward Thompson - *International Protection of Performer's Rights: Some Current Problems* - International Labour Review, April 1973.
(4) See 6 below
(5) *Cultural Workers and the Treaty of Rome:* Submission to the European Communities on behalf of the European (Common Market) groups of the F.I.A., F.I.M., and F.I.S.T.A.V. January 1977.
     See also
     Marie-Madleine Krust - *Droit de Travail et Problèmes d'Emploi des Travailleurs Culturels du Spectacle et de l'Interprétion Music-ale dans la Communauté Economique Européenne* - Brussels, 1977.
(6) *Community Action in the Cultural Sector* - Bulletin of the European Communities, Supplement 6/71. See also, *Select Commission of the European Communities:* Culture - House of Lords Session 1978-79 HMSO London, 1979, and *Arts and the E.E.C.* report of an I.C.A. Conference, May 1979.

A Piccolo Theatre player makes up for Giorgio Strehler's production of Goldoni's 'The Servant of Two Masters', Milan 1973.

Moving Being in performance at Chapter Arts Centre, Cardiff, 1980.

8. The Actor

The rogues and vagabonds tradition dies hard. Few professions have had to tolerate the contempt, the total social dismissal of the actor that began when Tudor legislation categorized them with rogues and vagabonds. 'Rentrons la lessive', the French used to say, 'les polichinelles arrivent!' (let's take in the washing, here come the actors); but a literal translation omits the added contempt of the word *polichinelles,* not even *comédiens* or actors, but those wanton and mercurial Italians.

The profession, however, has fought its way to respectability, partly because there have always been actors to command the respect of society, an impressive tradition that began with James Burbage and Edward Alleyn and has included Thomas Betterton, David Garrick (the close friend of Dr. Johnson), Talma, Bernhardt, Coquelin, Salvini and countless others.

But although the profession is no longer the subject of legalized discrimination, it still suffers from disabling public attitudes surviving from the 'bad old days'. British Actors Equity is unique amont unions in exercising a 'closed shop' policy while accepting, as it must, a lamentable degree of unemployment.

The actor today, though socially acceptable, is still suspect by those services of the modern state that create the silent structure of society: building societies examine his financial position in suspicious detail and insurance companies are hesitant to take risks on his life.

Why should this be? The answer lies in the fact that the life of many professional actors is as precarious as ever, while the very nature of his calling is one that challenges some deep-seated reserve in the heart of the respectable citizen.

The actor as artist
Nevertheless the immeasurably improved status of the actor is the result of the immensely improved status of the theatre itself. For this we have to thank not only such great players as those already mentioned but those who saw the theatre as a form of art and who both by precept and practice helped it to achieve its proper place as one of the main forms of artistic expression. One thinks of the supreme intellectual and artistic distinction of Constantin Stanislavsky, Edward Gordon Craig, Jacques Copeau, Harley Granville-Barker, William Poel, each of whom helped to create a theatre in which great actors could flourish and which society could view with respect.

The profession of the actor has now been put on an entirely new theoretical basis. He is treated and can begin to treat himself as an artist, not simply as a performer in the more derogatory sense of the word. It matters what he feels and the way that he works. His contribution to the ensemble is required and respected. The super, the spear-carrier, has virtually ceased to exist: it is now as important to get the small parts right, the 'walk-ons', the servants, the non-speaking roles, as the protagonists.

Nevertheless the change has not been total gain. The development in the 1930s, 1940s and 1950s of what is conveniently called the 'group ideal' was accompanied by an attack on the so-called 'star system'. The fact that today, in the 1980s, even the commercial theatre depends to a far lesser extent on 'stars' than it used to, is not only the result of a successful campaign by certain theatrical reformers, but of a profound change in the very structure of society which has tended to 'cut our giants down to size'. While the era of the anti-hero and the anti-memoirs, of de-schooling and do-it-yourself, may be helping to create a democratically acceptable society, in terms of the theatre it is tending to create a situation in which it is becoming increasingly difficult to cast the great classical roles. There is a danger that the classical actor will disappear along with the classical ideal and we shall be left with an intelligent social-democratic theatre which will offer us everything but those moments of intense insight which the plays of Shakespeare and Racine outstandingly provide.

Young actors and their attitudes
An example of the manner in which young actors are thinking is provided by a discussion that took place in 1977 at the Théâtre de Gennevilliers, a subsidized theatre *hors commission* to the north of of Paris (1). One of them began by saying that as long as an actor is treated as a *'sous-traitant du discours dramatique'*, a sub-contractor to the dramatic structure, nothing will change; but from the moment when the actor can assume *'un autre poids dans le discours lui-meme'*, some weight in the discussion, the situation changes and even becomes contradictory. The present structure of the theatre, he continued, places the director in a position of hierarchical authority and reduces the actor to the role of an employee or even a marionette. (We have already pointed out that the resentment of many young French actors for the director is based on the procedure by which contracts for subsidy are made between the Ministry and the director of the theatre, thus underlining the latter's position of authority, a subject to which we shall return in the next chapter).

Discussion of the role of the director led on to the subject of the *création collective*, a form of theatre of increasing popularity. (A good deal was said about it in the chapter on the alternative theatre.) One of the actors referred to a collective creation at the Théâtre National de Strasbourg, *Germinal*. The actors worked as dramaturgs, writers, and researchers but were neither given credit for their contribution nor opportunity to express their point of view on the whole spectacle. Participation was of a perfunctory kind. As a result they became extremely critical of collective creations since in many cases they are not what their creators claim them to be, but a method of working on the part of the director. They even take a swipe at the critics whom they say are less interested in the process of collective creation than in individual achievement.

A collective creation demands the greatest possible contribution from each actor concerned. But when one asks an actor to improvise he is beginning to assume the role of dramatist. If he begins to invent his own dialogue he has no need for anyone else's; and at this point the traditional division of labour begins to disappear: if the dramatist can be dispensed with, so can the director (whose role in the theatre is of recent provenance and whose limitations are evident). But to work in a collective has its own considerable difficulties and does not provide an answer to every theatrical problem.

The actors at Gennevilliers then went on to dicuss their relationship with the playwright. Actors 'think' in terms of their voice and their body and this can reduce them to the role of instrument. (It was the great French actor Louis Jouvet who said that the unique quality of the actor is that like the singer he is both instrument and intrumentalist.) This places him at a disadvantage in relationship to writers who 'think' in terms of words and are therefore more articulate. At this point in the discussion they saw a certain conflict between the actor's instrument, his body and voice, and the author's intrument, his words. One of them said that in spite of his belief in the primacy of the playwright he thought of the actor as his accomplice. The actor's voice and body are expressive instruments, capable of poetry, and if he does not use them in this way he becomes a marionette, a mouthpiece for the playwright's words. It is therefore important to see the actor, not as an instrument who gives life to the words of the playwright, but as another artist who carries on a to-and-fro dialectic with the writer.

So we find that the actor of today is expressing more of his personal authority, of his artistic potential, than he has in the past. He no longer sees himself as an 'interpreter' in the slightly derogatory sense in which the word is used in contrast to the creative artist, but as an essential contributor to the production, to the *création du spectacle*. This concept of the role of the actor makes it necessary to reconsider the organization of a company in order to provide for such a change of role. The actors at Gennevilliers claimed that it is not a question of democracy and authority within a company but of the creation of a new type of theatrical organization in which the problems related to division of labour in the present sense no longer exist. (One is left with doubts, perhaps, about the division of talent.)

Steps towards the creation of this new kind of company have been taken by the Italians with their co-operatives. These companies emerged not from the alternative but from the mainstream theatre. In the chapter on the alternative theatre we discussed a variety of companies from different countries many of which are organized on a co-operative basis and functioning for the most part in opposition to the established theatre. The Italian co-operatives, of which in 1979 there were over 100, have been carved out of the established theatre by actors who were tired of the traditional role of the actor and his relationships with management. Their radical ideology is not in doubt. They claim to have advanced a new socio-cultural policy in the theatre and a new method of work based on the self-determination of all theatre-workers. It has been argued that the extremely rapid development of the movement has resulted in a loss of homogeneity, with unfortunate implications for the credibility of the companies, which is to say, a lowering of standards. The accusation has led to much vigorous discussion of the professional status of their work, something which must be preserved if their socio-cultural aspirations are to be taken seriously.

An actor's conditions of work
The very concept of the collective poses some nice artistic problems. Does the collective require a director? That is really to question whether the collective is basically social and administrative or artistic. If the former, well and good; if the latter, is the collective sufficiently collected to be able to assume collectively the functions that are usually assigned to the director?

Experience and enquiry suggests that it is a matter of degree. Theatrical art in 1981 places high value on what is generally termed as unity of style within a production. This can often be achieved by hard work during rehearsals and sympathetic understanding between the director and the company. A more highly developed unity of style is the outcome of the ensemble or semi-permanent company. The collective which can wholly dispense with the services of a director and yet stage productions conceptually ambitious and stylistically unified must have committed itself in theory and practice to highly demanding and sharply focussed techniques and ideologies.

This is an area in which it is difficult for the private/independant theatre to compete with the subsidized.

But there are practical problems for the actors as well as the administrations. The first of these, security of employment, involves the union. Basically an actor, like any other worker, wants to be in continual employment. (A particular problem such as length of holidays is not one that we need discuss in the present context.) Membership of a collective might go some way to providing this security or continuity. We say 'might' because even a collective has to find the money to give its actors an annual salary or it is failing in one of the respects that justify its claim to be a collective. Some of the mainstream companies are moving towards the custom of giving a substantial proportion of its company one, two, and three year contracts. In some countries the union is pressing the point that a three year contract is virtually one for life with no possibility of dismissal. This point of view is becoming increasingly supported by government regulation which, particularly in Sweden, asserts that employment for a year constitutes a contract in perpetuity.

In terms of social security, such developments are admirable. But taking a strictly artistic point of view it could be argued that there are many directors who do not want to work with the same actors for more than three years, just as there are actors who do not want to work within the same company, collective or otherwise, for an indefinite period. The anarchical economic conditions prevailing in the theatrical profession in some countries is still a disgrace; but we must not confuse a sense of order and stability with an administrative rigidity leading to artistic frustration. From such a situation no one would benefit, least of all the artist for whose sake the reorganization is being carried through.

A further problem: if an actor from a collective applies for another job, especially if it is in a more conventional or traditional area of the theatre, he will be at a disadvantage in not being able to answer the inevitable questions about the roles he has taken, the plays in which he has performed, and the directors under whom he has worked, for he has probably not taken roles in the conventional sense, or played in plays that anyone would recognize as plays, or worked under a director of whom anyone has ever heard. He has ceased to be interchangeable. He has been identified with certain productions in which the whole is of greater significance than any individual part. And in that whole, in that collective, he may have been required to master a number of accomplishments, those perhaps of puppeteer, musician, teacher, raconteur, stage-hand, lighting-designer or sound-engineer. He has transformed his role; and society which has laboriously come to terms with whom and what an actor is, has now to face up to him being something or someone different.

An extremely interesting discussion on the problems of working within a collective is to be found in the Journal of the Standing Conference of Young People's Theatre, no. 4, 1979. The author, having worked with the Red Ladder group for ten years, analyzes with impressive honesty the problems which he and his colleagues faced: how to handle the complex administrative and financial problems; division of labour; are new members to be given the same rights as older members; the danger of the older members becoming the management and the younger ones the employees; and the fascinating revelation that ultimate power tended to devolve onto those who could write since this dictated what was said and done in performance. It is extremely important that such crucial issues be openly discussed without them being used as arguments against the whole principle of collective work. It is only by open debate of issues that matter that art can flourish in a democracy.

The professional life of the actor

By and large the appalling insecurity of the actor's profession remains. The statistics given below all emphasize the fact that in most countries actors earn an annual salary well below the national average and face an unemployment rate that is considerably higher. The sheer problem of finding work dominates every other consideration of an actor's life. And this is not a crisis that he must face, like many other workers, perhaps half-a-dozen time in the course of his life, but, if he is unlucky, a number of times a year. Most actors are far too familiar with the social security office; with the face of their agent; he spends a fortune in stamps; he must live where there is most work which is a large city or preferably the capital. London, Paris, Amsterdam, Brussels and Stockholm are each the theatrical as well as political capital of their country; and actors live in these cities, unwilling when unemployed to move far from a telephone, waiting constantly for a call from their agent, a manager, a producer, a casting director or a broadcasting company. It is an ignominious and demoralizing situation personally, artistically destructive.

The development of the co-operative and collective company is only a partial answer to the situation, for the artistic organization of an ensemble has nothing to do with its economic resources. In any case, as already emphasized, artistic development is unpredictable and the administrative structure of a country's theatre must allow the greatest possible amount of artistic flexibility.

The practice being developed by the major subsidized companies of offering one year contracts, renewable on both sides, would seem to be a proper development. Lifelong contracts cannot be in the best interests of company or actor. A company needs fresh blood; an actor needs artistic renewal. An actor's growth is closely related to his commercial value. No one wants to employ a poor actor.

The British National Theatre's practice of offering three year contracts while allowing periods when an actor can accept other engagements seems to be an admirable arrangement combining economic security with artistic freedom.

When British Equity, the actor's trade union, says that the predicament of the actor in the contemporary theatre is underpayment and underemployment, it is emphasizing the twin aspects of the problem. Most artists can go some way towards developing their skills whether they are employed or not. The actor almost not at all. Sir Henry Irving, who lived in the latter part of the nineteenth century when the expansion of the theatre was at its most vigorous, had played over 400 parts before he was 25 years old. Whilst being an achievement of which Stanislavsky might not have approved, he undoubtedly learnt more about the art of acting than most young people have the opportunity of ever doing in the contemporary theatre.

As to payment, we will give some specimen figures below. But it is lamentable to note that in Britain, where the theatre is generally held to be in a fairly lively condition, few actors earn a yearly salary equivalent to the national average for the country.

The film industry does little to help the artistic life of an actor. The stage can train an actor for films, never the reverse. A 'fat' part may provide an actor with economic security for a year but it will do little to help his artistic growth.

Similarly the commercial theatre is of limited value. We showed in a previous chapter that a play must run in London for three months if it is to 'break even'. This is about the longest length of time that is supportable to actors. Six months is the absolute limit. Even then it requires considerable discipline and expertise to keep the role fresh. That is why the major subsidised companies have espoused the limited run or the genuine repertory system. The latter is expensive but of unquestionable artistic viability.

Some practical problems
It is now proper to ask - who is responsible for the economic wellbeing of the actor? The profession? Its resources are limited. The state? Then how does the state organize its subsidies so that the actor will benefit? We will shortly look at some of the answers that are being proposed in various countries.

193

It is generally assumed that the professor and the school teacher are providing services more socially acceptable than the actor since they are better paid and generally better provided for. Their union enforces regulations prescribing the maximum number of hours they can work. They must have time for study and research when they are paid at the same rate as when they are teaching. Is is not reasonable to suggest that the actor, like the teacher, should have a guaranteed maximum salary? That he should work for not more than 40 weeks of the year and have 12 weeks in which to study, read, travel, see other productions, and to work on his voice and his body?

Is it not reasonable to ask that the income tax authorities should be a little more generous in allowing him to pay tax on unusual earnings, as a result of a film, perhaps, over several years, as an author can do, or over two years if he turns himself into a limited company, than in a single monster payment which will once again begger him?

Should not insurance companies be a little less discriminating against actors? Why should we take risks, the insurance companies will reply. And the answer is that if the state is to regard actors, as the state must regard all workers, as a potential source of wealth and well-being, then the state must ensure that he is not discriminated against through the nature of his employment. And if he is, he must be recompensed. And although it is an inevitable concomitant of a free-enterprise system than an actor shall depend for employment on an agent who takes 10% of his earnings, have we not reached the time when all countries should follow experiments that have been made in France and Germany where special employment agencies for actors and artists have been established?

Control of entry into the profession

It is arguable that the number of unemployed actors would be reduced if ways could be found of relating the number of young actors joining the profession to the number of available openings, as is done in the Soviet Union. The fact of the matter is that it is extremely difficult to find ways of doing this without the possibility of excluding real talent, and while preserving the rights of an individual in a free economy to enter the profession of his choice. British Equity exercises a system of control of entry that does little to help the students who have undergone a three-year professional training, or even those who have taken a degree in drama. A social democracy tries to keep open its freedoms, freedom of expression, of choice of career; even, as some students recently put it, freedom of the right to starve. But even when a pragmatic philosphy tries to find an equation between opportunities for training and employ-

194

ment, there lurks the underlying anxiety that genuine artistic talent is being curbed or frustrated.

There are countries in which vocational training is a pre-requisite for entry into the profession - Bulgaria, the German Democratic Republic, Finland, Iceland, Yugoslavia, Austria, Poland, U.S.S.R., Czechoslovakia, Hungary and the German Federal Republic. There are other countries in which the major theatres usually engage graduates of the drama schools - Denmark, Norway, Sweden, France, Switzerland, and Turkey (2).

The list is not exclusive. In Belgium, for instance, qualified professional actors in the Flemish-speaking sector are required to have followed a full course of study at a recognized drama school or worked as a probationary actor for a year or in the French-speaking sector to have taken part in 200 performances and earned a gross remuneration of at least 200,000 B.F., and so on (3).

The Swedes have come to the same conclusion as the British, that trained actors find employment more readily and remain in employment more consistently than untrained actors. It is interesting to note that significant improvement in the training of actors was the work of Ingmar Bergman while he was director of the National Theatre.

In Britain the issue of training for the stage is a contentious one. Actor's Equity exercises limited control of entry into the profession by means of a quota system, casting agreements with management which limit the availability of certain jobs to full members, and the imposition of certain salary levels, all somewhat complex in operation. At the same time the theatrical profession itself is assuming some responsibility for and interest in training through the newly created National Council of Drama Training, a body on which all aspects of the theatre are represented. Virtually all the drama and most of the major vocational drama schools were visited in 1979-80-81 by small panels of professionals. Their comments and advice should go some way to establishing standards and appropriate methods of training.

An already complex system is made even more complicated through the increasingly significant role the drama plays in higher education, with a growing number of single honours degrees in the universities and of BA's with a drama component in the newly created Polytechnics. Many of these courses are claiming to have a high vocational content, and there are those that see the universities as a valid form of training for directors if not for actors. It is to be hoped that both parties will be able to lay aside their vested interests while they discuss exactly what kind of training is necessary for the increasingly varied demands of the contemporary theatre. It is, at the same time, a ridiculous situation that students who have been trained for three years in a school accepted by the profession should not be given a union card on completion of their training. It is a question of what is to be accepted as professional training.

The employment of actors in the European theatre
Although unemployment is widespread it is particularly serious among young actors and, for obvious reasons, at the point of entry into the profession. It is after several years in the profession that lack of luck and talent begin to reduce the numbers; and it is in the late twenties that actors, with heavier responsibilities, will no longer be content to accept the minimum salary. There are more actors under 30 than over but more roles for the over 30s.

Figures suggest that there is less unemployment among actresses than actors. This may be because they can find work in a variety of secretarial positions, and there is loss among those who marry and have children.

Acting, however, is a profession that can be carried into old age. It is not surprising that it is the older actors, fewer in numbers, better established, and for whom suitable roles are reasonably plentiful, who earn consistently the better salaries.

There is no country that does not report considerable unemployment among actors, and increasing unemployment over the last few years. Where there is tight control of entry into the profession as in Belgium, the percentage of unemployed actors may appear to be high but the actual numbers will not be large.

Figures for unemployment are notoriously unreliable since a film star, who may have earned in a few weeks enough money to keep him in comfort for the rest of the year, may show up on returns as unemployed. In reply to a UNESCO questionnaire on unemployment among actors the French made the proper reply that although a figure of 80% would be roughly correct it did not make provision for the inevitable variables and so gave their reply in terms of employment. The figures showed that throughout the seventies there was a decline in opportunities for employment of something in the region of 30%. An EEC enquiry established that between 1968 and 1975, 25% of all actors, 32% of musicians, and 45% of variety artists ceased to perform professionally (4). Other surveys support these figures or make them slightly higher.

Employment, as well as unemployment, is highest in cities where there are both theatres and broadcasting stations but where a majority of actors tend to congregate. For this reason the theatrical life of Great Britain and France is centered on London and Paris to an unhealthy extent. Thus the centrifugal policy of decentralization must be a vigorous one and it is therefore all the more depressing to read in a publication of the Syndicat Français des Artistes Interprètes, *La Vie d'Artiste,* that only about 50 actors are employed in all the decentralized theatres and that contracts are rarely longer than four months.

Employment for actors in the Federal Republic of Germany is encouraged through the existence of over 200 subsidized theatres and eighty private companies offering a total of over 8,000 jobs for permanently employed theatre actors (5). This represents a drop of about 2,000 from the 1950 figure resulting from economies on the part of the subsidized theatres, fewer productions and smaller casts to accommodate inflation. The number of freelance artists is about 3,000 and this figure has remained steady.

The extent of the German subsidized theatre has reversed the situation pertaining in most countries where broadcasting is a major source of employment for theatre artists. In West Germany the theatres are the main source of employment, followed by television, radio and touring in that order. Unemployment in the profession has been running at about 11 per cent, very much higher among actors and actresses in the twenties, and 26% if stage technicians are included. The actors' unions put these figures higher. This situation partly reflects the dependance of West German television on American series and telerecordings from other countries.

There is a hierarchical structure of salaries, from a monthly salary of between 1,200 (£300) to 8,000 DM: (£2,000) in big theatres in big towns , from 1,000 (£250) to 4,500 DM. (£1,000) in the middle-sized towns; from 800 (£200) to 2,000 DM: (£500) in small towns, and anything between 100 and 1,500 DM. a performance for tours. The average earning is around 2,500 DM. (£600) a month. It will be remembered that these figures are related to salary levels in the public employment service. 70% of all performing artists are salaried.

A detailed picture of the professional actor in the British Theatre emerges from an Equity enquiry that was undertaken in 1978 by the Arts and Leisure Research Unit of the Polytechnic of Central London (6). The Annual Report of British Actor's Equity for 1979-80 establishes that there were some 26,000 fully paid members of the Union. The P.C.L. survey indicates that 91% of the total membership was composed largely of performers, of which about half were actors and actresses. The remainder of the membership were stage-managers, directors, dancers, singers, variety and stunt artists, circus performers, strippers, and so on. The entertainment industry in a capitalist democracy wears a coat of many different colours.

Members covered by the sample found 20% of their work in the mechanical media, predominantly television and radio, a rather smaller figure than might have been expected; most of the remaining work came from the 'live' theatre (53%), with the highest opportunities for employment being provided by the subsidized regional theatres (20%) and about 10% coming from the commercial regional theatres and the commercial 'west-end'.

The 'average' full member of Equity spent about 50% of the year working as a performer, 17% of the year wholly unemployed and 16% of the year engaged in employment outside the theatre.

The minimum Equity salary in London in 1981 was not less than £100 a week, in the regional subsidized theatre £67 or £78 according to the category of the theatre. It is depressing to note that of the full members of Equity who earn their living largely as performers, 70% earned less than £3,000 a year while only 11% earn more than £5,000 and a mere handful over £10,000.

A survey undertaken by Equity in 1971, the main findings of which were not notably different from those of the present survey, made clear that the profession is understandably a young one. Nearly 70% are under 40 and most of the women under 25. Only 4% of the profession is over 60. The peak age for earning is between 40 and 50 but the numbers involved are small.

The most stable areas of employment are in stage-management and directing, opera-singing and ballet-dancing, the latter categories reflecting the high standard of training required and the greater number of semi-permanent companies in the lyric than the dramatic theatre.

In Britain and France particularly the picture is one of chronic underemployment and underpayment; a majority of performing artists are engaged in what an officer of the union described as a 'poverty profession'.

There comes a similar story from the Netherlands. Increasing unemployment in the profession is the result of the subsidized companies employing fewer actors for shorter periods by choosing plays with small casts and curtailing their seasons (7).

There is a strong union but it does not exercise a closed shop. There is one contract for all subsidized companies. Most actors are on a one year contract which is mutually terminable with agreement of the Ministry of Employment. Actors, as in Belgium, have virtually the status of civil servants. Salaries, calculated on length of service, are agreed by the Union of Subsidized Companies and the Employer's Union.

Dutch actors, like their counterparts in Belgium, have virtually the status of civil servants as a result of subsidy being intended principally to cover the salaries of the artists.

There are some 3,000 actors and actresses in Sweden. In 1977 unemployment was running at about 6% against a national average of

1-2% (8). Most of the subsidized theatres offer contracts for one year but it is in Sweden that the Social Security Act of 1976, which requires permanent employment for any employee who has been in a certain job for six months, is cutting most sharply. We have already discussed the pros and cons of the arrangement; and it is in no way to contradict what has already been said about permanent companies to suggest that there may be a middle course between permanence and insecurity. The theatres and the government are said to be searching for such a compromise.

For membership of the Union actors must have worked professionally for six months in the theatre; but graduates of the country's three state drama schools are awarded a union card on graduation. One third of the union members work in a freelance capacity, which means in broadcasting or in the 'free' theatres; but union and managements are now trying to work out a scheme which will provide some freedom of movement between the 'free' and the subsidized theatres. It will be remembered that there is no significant commercial theatre in Sweden. In August 1980 there were 1,538 members of Swedish Actors' Equity Association of which 211 were 'passive' and 118 unemployed, a nice distinction. An agreement between the Actors' Equity Association and the Swedish Theatre Association lays down a minimum monthly salary of 4,753 Skr. (£500) rising after 24 months to 5,421 Skr. and then proportional increases, with individual variations and much higher salaries in the private theatre.

There is one contract applicable to all subsidized theatre with local variations.

The Swiss Federation of Actors reckons that in 1972 there were 710 in Suisse alémanique (German speaking Switzerland) and some 200 in Suisse Romand (French), but these figures are particularly unreliable since many Swiss actors look for work in Germany and France and at this time there were only 110 members of the union. But it is a two-way traffic with many German actors working in Switzerland. In fact the proportion of actors of Swiss nationality is in the region of 35%. In French Switzerland, on the other hand, the theatre has a far more regional character (9).

A very high proportion of Swiss actors have been trained for the profession; but owing to the limited number of professional theatres in the country and their modest repertory, few actors play more than 4 or 5 roles in the course of a year, or about 9 at the most. The Clottu Report states that salaries are far higher in the large German-speaking theatres than in Suisse Romand and the little theatres.

Swiss actors are controlled by special regulations that apply to different categories of workers, artistic, technical and industrial. The basic regulations control length of working hours, night work, breaks, overtime, Sunday working, employment of women, and so on. The special regulations are in the nature of privileges. It is clear that for the smooth running of a theatrical organization special regulations are necessary, but it is also clear that the nature of these special regulations, in so far as they apply to theatre workers, needs extremely careful consideration.

Let us give some examples of the difficulties that are met in over-organizing the life of an actor. His working week is laid down at 48 hours. Overtime, which for industrial workers must not exceed 80 hours a month, must not exceed 220 hours for the actor except with special permission. If an actor is not paid for overtime he is entitled to 10 weeks of paid free-time in compensation. But what constitutes working time of a theatre artist? Clearly rehearsal time and performance time; but how many hours should be allowed for study and daily training sessions, especially for dancers and singers?

Again: the special regulations give an actor four consecutive hours rest before the beginning of a performance. Exceptions are made only for foreign performances or when several performances are given on the same day. But under these circumstances the actor gets none of the rest that is allowed to the less burdened. Paid holidays are usually 4-6 weeks, varying in different theatres.

Discussions are proceeding between the professional bodies and the authorities. The former are demanding the removal of regulations that do not apply realistically to work in the theatre, while the subsidized companies are trying to ensure that regulations are appropriate to the nature of the profession while modifying the structure to meet socially justified changes in society.

Theatrical unions

Only a minority of actors are strongly union-minded. Most actors share the feeling of many artists that the union is for the industrial worker not for the artist. At the same time they are ready enough to admit the improvements which the theatrical unions have brought about over the last 50 years and to grumble only slightly as they pay their dues.

At the same time it is arguable that with the enormous financial involvement of governments in theatre, a political element has entered into the relationship between actors and management that cannot be avoided. It becomes almost obligatory that artists should have a representative body to speak for them in a situation of which by nature and by training they can have had no experience.

200

This is not to argue that unions must play a political role, though they must be prepared to do so if occasion arises. There is a strong case, for example, that governments should provide specialist agencies within the framework of the national provision of employment agencies. This is the kind of negotiation that can only be conducted by a body with the experience and authority to discuss what in general terms will be a political issue.

Broadly speaking an actor's union has a responsibility to provide for its members by negotiating level of salaries, conditions of work, security of employment and a variety of other benefits of which examples have already been given. But whatever power it may have as an industrial union, it must never forget that it is dealing with artists whose requirements are in many respects wholly different from those of the industrial worker. Economic security has to be balanced against artistic stagnation.

In creating opportunities for employment the union is largely dependant on management. But what it can and should do is to play a leading part in public debate. An example has been given (page 96) of the manner in which the French theatre unions commented upon ministerial policy and demanded greater participation in the framing of policy. A democracy is not a democracy by calling it such: a democracy must sustain the integrity of its forms through public debate, and yet in no country that has been covered in this book does there seem to be that vigorous debate over government policy between those who frame that policy and workers in the field.

Of course there are problems. On the matter of salaries it would be quite possible for a union to press for such high salaries for its members that no management could afford to employ them. But by pressing for a certain salary level a union is by implication ensuring a certain standard of professional competence. For if managements are obliged to pay their actors the most they can be reasonably expected to afford, they are entitled to demand 'value for money'. By this means a union, which could never impose a qualitative standard on its membership, can create conditions which by and large imply such standards. This is broadly the principle behind British Equity's recently imposed Middle Range Salary Level (MRSL).

Another problem facing a theatrical union in the 1980s is that in a situation of increasing unemployment among actors, increasing numbers are finding employment in a free-lance capacity, not, that is, as a member of an ensemble or a company but in radio and television; and in this capacity they cannot be so easily 'organized'. It is difficult for the union to speak for them collectively and the actors on their side feel isolated. It is a point made strongly by the French in their submission to a conference organized in 1972 by the Fédération Internationale des Acteurs, that the work of an actor is intermittent, itinerant, and subject to a variety of employers. There is no obvious solution for this problem but it emphasizes a point that has been made repeatedly in this book, that there is a constant dialectic between the structure of the theatre on all its different levels and the daily working conditions of theatrical artists.

Of particular concern to the unions is a widespread tendency towards 'deprofessionalization'. There are two principal reasons for this. One is the tendency for certain *avant-garde* directors such as the celebrated Herr Fassbinder to prefer actors 'off the streets' to the highly trained and widely experienced professional on the grounds that the former are wholly free from theatrical mannerisms and bring to their work an increased element of naturalism. The obvious comment on such a practice is that certain 'natural' actors might fulfil the requirements of contemporary neo-realism, especially as it is practiced in the cinema, but are likely to have difficulties in the classical repertoire.

The second reason is more complex than this. It is the gradual break-down of distinctions between the amateur, university, alternative and professional theatre. From a certain educational-socio-cultural point of view such a process of synthesis can be seen as highly desirable. It implies a conceptual unity of theatrical art among all those by whom it is practiced. It suggests a pyramidal structure in which the work of the amateur provides the basis and the most fully developed professional companies the apex. Anxieties stem from the obvious eroding of the precarious economic status of the professional actor who is bound to see the amateur, and, even worse, the semi-amateur (whatever exactly that means) as a threat to his livelihood.

The report by the General Secretary of the International Federation of Actors (1972), to which reference has already been made, points out that in socialist countries actors enjoy a standard of living well-above that of the average wage-earner; in Scandinavian countries one that is about equivalent to that of other wage-earners; in the rest of the world, and that most certainly includes France and Great Britain, a good deal lower.

Figures that we have already given emphasize very clearly that the status of the actor in European countries that pride themselves on the general level of their culture is that of a casual labour.

Theatrical employment agencies
This important aspect of the life of the actor can be considered under three headings.

First there are the efforts of the industrial countries to establish a national system of employment agencies for the purpose of paying social benefits. In professional and vocational terms these agencies serve the generalized needs of the employer and employed in the fields of industry, agriculture and the public service, but are of little help to the specialist artist. The art world has been familiar with agents acting on behalf of their clients since the seventeenth century with not always very happy results for society at large.

With the industrialization of the theatrical profession in the nineteenth century there came to be established a number of theatrical agents acting 'on behalf of their clients' and receiving remuneration by taking some 10% of the clients' fees. Legislation establishing some kind of control or supervision of such agencies was introduced in most countries in the early years of the century, confirmed in the years immediately following the 1939-45 War, and redefined in the late 1960s. This was followed by an even closer relationship between the artists and his agent in the form of the 'personal manager'; and while there is no doubt that the system has worked so satisfactorily that in most countries an actor considers it to be almost obligatory to have an agent working on his behalf, it is not a satisfactory principle that an artist should depend for employment on the exertions of a middle-man, or that an agent should live by means of exploiting the talents of his clients.

The position of the 10% agent became anomalous with the development of the subsidized theatre and the efforts of the more enlightened managements to create better conditions of work and greater stability of employment for the actor. (It is not the managements who are to be blamed if worsening economic conditions in the theatre have recently frustrated their efforts). It is clearly logical that if the state, through subsidies, is contributing significantly to the employment of artists, it should establish specialist agencies within the structure of its services for the employment of artists.

This has now happened in several countries. In 1967 the French government established the Agence Nationale pour l'Emploi, a special agency for the employment of theatre workers, staffed by people who understand the particular nature of the artists they are dealing with; but its facilities cover only one year of unemployment (19).

In addition there exists the Groupement National des Institutions Sociales du Spectacle, which offers an alternative or additional social benefit scheme to the national service. It has its own fund from the contribution of employers and employees and offers second retirement pensions, widow's second pension, financial aid in cases of hardship, a fully equipped medical centre and a great variety of activities for the elderly and retired.

A scene from 'The Oedipus Story' based on the dramas of Aeschylus, Sophocles and Euripides, at the Royal Dramatic Theatre, Stockholm, 1980.

Similar developments have taken place in the Federal Republic of Germany. In 1972 there were some 85 private theatrical employment agencies supported by a greater number of intermediaries operating in specialist fields. The national employment service was redefined in 1969 under the aegis of the Bundesanstalt für Arbeit (the ZBF), based in Frankfurt, with annexes in Berlin, Hamburg, and Münich, and subdivisions covering different aspects of the theatre.

The main task of the Frankfurt office is to centralize and coordinate opportunities for employment and this requires sensitive and up-to-date communication with theatres throughout the country. It is required to give special attention to the employment of young artists, and arranges for agents, managers and sometimes intendants to attend auditions at music and drama schools. It publishes annually lists of artists, with details of the parts they have played, and distributes them to all theatre directors. Many of the staff of the ZBF are themselves former artists from different sides of the theatre. Its efficiency depends ultimately on its agents and representatives, each of whom is responsible for theatres within a certain region and with whom all artists can get in touch (11).

Since 1971 the Bundesanstalt has been assisted by a Consultative Committee for the Employment of Artists representative of all aspects of the theatre. Lists of available jobs and opportunities for employment are published each month in an information bulletin by the Federal Labour Office in Nüremburg.

There is also in the Federal Republic a most interesting old-age pension scheme: every theatre seat sold, irrespective of its price, includes an additional 0.15 or 0.20 DM, depending on local regulations, which is paid into a pension insurance fund for performing artists (Bayerische Versicherungskammer). In addition the tax laws grant artists certain privileges such as a reduced rate of VAT on the salaries of self-employed persons, and allowances for 'publicity' costs (12).

The British Department of Employment was constituted in its present form in 1968 with headquarters in London, ten regional offices and considerable responsibilities in the whole field of employment and industrial training. Social benefits, of which a wide variety exist, are the responsibility of the Department of Health and Social Security. The Union has played a big part in ensuring that contracts between actors and employers entitle the former to claim all available benefits and that they are properly assessed in dealings with the Inland Revenue for the purpose of Income Tax. But neither the Department of Employment nor the Employment Services Agency make provision for special categories of artists.

Government regulations providing an employment service for all workers in Italy dates from 1949. In the following year a decree was passed creating a specialist office for performing artists but excluding instrumentalists, singers and dancers who had to make use of the existing services. The first of these specialist offices was opened in Rome and placed under the control of the Regional Office of Labour. In 1956 the Office was made an independant organization covering all theatre workers with offices in the larger towns. The service paid particular regard to the special and unusual nature of employment of theatrical artists and technicians, especially in films, an industry in which Italy has been outstandingly energetic. The operatic world is still excluded from the national employment service as well as being forbidden to run private agencies; but the law is frequently broken for agents are a necessary element in the complex world of operatic engagements (13).

In Sweden there are no private agencies taking 10% of an artist's salary. In a fairly small country in which, at least until recently, it was not difficult for an actor to keep in touch with what was going on in the theatre, there was little need for specialist agencies; but with the range of the theatre increasing, the growing responsibility of central government in all aspects of social security, and the need to provide employment for actors in a range of jobs other than acting (to counteract unemployment), the government has established in four of the larger towns, in addition to the usual government employment agencies, special agencies for cultural workers.

It is also encouraging to note that the theatrical profession itself is in some countries taking steps, either through the efforts of individual groups of artists, or through their union, to establish methods of putting actors in touch with available jobs and to provide such services as, for example, child-caring. There are interesting examples of such self-help from France and Great Britain.

Summary

It is arguable that in a free economy the performing artist, whose product is not an artefact that is subject to market laws of supply and demand, has greater need of the protection of union and agent than any other worker. Exploitation is possible in any industry and managers working within precise financial constraints do not have to be slavers or traffickers to demand the most work for the least pay. So it is reasonable that the union should assume responsibility for the general rights, privileges, and salary levels of the actor as performer, while the agent negotiates his salary on the basis of his individual skills and his quality as an artist.

206

Salary levels are thus negotiable in terms of such generalities as the minimum industrial wage pertaining at any one time and the financial constraints of the management which is offering him work. It is at least understandable that certain authorities, anxious to treat the actor like any other citizen, should have related his salary and conditions of work to those established by the unions of public employees. To treat him as a public or civil servant is arguably no worse, and in some ways much better, than to treat him as a casual labourer. But conditions of work are an irrelevance where work does not exist. The overriding necessity almost everywhere, is to increase opportunities for employment; but those who have read the first part of this book will understand that the implications of this are considerable.

Management, however, is operating within a total budget made up of box-office receipts and other earned income and whatever is accruing from subsidy or sponsorship. It is partly a policy decision, partly a matter of practicalities, how management shall divide total income between performer's salaries, technical salaries, production costs and administration. British regional theatres devote about 36% of their income to performers salaries, a drama touring company only 22%, the British National Theatre 17.2%. Proportions as well as actual salaries, are very much higher in the West German theatres which operate, as has already been shown, on a very much higher budget.

It is understandable that in these circumstances the 'star', whose drawing-power is ascertainable, should break-away from the subsidized sector and exploit his capacity to earn high fees in the open market. It is the ability of opera-singers to maximize their talent in this way that makes the international opera-house so costly an undertaking.

Sources
(1) *Théâtre/Public* - Théâtre de Gennevilliers - March 1977.
(2) International Federation of Actors - report on 1972 Conference, unpublished.
(3) Belgian Centre of the ITI
(4) The Stage 31.8.78, quoting on E.E.C. report on unemployment among performing artists by Marie-Madeleine Krust.
(5) Blätter zür Berufskunde: Schauspieler - Bundesanstalt für Arbeit-Bielefeld, 1977.
and
Joachim Werner Preuss - *Fostering the Performing Arts in the Federal Republic of Germany* - West German Centre of I.T.I., Berlin 1980.

(6) Preliminary findings of Survey of Employment and Earnings of Members of the British Actor's Equity Association - Arts and Leisure Unit of the Polytechnic of Central London, 1979.

(7) Actors Trade Union, Amsterdam.

(8) Svenka Teaterförbund (Swedish Actors Union), Stockholm.

(9) *Theater in der Schweiz* - Theaterkultur Verlag, Zürich, 1977.

(10) Antionette Chamberon - Reported in The Stage, May, 1978.
See also
Anon - *La Vie d'Artiste* - Syndicat Français des Artistes Interprètes - E.P.I., Paris, 1974.

(11) Z.B.F.

(12) Joachim W. Preuss (see 5 above)

(13) The Stage - 28.8.78.

9. The Director

Although the term 'director' is now used almost exclusively throughout the English-speaking world, the French term *metteur en scène* provides a better description of his function. It is clear and exact: the director is the man (or woman) who puts the play on the stage and organizes the ensemble.

The word 'director' strongly implies that directional attitude to which Peter Brook refers when he wrote - 'It is a strange role, that of the director: he does not ask to be God and yet his role implies it'.

The director is a comparative newcomer to the theatre. His predecessor was the stage-manager, that immensely practical man or woman responsible for the smooth running of the performance. There must have been stage-managers, or whatever they were called, as long as there have been stages and companies of actors to act on them. The Attic dramatists, who were their own directors, must have had a good deal of technical assistance, but historical records do not mention a division of labour. We have the names of Jean Boucher and Jehan Delachère in connection with the staging of the Mons Passion in 1508 and we know that the Elizabethan 'book-keeper' held a position of some administrative authority. Molière implies a good deal about his role as director in *L'Impromptu de Versailles*; Konrad Ekhof conceived what we might now call 'the group ideal' and David Garrick was clearly a directorial innovator of genius.

The likelihood is that much of the responsibility for the work that is now done by the director fell between the leading actor and the stage-manager, mostly the former, and that if we had seen a performance by one of the great players of the eighteenth century we might well have been highly impressed by the acting but critical of that element of the performance we claim so readily to be able to identify, but which is so often, and at its most successful, wholly absorbed into the performance, the production.

The director, as a man who was neither manager, stage-manager, nor actor, though he may have fulfilled any or all of these functions, emerged towards the end of the nineteenth century as a result of a particular concatenation of historical circumstances. Standards of presentation rose impressively, money became available for the building of new theatres, and the middle-classes gave their support to a new naturalistic drama. The attitude of the Emperor Louis Napoleon towards the money-making capacity of the grande bourgeoisie and their cultural tastes may have sickened Baudelaire, Courbet, Gaugin, and Flaubert but it helped to transform the theatre, and the director was a product of this transformation.

The fact was that the capitalization of the theatre resulted in the need of the manager or entrepreneur, who put money into production as an alternative to other forms of speculation, for someone to stage his plays and ensure they were attended by as large an audience as possible. But there was a powerful movement afoot within the theatre itself. The Duke of Saxe-Meiningen with his stage-manager Ludwig Chronegk, Tom Robertson in London, André Antoine in Paris, each in his different way, envisaged the necessity for new theatrical methods. The great names emerge - Constantin Stanislavsky and his colleague Nemirovitch-Danschenko, Gordon Craig, Jacques Copeau, Max Reinhardt, and show us the shape of things to come. Adolphe Appia wrote in his *Staging Wagnerian Opera*, 'There is only one way to emerge from this blind alley (the various specialisms in the theatre) and that is to entrust the entire interpretation of the drama to a single person'. The same proposal was vigorously advanced by Gordon Craig who wanted his stage-director to have dictatorial powers in all artistic matters. And to a certain extent this is exactly what has happened, and the shape of the contemporary theatre is marked by the Revolt of the Actors against what they believe to be an unwarranted assumption of authority.

A final point on this subject. A further reason for the emergence of the director as a dominant person in the theatre undoubtedly results from his position in the film industry. Here he became 'top dog' because the medium is visual rather than literary and someone in a directorial capacity was required to control the operations of the camera as well as the technical paraphernalia and complicated techniques that go to the making of a film.

So the director, the *metteur en scène*, the *régisseur*, has emerged as the man who can impose his vision on that of the playwright and the actors. He has become a creative artist in his own right and it is a right that is often disputed. This autocracy may not generally be as extreme as that of such great figures as Vsevold Meyerhold or Max Reinhardt, but it is still considerable, and the point that was made by the actors at Gennevilliers is true, that if the director is now more interested in collective techniques than in authoritarian methods, this is his chosen method of directing: he is still the director.

The director and the actors

The director requires no very precise form of training - and indeed he rarely receives it. He is usually a well-educated man or woman with a

210

broad interest in and knowledge of art and culture, capable of finding his way through the whole range of dramatic literature and coming up with an 'interpretation' of the play he has undertaken to stage. He must be able to thrust his way to the heart of a play and to transform the text into theatrical terms through the agency of actors, designer, musicians and any other technician or artist whose skill may be required. He must therefore understand actors and the art of acting intimately, for he has to accompany them, in a capacity which he will have evolved for himself, through the fascinatingly difficult period of rehearsals, when almost uniquely among artists, actors and actresses have to carry out their exploratory and creative work in public. Since he has to create an ensemble not only of the actors but of designers, musicians, and who knows how many other technicians, he must have sensibilities in the visual and musical field and an ability to interest himself closely in the intricacies of staging.

It is hardly surprising that with so many talents demanded of him and so much potential authority at his disposal, he should have become the dominating figure in the contemporary theatre. Yet, as we have said, it is an authority that is challenged. It is challenged firstly by the actors who claim that many directors are highly intelligent people but often do not know the way actors work, providing the worst of both worlds, interference without real understanding of the actor's creative process, lack of support when the actor is coping with crucially important problems in the creation of his character. Many professional actors have learnt to adapt their methods to that of a particular director; but unless we accept that the dominating role of the director is the proper way of things, as Craig would have had us do, it can equally well be argued that the director should adapt himself to the methods of the actors. But in the free-for-all of a *laissez-faire* theatre, such as still largely exists in Western Europe, actors have become accustomed to suppressing what may be their own style in favour of adaptability. They have realized bitterly that it is not they who call the tune, as the director in turn knows that he must play the game according to the rule (or taste) of the manager who employs him. With unemployment running in some countries at 80%, actors must be all things to all men, or at least to all directors and producers.

The director and the playwright
The director's authority is challenged not only by the actor but also by the playwright. There appears to be a fairly widespread resentment of directors by playwrights based on a suspicion of, and even hostility towards, what has come to be called the 'creative' director. This term is

used, often pejoratively, when the director employs the text of the play and the agency of actors and designers to create his own visions, his own theatrical fantasies. It is not the purpose of this book to criticize or even discuss this attitude; but we can point out that factually some of the recent outstanding productions of the leading directors have been of slender, documentary, or basically undramatic texts. One thinks of Luca Ronconi's *Orlando Furioso*, Ariane Mnouchkine's *1789*, Gerald Savary's *Le Grand Cirque de Monde* or Jean-Louis Barrault's *Rabelais*.

When, however, the director transforms a classic text into a major production, we have the art of the theatre at its finest. One recalls Peter Brook's *A Midsummer Night's Dream*, Louis Jouvet's *L'Ecole des Femmes*, Barrault's *Christoph Colomb* and Terry Hands' three parts of *Henry VI*. The creative director at his most successful takes a script and transforms what are largely literary images into theatrical images. When these images transpose and extend the author's evident meaning and intention we have a successful or even a memorable production: when they obscure or twist the author's meaning, critical pens are dipped in vitriol.

The problem has been fully aired by John Arden (1) who makes a distinction between the meaning of a play, which is the playwright's responsibility, and the interpretation of the play, how the meaning is classified in performance, which is the director's. Mr. Arden suggests that some directors tinker with the structure of a play without knowing what the structure is intended to express, and by imposing their own meaning on a play assume the author's responsibility. It is when the author is no longer alive to let people know what he intended his meaning to be that a director can use a text for his own ends. In the same spirit an Italian critic has claimed that the *regista* has become a kind of *drammaturga* by virtue of his identification with a text, and that this relationship becomes all the more intimate when, as in the case of a classic, the author is dead.

The director and the ensemble
It is not, however, the past with which we are so concerned as the present and the complaints of authors about the man who should be their closest ally and, to be fair, who often is. There are many examples of directors who have become closely associated with the work of particular playwrights such as Peter Hall and Harold Pinter.

There is another role for the director in the contemporary theatre and that is as artistic director of a company in his own theatre. Some of the most productive work of the century has been the outcome of what was known in the 1930s as 'the Group Ideal'. This was exemplified in the work of Stanislavsky at the Moscow Art Theatre, of Jacques Copeau at the Vieux Colombier, Harold Clurman with the American Group Theatre, and the productions of Louis Jouvet at the Athénée and Charles Dullin at the Atelier. More recently there have been Giorgio Strehler at the Piccolo Theatro, Milan, Peter Stein at the Schaubühne am Halleschen Ufer in West Berlin, and the group of directors who are associated with the Royal Shakespeare Company in England.

It is a curious phenomenon of the recent theatre that the Group Ideal has become transformed into the concept of the collective. This is not, as we saw in the last chapter, an old wine in a new bottle. We are not dealing simply with a change of artistic method, but with a basic change in theatrical organization. The same Italian critic claims with a mixture of approbation and disappointment, that the *regista* has put a limit on the excessive individuality of the actor. But this can go too far. The individuality of an actor counts for much. Even if we accept that the European theatre is better for absence of giants, in any case a questionable assumption, no one is going to glory in a theatre of pygmies.

The role of the director as artistic director of a theatre is very closely related to the artistic policy of the regional theatre. It is the conviction of many directors that a regional theatre, in order to fulfil its obligations to the community, should employ at least the basis of a permanent company, a small group of actors under contract for at least a season. If the director is also on a permanent or semi-permanent contract this will at least allow some kind of artistic policy or house-style to emerge. Experience suggests that it is unity of approach among director, actors, designer and everyone else involved in the production that provides a certain guarantee of quality. A director anxious to achieve this unity will remain attached to a theatre or a company for a considerable length of time, three years perhaps as the French regional contract stipulates. But commercial pressures are often irresistible. The highly successful creative director tends to be lured away from this kind of discipline by the financial inducements of working as a freelance in a 'star' capacity. It is a danger to which the directors of the big German subsidized theatres are subject. The freelance director is in danger of destroying the ensemble of the theatre in which he has been invited to direct. Peter Stein is conspicuous in having stood out against this tendency.

But in the present structure of the theatre the director has often to choose between an artistic and administrative function. If he spends a large amount of his time directing plays he may not have adequate time for the responsibilities of artistic leadership, for directing the artistic policy of the theatre, an area in which he must work closely with the administration. If this kind of work absorbs too much of his time, his

talent as a director may run to seed. But it is work of the highest importance, for it involves selecting his actors, designers, his administration,
his staff; evolving an artistic policy which means choice of repertory and
many related decisions, some of which came under the heading of
marketing. He will have to negotiate subsidy, show political astuteness
to politicians, loyalty to his company, sensitivity to the public, alertness
to the complex problems of selling his product. In his very person he is
a kind of guarantee of the professional competence of his theatre,
better than that, of its artistic excitement.

The director and society

Directors, understandably enough, have their own views about their
responsibilities, and among the most demanding is that of their relationship with the community, a phrase that has cropped up throughout the
book; and it has done so because in some ways it lies at the heart of
the problem; the role of the theatre in our society. Jean-Paul Vincent,
for example, director of the Théâtre National de Strasbourg, expresses
some of the anxieties of other directors when he rounds on the principle
of decentralization and claims that it is only a political heading for a
much deeper problem, which is to find the form of theatrical creativity
which will develop the art of the theatre as a properly social art. The
enemies of the theatre include the imbecile glut (*engorgement*) of the
mass media; the *prétise* (holiness?) of contemporary culture; the
growing polarity of mass culture on the one side against the so-called
élitist creativity of the intellectuals on the other. His own comment at
this point is *'pouah!'* (2).

Every cultural issue, he goes on to say, is turned into a contradiction:
Beaubourg or the regions? alternative theatre or opera? professionals
or amateur? Since we no longer believe in progress the best we can do is
define artistic creation in terms of its 'cultural context' (his actual
phrase is *'un milieu populaire'*).

It seems appropriate that we should emphasize the problems he
poses, for, as we have said, they are problems for which there is much
general sympathy, though other directors might pose them in different terms. M. Vincent rightly insists that we should accept that the
public is not as idiotic as the apparent success of the mass media seems
to make them out to be. The problem of artistic creation in the theatre is
a profoundly difficult one. For the means of creation must be found, not
in isolation, but in terms of the public for whom and among whom the
act of creation is taking place. The public is not a sort of monster with
definable appetites which can be identified by means of public opinion
polls, but a part of the culture of which the artist is also a part, aspects

of which he expresses and transforms in his work. M. Vincent describes artistic creation as a kind of 'confrontation' in the process of which the participants do not leave their class or social differences in the cloak-room. There is no difficulty for a director with a large subsidy to fill his theatre with popular productions and in doing so make a lot of money; but in the process he will destroy the possiblity of research into new forms. The unproductive artist risks being alienated not only by the survivors of the nineteenth century bourgeoisie but the excellent cultural sensibilities of the masses. It is, in short, not merely a matter of filling one's theatre, for at a price that is not difficult to do: it is filling it with the right kind of material on both sides of the 'curtain' (2).

Of the creativity of the playwright there can be no question: it is discussed in the next chapter. Of the creativity of the actor there has traditionally been some doubt. He is often held to be interpreter, no more; but his present assertion of his right to be considered a creative artist and to play the part of one in the contemporary theatre can only be for the good.

The role of the director is the most open to discussion. By the nature of his work, and as a result of the developing structure of the theatre, he has found himself in a position of outstanding authority. He is at the same time a creative artist in his own right, and a key man in the organization of the theatre, the link between artists and administration.

We have referred more than once to the criticism that is commonly expressed of the practice of the French Ministry of Culture of awarding subsidy to the Centres Dramatiques in the form of what amounts to a personal contract with the director. This, it is said, emphasizes, under-lines and gives authority to his privileged position. Yet the practice has been established with the very best intentions. The Ministry's rubric reads:

The contractual system, established in 1972, is extremely flexible. It establishes two permanent characteristics of ministerial policy with regard to the theatre: firstly, the wish to encourage the init-iative of individuals in leaving to them responsibility for the admin-istrative organization (*forme juridique*) of the company and its administration, so that they may enjoy absolute freedom in organiz-ing their company and technical staff and arranging their pro-grammes; in the second place, the need to limit (for a certain length of time) the preferential position granted to a small number of '*hommes de théâtre*' in order that new talent can in turn emerge to benefit from the same conditions (3).

The matter is an important one. Is ministerial involvement in any form whatever to be deprecated? or are there dangers, similarly threatening though of a wholly different kind, in the British procedure of keeping governmental participation in any direct way at all to an absolute minimum?

In discussing the role of the director in the contemporary theatre it is also necessary to take note of his position in contemporary society. For while on the one hand our society is tending towards constantly greater specialization, there is a contrary trend for frontiers to be destroyed and human activity to be seen in the framework of a living social context. We have an indication of what has been happening in the theatre from increasing use by the French of the word *animateur* to replace that of *metteur en scéne*. Now the word *animateur* has educational antecedents. It is used to describe a form of activity, in our case theatrical, in which dramatic methods and techniques are used in an educational setting. (We shall devote a large part of Chapter 11 to the subject). The use of the word by the professional theatre indicates clearly the extent to which the profession is moving in the direction of education. This will surprise no one who is familiar with recent trends in the two fields. The fact of the matter is that the teaching of the great theatrical innovators like Constantin Stanislavsky and Jacques Copeau and that of the great educational reformers like John Dewey and A. S. Neil have a remarkable amount in common. The new relationship with the director which has been demanded by the actors is extraordinarily similar to the new relationship demanded by teachers towards their pupils. We have reversed the emphasis only because the actors are on the whole older than pupils and somewhat more articulate in the formulation of their relationship. But from whichever group comes the stronger dynamic, sometimes from the one, sometimes from the other, the actor-director relationship has much in common with the pupil-teacher.

What in fact this implies is a new concept of directing, using the word in the broadest sense. Just as the teacher no longer considers it to be his main task to fill his pupils with a body of knowledge, something which a well-educated young person can do much better for himself by reading books, so the contemporary director no longer considers it to be his task to dictate to his actors exactly where and when they should move and how to speak their lines. The education of a pupil is now considered to be a process by which the teacher helps the pupil to think for himself, to cultivate an insatiable curiosity, to handle facts and to see their relevance to the tortuous manifestations, intellectual as well as affective, of the human spirit. The directing of a cast of actors is now seen to be a process of stimulating the greatest possible artistic and creative potential in every member of the cast, and to help order the results into an artistic unity related to what the whole company believes to be the interpretation of the author's meaning.

Pressing this whole argument a stage further we can begin to see how and why it is that professional actors have become increasingly interested in education and why one of the most original developments to have taken place in the theatre in recent years is the policy towards education which is clearly of overriding interest not only to the alternative theatre groups but to some of the leading continental companies.

The education of the director

We use the word 'education' in preference to 'training' as seeming to be more appropriate for a profession that requires a kind of wide-ranging understanding rather than a limited range of technical skills. This aspect of the work of the director is reflected in the shortage of courses for his training. There seems to be a good deal of support for the English belief that universities may fill this need. Yet perhaps it is this basic lack of understanding of the nature of the actor, not an intellectual understanding but a deep-seated intuitive sympathy with the way the actor works, that has helped to create this sense of animosity between the director and the people he most intimately works with.

In this connection we should draw attention to the most interesting practice in Belgium which enables a young director, on leaving drama school, to propose to the appropriate committee an experimental project which on acceptance will receive subsidy towards its realization. This practice seems to provide an admirable link between the idealism of a young would-be director and the practicalities of the professional theatre.

It is in this context of the further practical training of the director that the bursaries offered by the Arts Council of Great Britain for 1980-81 establish an admirable precedent. The Director's Scheme is divided into three parts:

1 is intended for young directors to enable them to study all aspects of directing and the artistic direction of a theatre or opera company for a period of up to one year, with occasional possibilities of a longer period;

2 consists of in-service training for directors who already have some directing experience in professional theatre or opera, to extend their knowledge in specific areas of work in this country or abroad for a period of up to six months;

3 is to enable an experienced director who has not been responsible for the artistic direction of a theatre, to be appointed as an associate director at a theatre for a period of up to one year.

The director in broadcasting

As for other artists in the theatre, generous opportunities are offered to the director in broadcasting.

In sound broadcasting the role of the director is a fairly straight-forward one. The scope for highly individual work is limited by the constrictions of the medium; it is really only the writer and the composer who can develop their creativity to the full. Most people will be able to name a distinguished broadcaster but few a radio producer (or director).

It is quite another matter in television broadcasting where the inter-vention of the camera creates an altogether different creative medium. The television director has the opportunity of making a variety of choices and establishing a variety of relationships through all of which he exercises a powerful creative function. His choices include the use of studio or 'real life' locations, film or video-tape and recording techni-ques. He must establish relationships with his actors and his technic-ians. In television as in film the latter constitute an essential element in the ensemble of the production. And thirdly, he must establish a relat-ionship with his producer, the channel through which he makes further relationships with both the artistic and financial management.

In general, the bigger broadcasting companies do not carry a large number of staff directors but employ them on contract; this in turn encourages the current tendency for directors to make small low-cost films in an independant capacity and sell them to the major companies.

Whether he is functioning independantly or under contract to a broad-casting company his most important relationship is with the playwright. In company with the producer, or according to the structure of the organization, it is his responsibility to supply the plays, filmed or telerecorded as the case may be. It has been one of the main themes of this book that in spite of the existence of a huge number of plays, a living culture depends on a steady flow of vigorous contemporary work. And it is the responsibility of the director/producer to find or commission the plays and to produce them in the appropriate medium as it is for the broadcasting companies to provide facilities for their transmission. To emphasize the extent to which broadcasting companies are a helpful employer of theatrical labour is firmly to put the cart before the horse. The very term 'mass media' as applied to broadcasting throws emphasis on the responsibility of broadcasting companies to make a vigorous contribution to the cultural life of their contry; and this contribution, so far as drama goes, is largely in the hands of the director/producer and the playwright.

The role of the producer and his relationship to the director is often ill-defined. Lord Annan says (4) that in many countries 'the profession of programme-making is the core of the system and management consists of a set of procedures and structures rising above the level of programme-making'; but in Britain, for example, 'the whole production function is buried within the managerial process: the producer occupies

218

one rung on an institutional ladder'. Placing the producer closer to management has the effect of giving management itself far more collective experience in production than is usual elsewhere. Direction is as it were at the top of the pyramid of craft skills; producing programmes (i.e. making the primary creative and intellectual choices along the line) is the function which is placed within the management grades; but the present feeling within the BBC is that producers are more closely related to the production team than to management although they have managerial responsibilities. Producers are expected to combine considerable organizational and financial genius with outstanding artistic flair, and the ability to work closely with a great variety of technical experts.

It is clearly a matter of the greatest importance that neither the extent, the popularity, nor the commercialization of the television industry should lead to a lessening of the fullest creative opportunities for the artists it employs. It is a problem that has to be faced at every level of creation, from the producer who initiates a programme, to the floor- or studio-manager who is responsible for the smooth running of an immense technical apparatus within the middle of which the actors carry out their creative work. In evaluating new techniques in production it is essential to consider their relevance to artistic creativity as much as their technical or economic advantages.

There is a broader issue, however, than the creative opportunities for the director in broadcasting, and that is the comparative function of the director. Acting and directing are very closely related. Many distinguished actors have proved themselves to be directors of considerable ability. The actor-managers combined the two functions with considerable success: Henry Irving, George Alexander, Herbert Beerholm Tree; and similarly in France: Louis Jouvet, Charles Dullin and Jean-Louis Barrault. Many other names could be added such as, in more recent times, John Gielgud and Laurence Olivier.

The actor-director directs as an actor; therefore he is rarely what we have described as the 'creative' director and some would add 'thank God for that!' The Peter Brooks, Peter Steins, Ariane Mnouchkines are not actors and their productions have a different emphasis.

There is not a very close relationship between theatre directing on the one hand, and film and television directing. There are men and women who do both. But the outstanding film and television directors do not on the whole move outside their own medium, although some have been actors within that medium. The reason for this is that the two media are far more different than superficial similarities lead one to suppose. The three dimensional element of the one art-form, and all that this implies in terms of relationships between the performer and his audience, is of a wholly different kind from the two-dimensional nature of the other, which requires the audience to face the screen and watch the moving pictures. A temperament which functions creatively in the one medium does not do so readily in the other.

Sources
(1) John Arden - *To Present the Pretence* - Eyre-Methuen, 1978.
(2) Théâtre/Public - Théâtre de Gennevilliers, January, 1978.
(3) French Ministry of Culture.
(4) Lord Annan, *Report of the Committee on the Future of Broadcastcasting* - HMSO, 1977.

10. The Playwright

The nature of the artistic experience

This book is about creativity in the theatre. Creativity is a two-sided activity: it involves the creator, the artist, on the one side, and the people who are interested in what he creates, the audience or spectators, on the other.

It is in the nature of an act of creation that it is both a disturbing and a placating experience. The artist is disturbed or excited by some experience, by the impact of something that he has seen or heard or thought and so undergoes a process, part volitional part subconscious, in which he transforms this experience into a new reality, some kind of expressive or symbolic form. Critics may disagree with this oversimplification of the creative process but so complex is the subject that a whole book would not ensure agreement. It is simply necessary in the present context to establish that the creative process involves a very close symbiosis between an individual and his environment.

It is also necessary to establish that this reordering of reality into a new, artistic reality, can have a very disturbing effect upon an audience. People have been greatly disturbed by the reordering of visual reality by the impressionist painters, then by the cubists, the surrealists, and so on. They have been disturbed by the reordering of sound by Stravinsky; by the reordering of Irish life by Synge and O'Casey. Flaubert was prosecuted for having written *Madame Bovary; Ghosts* has been received with every calumny. When nineteenth century society saw that its artists were drawing attention to its prejudices, its profligacies, its materialism, it replied with screams of protest and invoked the protection of the law.

But there is also a sense in which an audience is soothed, placated, satisfied, because the ordering of a work of art, however disturbing in its reordering of reality, has reduced the apparent chaos of that reality to a form that can be encompassed by human experience. The greatness of such plays as *Agamemnon, King Lear,* and *Phèdre* lies in the success of their authors in making coherent aesthetic form out of tumultuous and seemingly uncontrollable human emotions, emotions which if continuing to be uncontrollable might be thought to endanger the very fabric of society. Diderot says in his celebrated *Paradoxe* that at the end of a theatrical performance the actors go home refreshed, the audience exhausted. There is some truth in the observation.

Some writers, particularly those of recent times, have eschewed the possibility of satisfying their audiences and done their utmost to infect them with such dissatisfaction with society that they will leave the theatre determined to take action. Brecht was particularly articulate in his attitude towards actor-audience relationships.

Audiences on the whole prefer the theatre to be placatory rather than disturbing. This is understandable enough. Daily life itself tends to be so intensely disturbing that we turn to art for a confirmation of traditional values, not a challenge to them. That is why theatre audiences accept so many poor plays, which they know to be an insult to their intelligence, without comment. They may be drivel but they are relatively undisturbing. It is understandable that we will pay money to be assauged, amused, astonished rather than to be disturbed.

But it has become evident to those in authority that if a theatre, like any other art, is not injected with, and does not in turn inject into its audiences, new and inevitably disturbing attitudes, it will become moribund. If no new plays were written the theatre could survive a considerable time on the plays that have already been written; but it would loose its vitality with increasing rapidity, for the reality expressed by those plays would become increasingly remote from existing reality.

One of the arguments running throughout this book is that since audiences will pay to see the classics, which they know will not be unacceptably disturbing, rather than contemporary plays of a challenging kind, steps have to be taken to sustain the vitality of the theatre by ensuring the production of contemporary and possibly disturbing plays even if they offend the taste of a majority of the theatre-going public. The income-gap, the difference between what it costs to stage a play and what the public is prepared to pay, is paralleled by an appreciation gap, the difference between plays that confirm or challenge existing social values, as well as by the culture which tends to polarize different kinds of artistic experience.

The popularity of drama

We have already discussed the proposition that if people do not want the art of the theatre and disturbing plays enough to be ready to pay for them, the state has no business to interfere. We will assume, however, that the state has a certain responsibility to encourage services that seem to be socially justified but which cannot be sustained by the market-test, that is to say, cannot be made economically self-sufficient by the purchasers of that service.

If the theatre is indeed a service of this kind, and the writing of plays is a crucial part of this service, it follows that some special considerat-

222

ion must be given to playwrights. It is by no means uncommon for a British theatre to receive 500 unsolicited manuscripts a year and for the BBC to receive that number every week. But of this heap of material only about 2% is usable. Indeed it might be said that the number of potential authors increases in exact proportion to the decrease of readers, just as the number of potential actors increases while that of committed audiences declines.

The Nature of Writing Plays

The difference between writing plays and a poem or work of fiction is a significant one. Prose fiction involves the transference of experience, expressed in the mental image, into visual symbols such as calligraphy, the typewriter's lettering, the printed page. These symbols are picked up by the eye and transmuted into mental images which produce thoughts and feelings. The visual symbols of the playwright's dialogue are taken one stage further. They are transmuted into mental images which are then transformed into speech, that is, sound symbols, when they are picked up by the ear. It is this difference in the nature of the final experience that constitutes the distinction between the two expressive forms, the narrative fictional form and the dramatic. The reader of prose fiction sits comfortably in his chair, often alone, often in silence, or at least enclosed within a world of his own imagination as prompted by the visual symbols of the author whose book he is reading. But the audience at a play is largely engaged by the words it is hearing and the actors it is watching. The skill of the playwright therefore seems to lie in his ability to write words which, when spoken by the actor, help to create an imaginative world in which he can participate, and to create actions which, when accomplished by the actor, complete this sense of imaginative conviction. This means that the playwright, by training, intuition, or experience, must be able to identify with the physical life of the actor, giving him words that he can speak and actions that he can act. He must be vicariously an actor himself.

It will be remembered that in the chapter on actors we drew attention to a variety of claims they now make, how they have a powerful creative fantasy, how they can contribute creatively to 'collective creations', how there is a kind of poetry in their power of gesture, in the way in which they use their bodies. It was clear that many actors see themselves moving towards the condition of the playwright. But we have now seen that the playwright is moving towards the condition of the actor. He too has a creative fantasy; and although he may not be able to express poetry in his movements, he writes a verbal poetry which by virtue of its speakability involves a quality of moveability, permitting the mover, who is the actor, to exploit that poetry of gesture on which he prides himself.

It is therefore not surprising to find that in the course of theatrical history most great playwrights have been actors or very close to the practicalities of the theatre. The Attic tragic dramatists directed their own plays. Sophocles is said to have been an accomplished dancer. Shakespeare and Molière were actors, men of the theatre through and through. Racine had a rigorous education in rhetoric. And when an era of specialization laid greater emphasis on individual skills we find that the playwrights, though no longer associated closely with the work of the actor, were associated closely with the work of the theatrical company. It is very much open to doubt whether Chekhov would have continued to write after the disaster of *Three Sisters* at the Maly Theatre if the Moscow Art Theatre had not succoured him. Ibsen had a firm grounding in theatrical art at Bergen. The Irish playwrights have been closely identified with the Abbey Theatre, Giraudoux with Jouvet, Shaw with Barker, and many American playwrights of the 1930s with the Group Theatre. Perhaps the relationship should not be pressed too exactly. But it is possibly true to say that whatever the detailed nature of the relationship, the playwrights have known where they stood in relationship to the theatre. They have enjoyed a personal and professional identity. And this, curiously, is what they claim to lack today.

The theatre of the last 100 years has seen many more changes of style than that of the previous 500. The contemporary playwright does not know where he is. In Britain he is carried along by a cultural revolution that allows him such moral freedom that he no longer knows the difference between liberty and license. In Germany he is the victim of both a national guilt and a determinedly materialistic society. In Italy he is involved in a struggle for political identity, and in France in a struggle between a traditional autocracy and a still centralized policy of decentralization. Within such uncertainties he finds that he has lost his traditional relationship with his audience, his directors and his actors. He is obsessed with social problems. But his inherited form of expression is a rather limited form of naturalism. There is no longer a living popularly-accepted poetry, nor a poetic theatrical convention. Yet this is what is eagerly sought for by directors and actors - a theatre of gesture, as they call it. But playwrights cannot think in terms of gesture because their education is largely in terms of the word, and for the most part the prosaic word.

Nevertheless before a playwright can write plays he must be able to write. He must have the facility, the gift for transmuting human experience into words, and he must be able to handle the words themselves. And the problem with which we are faced is that all the subsidy in the world cannot endow a man or woman with either of these essential gifts.

If this apparent isolation of the playwright is less pronounced in Britain than elsewhere it may be the result of bursaries provided by the Arts Council of Great Britain (details below, page 249/50) which enable playwrights to be attached to a regional theatre for upwards of a year, during which time they are expected to write a play, even if they are not directly commissioned.

It is also possible that the general practice of attaching literary editors, what the Germans call the 'dramaturg', to every subsidized theatre is a policy that should be more widely examined. The high level of subsidy in West Germany enables the bigger theatres to employ as many as five dramaturgs, one of whom is assigned to each production; but they often assume a wide variety of responsibilities, working closely with the directors of the theatre and the intendant. It will be objected by many British directors that this is a luxury they cannot afford. To which we would be inclined to answer that so crucial is the contribution of the playwright to the vitality of the theatre that nothing which might lead to the writing of more and better plays is a luxury. If the playwrights are likely to respond to a greater interest in their problems by the personnel of the subsidized theatre, they should be given that interest. If anyone suggests that this is to pamper them we would reply that the creative spirit may well respond to some pampering. We are not dealing with an assembly line of farm tractors. Nevertheless, the prevalence of dramaturgs in the German theatre has had no effect in stimulating playwrights of distinction, and there lies the rub.

It is perhaps perverse and certainly digressive to suggest at this stage in the argument that success can bring its own dangers, but this has been most emphatically pointed out by several young dramatists. When a playwright finds overnight that his latest play is a success, the operation of the market is immediate and overwhelming and can do much to destroy the very creative instinct that success might be thought to foster. The broadcasting companies want interviews, the popular press wants articles, the theatres want more plays. And under such sudden and unexpected pressure the mind suddenly seems to be empty of ideas. Ibsen at the height of his creative powers took two quiet and isolated years to write a play. And now the media want a pile of them and at once. And if I don't oblige I shall miss the chance! And starve! No wonder the Americans in their cynically realistic way have designated her the 'Bitch Goddess - Success'. Success should never be as destructive as failure; but the demands of a consumer society for the products of the human spirit can be very destructive of that spirit.

Edward Bond

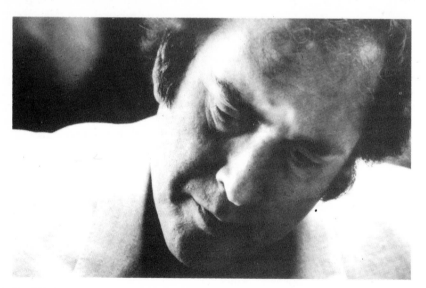

Harold Pinter

226

Problems of Language

A particular difficulty the contemporary playwright has to face lies in the present devaluation of language. The collapse of traditional confidence in the communicative power of language is a phenomenon that has pervaded the whole of European literature throughout the present century. The subject has been fully discussed by George Steiner in a number of books (1) but not in terms of the theatre. Drama is even more responsive than other forms of literature to the reverberations of contemporary speech. If the playwright creates his own language, his own verbal imagery, as poets have tended to do, the resulting obscurity will simply alienate audiences. If he throws back at his audiences the language of the streets, they will complain that this is not what they have come to the theatre to hear. One regrets that few if any playwrights are pursuing the experiments of T. S. Elliot in trying to find a language for the theatre that is at once poetic and at the same time of a contemporary resonance. Perhaps we should include the Italian writer, Giovanni Testori, but of him more later.

This devaluation of language has been accompanied by attempts to upgrade the significance of non-verbal forms of communication. In the art of both the actor and the playwright there is a delicate balance between the physical and the linguistic. The history of the Commedia dell' Arte shows us both the splendours and the dangers of a theatre that is based on physical skills without support or extension from the spoken word; while emphasis in the drama of the present century on a naturalistic and literary register to the almost complete exclusion of the physical shows the dangers of bias in the other direction. The enormous popularity of Shakespeare and Molière throughout the European theatre of the 1970s seems to be attributable not only to the contemporary significance of their plays but the superb integration of a rich and resonant text with strong physical characterization.

Here are two quotations to show the way things are running. Donald Kaplan, an American psychologist, writes:

On the face of it, scripts have not been a compelling preoccupation of current experimental theatre . . . Their fate has been the aspect least provided for, seeming at times a curruption of the whole point of avant-garde theatre, which believes itself to be striving for a kind of reclamation of gesture from diction.

And Paul Epstein, an American composer:

Just as new music has reacted against the tyranny of the printed score, new theatre has rejected the supremacy of the text in favour of a complex information structure that includes movement, gesture, and non-verbal sound (2).

227

One might even question whether the theatre is the invention of the dramatist - the innovatory genius of Aeschylus suggests that this might have been the case - or whether the dramatist is the invention of the theatre, which has shaped him for its own ends and will wish, in due course, to dispense with him.

The Playwright and the Director

The 'creative' director has clearly made an enormous contribution to the European theatre; but whereas most people might agree that the influence of such men as Stanislavsky, Granville-Barker and Copeau has been entirely for the good, there are those who can be seen as imposing their own interpretation upon a play; those of whom John Arden had hard words to say; of whom Swedish playwrights have complained that they see *The Tempest* as an essay on imperialism or a piece of space fiction.

The problem is unfortunately widespread. There have come to our notice two further discussions about the position of the playwright in the contemporary theatre, one French (3) and one German (4), both written in 1973 and both beginning with similar complaints against the director. The French writer sees the director as increasingly assuming for himself the role that is the right of the dramatist. The policy of subsidy, the application of the policy of public service to the theatre, and the pressures of decentralization have projected the director-animateur to the forefront of the scene and contributed to the present disarray among writers for the theatre.

The German writer complains that the theatre is dominated by the director for whom a comfortably large number of plays exists even if no new ones were ever written. The playwright is rarely involved in any kind of discussion of a theatre's policy, and when one of his plays is staged the director's interpretation seems to take precedence over the author's meaning.

The French writer argues that the artistic dominance of the director is both made possible and heavily underscored by the manner in which, in the French theatre, subsidy is granted on the basis of a contract between the Ministry of Culture and the director. Yet it must be remembered that powerful though the intendant of a German theatre may be, he is in direct control of only 20% of the theatre's budget, the remaining 80% being paid out in salaries on the basis of arrangements made between governments and unions.

On the other hand it must be firmly said that many playwrights are ready to express their gratitude for the help they have had from directors and the extent to which their play has succeeded through collaboration.

228

Referring in his autobiography to the isolation of the playwright and to his work in St. Etienne, M. Jean Dasté, that splendid man of the theatre, writes:

We always lacked an author who could live long enough with the company. We made application a number of times to the Ministry: the director of theatrical activities was always sympathetic but short of funds. A dramatic work, to reveal its inner life, must be written for a company and a public: it is an ancient truth; the talent, the inventiveness, or genius of the author and of the stage director most often develop as a result of an encounter, a confrontation which causes sparks to fly! (5)

The repertory of the subsidized theatres

An examination of the annual repertory of the European subsidized theatres shows certain fairly consistent patterns. Most theatres stage between five and eight productions a year, usually new ones. In exceptional circumstances an outstandingly successful production is revived for a second year. This number is explained by the fact that most are scheduled to run for three or four weeks, or some thirty performances, as part of an eight month season. In the Federal Republic many theatres stage more than eight productions annually for reasons that were explained on page 135; in the Italian Stabili the number tends to be slightly less owing to the shorter theatrical season.

It is possible to analyse the repertory of many European theatres into four rough categories:

1 there will be at least one production from the European classical repertoire; Shakespeare features in the programme of an extraordinary number of theatres. In Germany there are likely to be at least two productions in this category;

2 there will be two or three productions of what might be called 'Contemporary classics' of which at present Brecht provides an outstanding example.

3 most theatres stage on *création*, a new play by a contemporary author, éach season. As we have noted, there are usually financial inducements. We note that the Comédie de Saint-Etienne is outstandingly enterprising in its support for new plays; a legacy, no doubt of M. Dasté.

4 There may be at least one experimental production or *création collective*. In this respective the Théâtre de Strasbourg seems to be outstandingly enterprising. Its repertory for 1978-79 included: Bernard Pautrat (*dramaturgie*), *Théâtre Complet de Kafka*: an adaptation for the stage of excerpts from the work of Kafka;

Bernard Chartreux and Jean Jourdheuil, an attempt to sketch a portrait of Jean-Jacques Rousseau from his own writings; Création du Groupe regional d'Action Théâtrale, *Ca Respire Encore*, 'Spectacle Satirique', from the works of Büchner, Dario Fo, Karl Valentin, and Michel Deutsch; Création Collective by Le Théâtre de a'Aquarium, *La Soeur de Shakespeare*.

It would seem that the young playwright must cultivate patience until he becomes a 'contemporary classic'. Unfortunately he is unlikely to attain such eminence without having first been a contemporary *création*.

Let us consider this question a little more closely and try to ascertain how often playwrights are performed in their own country.

There is a very interesting comparison to be made between the French commercial theatre of the 1970s and the French subsidized theatre in the early days of decentralization. The establishment of regional theatres in the 1950s was a slow and deliberate policy, the result of support by the visionary Jeanne Laurent in Rue Saint Dominique, of determined and similarly visionary men like André Clavé in Colmar, Jean Dasté in St Etienne, Maurice Sarrazin in Toulouse, Hubert Gignoux in Rennes, Gaston Baty in Aix, Roger Planchon in Lyon and Jean Vilar in Avignon.

If we take note of the repertoire of the first five of these centres between 1946 and 1952 we find the percentage of classics as follows (6): Colmar, 35%, St Etienne, 68%; Toulouse 56%; Rennes, 50%; Aix, 100%. The rest of the repertoire consisted of what might be described as 'modern classics', the works of playwrights who even in 1946 were fairly well established in the mainstream theatre — Armand Salacrou, Jean Anouilh, François Mauriac, Jean Cocteau and Paul Claudel with their counterparts from abroad — Bernard Shaw, Sean O'Casey, J.M. Synge, and Garcia Lorca. Of the French classics by far the most popular was, and still is, Milière.

The young French directors of the 1950s and 1960s pursued a policy of decentralization which envisaged the education of new audiences for the theatre. Thus they had to give them the best the theatre had to offer. They considered their aims would be served by showing these audiences productions of classic masterpieces of the excellence of which there could be no question, rather than contemporary plays of the quality of which there might be some doubt. The policy was violently attacked at the time by popular playwrights like Marcel Achard and André Roussin and it is understandable why they did so. They pointed out that Gaston Baty directed *Arden of Feversham* and two plays by Alfred de Musset, and Gignoux at Rennes had staged *Cymbeline* and *The Taming of the Shrew*, all plays of the greatest interest but not among the masterpieces of dramatic literature. M. Gontard, in his admirable book on decentralization (6), argues that such plays, together with Molière, provided a more acceptable theatrical diet than *Patate* or *The Little Hut.* The controversy is interesting. We are dealing with the years immediately following the war and the liberation. The most popular play in Germany at the time was Zückmayer's *The Devil's General;* but it should be added that the next most popular plays were by Goethe, Schiller, and Lessing. It is a possible argument that in times of trouble society requires a reaffirmation of civilized values such as are represented by the classics, and that it is not until society is stabilized that it can absorb the challenge of a new and perhaps disturbing art. The controversial playwrights of recent times were the product of a relatively stable society in the 1960s, until the events of 1968 created a wholly new situation.

The work of the so-called 'commercial' playwrights is so intensely alien from the ideals of the subsidized theatre that it tends to be rejected out-of-hand. Thus there is danger of a curious polarity, the Parisian bourgeoisie being entertained with one kind of theatre, the regional bourgeoisie with another. We must repeat the surprising fact that a court dramatist who wrote over 200 years ago was considered to be more acceptable to uncommitted theatre audiences than any contemporary dramatist.

The process of decentralization in France is all the more interesting when we compare it with what happened in England — and the comparison is not altogether complimentary to the latter. The British repertory movement, as we have already seen, was an entirely spontaneous growth, unassisted by government subsidy, advice, or policy. It staged a heterogeneous repertoire of plays many of no great artistic worth; but some of the directors were men of considerable professional distinction: Geoffrey Ost at Sheffield, William Armstrong at Liverpool, H.K. Ayliff and Herbert Prentice at Birmingham, Nugent Monk at Norwich, J.B. Fagan at Oxford and Terence Gray at Cambridge. They brought a classical and contemporary repertoire to the regional public for the first time.

In 1973 a special number of ATAC/Informations recorded all the productions of the decentralized movement over the previous 25 years. The list of 412 playwrights produced was headed by Molière (136 productions), Shakespeare (84), and Brecht (48). The first living Frenchman was Ionesco (30 productions, 6th place), then Obaldia (20 productions, 13th place), then Anouilh (18 productions, 17th place). Of the 54 playwrights produced more than five times, only three are authors of original texts who can be said to have been discovered by the decentralized movement; they are Foissy, author of light modern satires (13 productions, 22nd place), Gatti, the anarcho-humanist poet, (9 productions, 34th place) and Planchon, the actor-producer-director

(7 productions tying with Aristophanes at number 43) . . . The 412 included 126 other contemporaries first produced within the decentralization, but of these only 30 had more than one play produced (7).

A further analysis published in ATAC/Informations of December 1976 shows that during the season of 1973-74 few living French playwrights had had more than one play produced during the year and that such plays were staged only once each. A subsequent article analysing the two sets of results (1973 and 1976) reveals that only 47 living authors appear in both. Three out of every four authors who appear on the first list do not appear on the second. It is not surprising, of course, that the classics should be played more frequently than contemporary plays and show more staying power since they have stood the selective test of time; but it is important to note that both theatre directors just as much as the general theatre-going public are more consistently interested in plays of the past than of contemporary dramatists. We shall return to this surprising phenomenon in the next section.

The Theatre Yearbook of the Flemish Theatre for 1974-75 lists 15 productions of plays by 14 living Flemish authors against 341 productions of plays by 260 past authors, many of them foreign. This is to say, 4% of all productions in the Flemish theatres were by contemporary Flemish authors. The figures for the following year show a slight decrease in *créations*.

In French-speaking Belgium, with a smaller population than Flemish-speaking Belgium, about eight new plays by living dramatists are staged each year. (The manner in which productions are categorized preclude a detailed analysis.) That is to say the 13 main subsidized theatres do not produce one new Belgian play each a year in spite of considerable incentives for *créations*.

The anonymous author of a note on playwrighting in the same publication suggests that an appropriate climate for playwrighting is created by a mixture of intellectual freedom and a strong but liberal central authority such as did not exist in Flanders until the nineteenth century when Belgium became independant. A writer should be actively involved with a theatrical company. Administrators and theatre directors have a responsibility for developing the talent of potential playwrights; but he does not consider that the commissioning of plays is the answer. Flemish plays should not be staged simply because they are Flemish: they must be worth staging for their own sake.

M. Delsemme (8) has analysed the repertoire of 13 French-speaking theatres in Brussels between 1970 and 1975. Of the 539 different plays that were staged, 258 (47.9%) were French; 171 (31.7%) British and American; 40 (7.2%) Belgian; 16 (2.9%) Italian; 13 (2.4%) Russian; 9

(1.6%) Dutch; and 5 (0.9%) German. There was a preponderance of British - American plays at the National Theatre, which selects an international repertory, and the Comédie des Galleries. French plays predominated at the Théâtre Royal du Parc, the Théâtre du Rideau de Bruxelles, and Théâtre Royal du Gymnase, the leading subsidized theatres. Belgian plays made a better showing at the small theatres, the Théâtre du Poche (18.3%), and the Théâtre de l'Esprit Frappeur (18.9%). Perhaps even more telling is the fact that out of 287 authors, at least one of whose plays was staged, 191 had only one production, 43 had two, nine had five. The only playwright who might have made a living from his royalties was Molière!

Of the foreign plays in French, 33% were adapted or translated by Belgian writers but in the Thèâtres Agréés (major subsidized theatres), where Belgian adaptation is a source of increased subsidy, the figure was 65%.

40 new Belgian plays in five years, eight a year among 13 theatres where there are financial inducements to stage such plays! A common explanation is that in a small country there is so small a demand for a native play that financial inducements are negligible. The argument would apply with greater force to Flemish-speaking theatres; but French is French and there are no import restrictions on culture. If the Belgians can stage over 50 new Flemish plays a year, there is no apparent reason why Paris should not stage a few Belgian plays, if they are good enough.

Again, we find that the German subsidized theatre is dominated by the great classics. Between 1955 and 1975 the most frequently performed playwrights were Shakespeare, Schiller, Bernard Shaw and Bertolt Brecht. The latter has increased in popularity over the years until in 1971-72 he topped the list. Zückmayer is twelfth with 10,333 performances of 17 plays. Living German playwrights are rare. Hauptmann is seventh, Sternheim sixteenth, and before we come to any other German names we find Giraudoux, Priestley, Arthur Miller and Tennessee Williams. Woman dramatists are conspicuous for their almost complete absence (9). Of the 41 plays with more than 200 performances, 26 were classics and the remaining 15 were occasional entertainments (*Zeitstücke*) by contemporary playwrights.

Of the 40 most frequently performed plays, Brecht comes well down the list with *Mutter Courage und ihrer Kinder* followed closely by *Die Dreigroschenoper*; but *Charley's Aunt* had 167 more performances than either.

In 1977-78 the most frequently performed plays were Alan Ayckbourn's *The Norman Conquests*, a monologue about Goethe by Peter Hacks, and Kleist's hoary classic *The Broken Pitcher*, with strong support for Sartre, (then living though French), Chekov, Pinter, (still living though English) Strindberg and more Kleist. The sixth most frequently performed play was Shakespeare's *A Midsummer Night's Dream*. But apart from the present popularity of Brecht, it is Shakespeare who consistently tops the list with Goethe and Schiller as runners-up. And in analysing the fact we should not forget the great acting parts which these old plays offer.

During the season of 1977-78 in the German-speaking theatre of the Federal Republic, Switzerland and Austria there were 1,500 productions of which 163 were given over 75 performances. Of this number 67 were by German-speaking authors, of whom 47 were deceased, and of those still living 14 were by 11 German writers, two by an East German, three by Swiss, and one by an Austrian. Of the 1,500 productions, 977 were new, the remainder revivals.

It has been suggested that the proportion of foreign to German authors staged in the German subsidized theatres is about 60:40, but this is difficult to prove. In the seasons 1978/79/80, 4% of the productions in the subsidized theatres where first productions of new, largely German plays. What is clear is that the number of contemporary German playwrights whose plays are regularly staged is extremely small, that the German-speaking theatre is dominated by the classics, and that the repertory is predominantly international rather than German.

One has only to press the argument, however, for it to become exceedingly parochial. One may lament the shortage of living German playwrights; but at the same time one must applaud the internationalism of the country's theatre as much as one must deplore the lack of interest of the British theatre in the European drama past or present. Subsidies are in no way bound by conditions for the special promotion of German authors. But remembering the two sides to this important argument we should refer to our constant emphasis on the cultural and social importance of a living art. If the Germans bring an original vitality to the theatre through direction rather than through playwrighting, that is an area for speculation beyond the limits of this book.

There is a considerable number of playwrights in Britain at least scraping a living out of the theatre. One agent has suggested there may be as many as a hundred. The British Alternative Theatre Directory of 1981 lists 373 playwrights, most of them working largely for the Fringe. It is also fairly clear that Britain has a thriving export of plays to Europe. While French and German playwrights complain that their subsidized theatres stage far more foreign plays than native, a complaint for which there is a great deal of justification, critics in Britain lament the parochialism of the British theatre and the absence of European plays from its stages.

It is difficult to analyse this outburst of playwrighting. Britain's recent social revolution may have had something to do with it, but this too is difficult to analyse. There was clearly a dynamic in the seventeenth and eighteenth centuries which led to the creation of an Empire and made Britain for a time the leading industrial country in the world. This dynamic was a Protestant one, perhaps it would be truer to say a Puritanical one with *Laborare est orare* as its driving force. 'Be wholly taken up in diligent business of your lawful callings', wrote an eighteenth century divine (10), and 'God hath commended you . . . to labour for your daily bread'. Religion was an active experience; prayer and meditation were a form of self-indulgence. The drive has collapsed and so has Britain's economy, though it is difficult to say how far the reason can be attributed to two world wars and the final separation of secular from religious life. Visitors to the country are both amused and horrified by the vestigial remains of a class structure that has enjoyed 700 years of stable evolution. The final crumbling of that structure is painful for the participants although enough stability survives for the country to have been able to develop a cultural freedom of remarkable flexibility. Inspite of the criticisms and animadversions that are constantly levelled against the English educational system (English, for they do these things differently in Scotland), for its élitist nature, many of the young writers whose plays are contributing to the rich output to which we have already referred, are of working-class origin, the children of families who until recently would not have remotely been considered likely to contribute to the nation's culture.

Partly as a result of the considerable encouragement that is given to all kinds of creativity in schools; to the cultural climate in society as a whole; to agents who are ready to handle new and unconventional plays and theatres ready to stage them; to the financial help that is available to young playwrights from the Arts Council of Great Britain, many young writers have been able to earn a pound or two from the production of their plays.

The London commercial managements, wilting in the face of economic difficulties, are far less enterprising in the staging of new plays than they used to be; but in London there are a number of small theatres associated with the Fringe, specializing in new plays and each creating a regular audience. There is also a good deal of interchange between the Fringe and the subsidized theatres (see page 35). The subsidized regional theatres rarely draw good audiences for a new play unless the author is uncommonly well-known.

The National theatre is both generous and sensitive, within the limits of its budget, to new playwrights. The same is true of the Royal Shakespeare Company. Both organizations commission new plays. A somewhat disturbing situation, however, is arising in the demands that are being made by young playwrights for a downpayment in excess of what the theatres say they can afford. Their reply is to exercise a control of the play beyond what can be in the best interests of the playwright.

The Writers and Artists Year Book for 1980-1 lists 78 agents specializing in plays, films, television and radio, 15 publishers interested in plays, together with 32 production managements in London and 80 in the regions. The same book provides an impressive list of B.B.C. and Independant Television channels and keeps radio stations ready to receive manuscripts with details of requirements.

Next the Italian theatre. In the season of 1975-76 the private theatres gave 6,764 performances of 109 different plays of which 88 were Italian, 21 foreign; the Stabilii gave 2,065 performances of 47 plays, of which 26 were Italian and 21 foreign; the co-operatives gave 8,714 performances of 179 plays of which 146 were Italian and 33 foreign; the experimental theatres gave 2,594 performances of 106 plays of which 91 were Italian and 15 foreign.

These figures give us a total of 20,137 performances of 436 plays of which 90 were foreign. And since the Italian theatre has not a body of classical masterpieces anything like as substantial as that of Britain, France or Germany, a very high proportion of Italian plays must be by living playwrights. How are we to account for the preponderance of the homegrown product when every other country in Europe, with the single exception of Britain, is living on imported plays?

The figures show a consistent rise in the proportion of Italian plays being staged from 54.4% in 1969 to 69% in 1979. English plays have dropped from a recent 10% to 5%, French, partly owing to the popularity of Ionesco, have risen from 4% to 10%, while German, with the fading popularity of Brecht, have dropped to 3.9%.

Of the 20 most successful plays in 1974-75, five were written by living Italian authors, one being a new play by Edouardo de Filippo. In the following year there were seven new Italian plays among the first 20 including another by Edouardo de Filippo, another by his brother, and one by the prolific Dario Fo. The rest tended to be prolonged vaudeville turns.

Many Italian plays are given by small companies in small theatres, the more successful touring the left-wing political clubs where they play for one, two or three performances. A very large number of plays are being written but evidence suggests that not many of them are of impressive quality and few that could survive export.

The Dutch themselves say that their genius has never expressed itself successfully in the theatre, an omission for which a variety of reasons

236

have been advanced - Calvanism, the exclusive nature of Dutch bourgeois society, high priority given to earning a living, and so on.

Figures seem to support the claim. Between 1946 and 1970 some 3,000 foreign plays were staged in the Netherlands together with 104 plays by 69 living Dutch dramatists and 63 plays by classic Dutch dramatists (13).

Since 1969 the situation has improved, largely as a result of the emergence of a vigorous educational and alternative theatre (see pages 6, 11), supported by a more liberal and flexible policy towards subsidy. 40% of the plays now staged in the Netherlands are by Dutch authors but the political and social element in them is so strong that people doubt how far the theatre is benefitting as a form of artistic and aesthetic expression.

A writer on contemporary playwrighting in the Yearbook makes the interesting point that it is a result of having to work collectively on new scripts that actors have found their way towards collective creations, but doubts whether this is in the best interests of an actor's technique. Is, therefore, a theatre company the best training ground for a new playwright? The question is a valid one. But if it isn't, what is?

The Swedes are similarly self-critical about the state of playwrighting in their country. Their critics have expressed the view that the general attitude towards the theatre is too educative and too solemn. In this respect they feel themselves to be as inhibited as the Germans, by whom in cultural matters they are greatly influenced. Even the work of the Free Theatre groups is held to be unduly puritanical.

Would-be playwrights are isolated; they have no living contact with the theatre. The most successful playwrights appear to be actors and critics who maintain a contact with the theatre through the nature of their work. They instance Kent Anderson, an actor; Allan Edwall, another actor; Goran O. Eriksson, a critic. The Swedish Union of Playwrights states that the number of new plays is declining and represents no more than a quarter of the total repertory, and this includes many children's plays that are not full-length.

The Swiss Clottu Report provides us with some useful basic information. How, the anonymous author asks, does one define an author? Does he need to have a book published or a play produced? Does he have to live by his writing? Of those who were asked whether they considered themselves to be professional writers, 60% said yes, 21% said that writing was an essential part of their life, though they did not wholly depend on it for a living; and those who did earn their living by writing did so mostly from television and radio, from broadcasting rather than traditional forms of literature.

The report establishes that writing is not for the young: a mere 4% were under the age of 30, 7% in Suisse Alémanique, a negligible percentage in Tissino. This is not a reflection of disenchantment in literature among the young but evidence of the difficulty in getting published. A high proportion of professional writers - 66% in Italian Switzerland - are between the ages of 40 and 65 - and in general 83% of the professional writers are men, 17% women! 85% draw an income of less than 5,000 F a year, 10% earn between 5,000 and 10,000 F, and 5% more than 10,000 F.

The Report includes a very useful table of the form of subsidy that authors would most appreciate. The majority want help with sales (diffusion); then a commission. A good deal below comes a guaranteed minimum income and paid holiday. These figures show the loyalty of a writer to his work. He wants to be helped through his work, not with a kind of social service. Moreover in their anxiety to be recognized as writers we find a futher response to that sense of isolation and loss of identity that has already been discussed.

The particular problems of the playwright are understandably different in the various linguistic regions according to the strength of the theatre. In German-speaking towns, playwrights are paid good royalties which are negotiated by the society of theatrical publishers who protect their rights. The theatres in Basle offer courses in playwrighting.

Although about a quarter of the plays produced in Switzerland are of native origin, the position of the playwright in the French-speaking area is less satisfactory than in the German since permanent theatrical companies are of more recent origin and traditionally depend on Paris for their plays. The Foundation Pro Helvetia offers grants to theatres that stage original Swiss plays but it is generally felt that a more direct form of subsidy to playwrights is desirable.

The Report draws attention to the situation we have noted particularly in Germany. When a theatre offers reduced seats to season-ticket holders or a party-booking, this reduces the gross receipts on which royalty is based. The Report poses the question whether playwrights should not be guaranteed some kind of minimum wage in line with that of the industrial worker. The interesting proposal of the Irish was described on page 184.

Some problems of the playwrights

It is only too easy to summarize the complaints of the playwrights. But it will be clear from all that has already been said that there are no ready solutions. Original creative work is not easy in any society since, as has been emphasized, it contains an element of dissatisfaction, of the will to transform existing reality into a new fictional, but nevertheless in many respects even more living reality. Creative work in the theatre is particularly difficult in that it involves an element of co-operation with other workers and a complex administrative process before even the simplest 'spectacle' can be staged before a public.

Complaints can be summarized under a number of headings. First, the straightforwardly administrative. It is clearly the responsibility of every director of a theatre or a company to provide for the reading and assessment of manuscripts. We are not suggesting for a moment that he should enter into critical discussion - this may or may not be the province of the literary editor or dramaturg - but letters should be answered immediately, manuscripts acknowledged and read within a reasonable time.

Also important is the question of paying the playwright. The system of payment by royalties on box-office receipts is outdated in the subsidized theatre. It is both important and urgent that new procedures be discussed. This is an artistic matter as much as financial, since the method of paying the playwright must depend upon his relationship to the theatre in general and the company that is staging his play in particular.

Young authors often express the view that they are not receiving adequate support from the authorities responsible for culture. We shall describe in the next section what many authorities are doing and in some countries have been doing for many years. It is perhaps necessary to point out to the authors that in the first instance the responsibility is that of the theatre, not the bureaucracy. Artists are the first to bewail lack of understanding of their work on the part of the government inspector. But having said this we should emphasize the point that lies behind the whole writing of this book, that nothing is more important for any art than the production of vigorous, original, contemporary work. The preservation of the heritage is important; but it is arguable that the work of the greatest masters would lose something of its significance if it were not sustained and complemented by new visions of artistic reality. And we would therefore argue that any public authority concerning itself with subsidy must place the policy of the company with which it is dealing towards original work and 'creations' at the top of the agenda.

Finally there is the question of the collective creation. This, as has been shows, is a phenomenon common to the whole European theatre. The process of creation by the collective works in many different ways and produces many different results. It is a form of theatre that includes Peter Cheeseman's musical documentaries which he has staged over the years at the Victoria Theatre, Stoke-on-Trent; Ariane Mnouchkine's work with the Théâtre du Soleil; the interesting relationship between writer and company that has been developed by the British Joint-Stock Company; and, in fact, a large proportion of the productions of the whole European alternative theatre.

To those who would argue that the collective creation is unlikely to give rise to a work of genius, we would argue the reverse. The deep involvement and personal concern of actors for the text they are interpreting, or recreating, is a development of the greatest importance for the theatre. It is creating a milieu in which the potential playwright can participate and help to escape that sense of isolation which is evidently a basic inhibition to his creative impulses. We are in danger of regarding the actor and the playwright as different species, whereas it is probable that each of them carries within him something of the other's disposition. Shakespeare and Molière were not the only playwrights of distinction who were clearly no mean actors.

Of the greatest interest in this connection is the work of at least one of the Italian co-operative companies. Signor Parenti's company, based in Milan, exploits to the full the creative fantasy of the actor. Signor Parenti himself asserts that the actor has a creative potential which traditional methods of creating a character, given him by a playwright, in a manner that has been given to him by a director, does not satisfy. He has therefore tried to reassert the basic qualities of drama as an action, or a series of actions constituting a story which is the province of the actor. But the drama additionally needs words, and it is in this capacity that the actor needs the collaboration of the playwright. He has therefore sought that of the distinguished Italian novelist, Giovanni Testori who provides a structure of narrative and words which the actors can develop with their own mastery of gesture and in particular with their own creative fantasy (14).

This is not the place to enter into a full discussion of Signor Testori's experiments with language. But the confidence of Signor Parenti in the power of language in the theatre is in itself a source of immense encouragement at a time when dramatists are denying themselves the use of language, or, even more seriously, denying the power or value of language as a civilizing influence.

The economics of playwrighting

With the invention of printing by Gutenburg of Mainz in 1451 the control of an author's work fell into the hands of his printer. It was a considerable time before there emerged a distinction between printing and publishing and before there was any effective control that prevented the indiscriminate copying of an author's work and ensured him adequate remuneration.

240

The control of performing rights by the playwright or his agent took even longer to establish because it was more difficult to enforce. In this the French took the lead. The first Right of Performance was enacted by the French Assembly in 1791 following years of agitation by Beaumarchais. The French continued to be so far ahead in the collection of performing right royalties that French agents established themselves in London and acted for British authors until at least the end of the nineteenth century when the Dramatic Authors Society, established in 1832 largely through the efforts of Edward Lytton, began to acquire real power. With a long history of piecemeal legislation it is hardly surprising that the present vast changes in the economic structure of the theatre should have put the payment of the playwright once again in question (15).

Since the act of 1791, playwrights have almost everywhere been paid on a percentage, usually 10%, of box-office receipts, while actors have traditionally been paid a salary and directors a fee and/or a percentage of receipts. This practice, as we have already implied, places them firmly within the market-mechanism. The playwright stands to make money according to the success of his play with the public and the willingness of the theatre staging his play to 'milk' his success to the full. It is in the nature of the private theatre to indulge in such milking and for the subsidized theatre to spurn it.

A simple calculation will show that a play running at 75% capacity in a theatre with 800 seats at an average price of £4 with eight performances a week will draw royalties of about £2,500 a week or £30,000 for a run of six months. And since in the world of commercial entertainment nothing succeeds like success, a popular production may well bring film, television and publication rights as well as productions throughout Europe and the United States.

Even if £30,000 is the limit of the returns for the first production of his play our playwright is not likely to feel wholly dissatisfied. A London bus driver in the summer of 1979 earned little short of £100 a week or £5,000 a year. If the playwright has a standard of living no higher than that of the driver he will have earned enough to live on for six years. But how long does a full-length play take to write? Ibsen who was no duffer in these matters took about two years, Shakespeare a good deal less. It is, however, impossible to generalize, for it is not the actual writing of a play that takes the time so much as its gestation; but no one is going to accuse a playwright of malingering if he claims that it takes him the best part of a year. If, therefore, his standard of living is that of a bus-driver he must hope to earn at least £5,000 from a play; if he considers that it is higher, proportionally more.

241

The anomalous position of the playwright in the subsidized theatre first came to a head in Germany where subsidy was practiced long before it was introduced in other European countries. In the past 25 years this subsidy has consistently increased, while box-office receipts as a proportion of total expenditure have decreased to a figure which provided the playwright with a royalty only fractionally higher than he was receiving in 1926 but which in terms of the value of money was considerably lower. An article in the Dramatiker-Union *Mitteilungen* (Information No.3 1977) sums up the situation like this:

... The individual income of the State, municipal and Land theatres ... supplied only 17.8% (ticket sales, cloakroom, radio and television fees, programme sales, advertising income, and so on) while the subsidy requirement had reached 82.2%. Everyone on the theatre staff from intendant to doorkeeper, from guest star to dayman, profited from the budget, the dramatist received royalties on the basis of a mere 12.4% from the sale of tickets.

Since there was no logical reason why in due course subsidy should not reach 100%, a possibility which has in fact been seriously considered in Sweden, it was clear that something would have to be done.

Another problem arose from the fact that royalties were calculated on the basis of full-price tickets which for many years were bought by less than one third of the play-goers, the rest being accounted for by season-ticket sales, party-bookings and reductions for young people. Subsidy was payable to offset such reductions as well as to lessen the cost of full-price tickets.

The problem is exacerbated by the fact, already emphasized, that the subsidized theatre does not exploit a successful play in the manner of the private theatre. The fairly close and often mutually profitable relationship between subsidized and private theatre in Britain, which enables the private sector to benefit in a number of ways from the public, does not exist in other European countries, except perhaps in the Netherlands where the structure of the theatre is wholly different.

It has already been pointed out that a subsidized theatre is likely to stage about eight priductions a year, each being given about 30 performances. Not more than one of these productions is likely to be a *création*. Owing to the manner in which seasons are planned in advance, and especially if productions are running in repertory and there is a season-ticket scheme in operation, there is no way in which a successful *création* can be exploited except by transferance to the private sector, which is unlikely to happen in most European countries where the gap between the private and public sector is unbridgeable, or where there may not be a private theatre at all (as in Belgium). The most a playwright can hope is that his play will be revived the following season, or in Germany,

242

that it will be promoted from the studio, where most new plays are tried out, to the main house.

The point need not be laboured. In Britain the playwright in the subsidized theatre receives 7½% of box office receipts which represents something in the region of 50% of gross costs. The Dutch point out that a native dramatist can derive from his native theatre, if he is lucky, an annual income equivalent to the minimum monthly wage of an unskilled worker.

Let us make the situation absolutely clear. A British regional subsidized theatre may have 700 seats. With an average price of £2 it will have a capacity of £1,400 a night or £11,200 for a week of eight performances. But it is unlikely to play to more than 60% or around £6,000 from which the author will benefit to the tune of £600 or £1,800 for a run of three weeks for a play which may have taken him a year to write.

In Germany there were long and arduous discussions between the theatre authorities, and the Association of Authors and Composers (Dramatiker Union), and the play agents (Verband Deutscher Bühnenverleger); but agreement was finally reached and has now been put into practice with considerable success. The crux of the new system is that the subsidized theatres pay a fixed royalty fee per visitor for every occupied seat, whether the seat is sold at full or scheduled price. The amount is graduated according to the theatre's expenditure on its artistic personel, which in turn is related to a number of other factors such as size of theatre and local population. In 1967-77 the figure was between 1.70 DM. in the larger theatres and 0.75 in the smaller. In English terms this would work out at between 40 and 20p or £150 a performance in a theatre seating 500 and around a £1,000 a week of seven performances playing to capacity. In Germany the sum of these fees must equal at least 12% of gross box-office receipts but may not exceed 18%. The fee is adjusted from time to time in the light of general price and wage increases. Special guarantees have been made for studios and theatres with a capacity of less than 200. The whole arrangement is now supervised by an association that combines the authors' and agents' organizations mentioned above, (the Neue Zentralstelle der Bühnenautoren und Bühnenverleger, Bismarckstrasse 17, 1000 Berlin 12.) (16).

Sweden is another country which, with the level of subsidy running extremely high, has broken away from the royalty system and come to an arrangement by which the playwright is paid at a fixed rate. Depending upon the length of the play he receives a salary corresponding to the minimum salary of a theatre director (1976-77, about 6,000 SK. or £750 a month). For a play of more than 90 minutes played for 30 performances the playwright receives the equivalent of a five month salary at 6,000

Alessandro Fersen,
director of the Teatro Stabile di Bolzano.

Franco Parenti in his own company's 1976 production of Olescia's 'La Congiura dei Sentimenti'.

244

SK. a month, increased to six months in 1978. For a play of between 45 and 60 minutes the playwright receives the equivalent of three months salary of the director for the first 50 performances. For revivals, the playwright is paid for a smaller number of months. But when the number of performances exceeds the stipulated figure, the playwright is paid at the rate of 1/20th of a month's salary (at 6,000 SK.) for a 90 minute play, 1/45th for a play lasting between 45 and 60 mintues, and so on. A similar agreement covers translator's fees. For example, for a play of more than 60 minutes the translator receives a month's salary of a director and 1/60th of his salary for each subsequent performance (17).

Among a variety of contracts at present being negotiated in Britain, there is one which relates payment to playwrights on the basis of six month's work (for a full-length play) 'at a wage not lower than that of anyone else working for the company at a recommended rate of £80 per week'. Other negotiations are based on a proposed down payment of £2,000 (to represent about six months' work) followed by royalties at a higher rate than the present 7½%. (In 1981 the usual royalty was 10%). But this figure is well beyond the means of any but the larger companies, and likely to remain at the present £750.

The attempt to relate the payment of a royalty to the wages of other theatre personnel breaks down on two issues. It is only fully relevant when the playwright is working as part of an ensemble, a practice which only a limited number of companies follow, while once the initial production is over the playwright has a property on his hands which might produce an income for many years without him having to raise a further productive finger.

Another contentious issue is the demand by certain playwrights' organizations that a theatre should have no control over or interest in a play after its first production. While there is a strong case to be made that a play should remain the exclusive property of its author, it is a little hard that a small theatre should lose money on the first production of a play and not be able to recoup if the production is staged by another management. The fortunes of a playwright are closely related to those of the theatres on which they depend to stage their plays.

Methods of helping the playwright
Perhaps the most serious of the contemporary playwright's anxieties is this sense of isolation, of not being really wanted by the theatre for which his object is to write plays. Since it is probable that not even the young actors and actresses of Gennevilliers would vote for the absolute rejection of the playwright from the theatre it would seem to be nec-

essary to reintegrate the playwright into the ensemble, perhaps, as was suggested, on the basis of a new division of labour. It is this reintegration which is the outstanding feature of the new contracts at present being negotiated by such an organization as the Theatre Writers Union. The principle of these new contracts is that the playwright is paid for a certain number of weeks as the member of a company and that he may attend the rehearsals of his play 'at a wage not lower than anyone else working for the company'.

Next in importance is unquestionably the financial return due to a playwright. A conference of playwrights held in Budapest in 1974 made a number of practical suggestions based on the continuing practice of royalties: that they be paid on a percentage of subsidy as well as box-office receipts; that they be increased well above the long established 10% (12% in France and 7½%-10% in the British subsidized theatre); that 1% or more of all subsidy be put aside to create a fund to help writers; that a percentage of subsidy be put aside to help all *'créations';* and so on.

Subsidies to theatres in French-speaking Belgium can be increased by 50% for the Belgian adaptation of a foreign play; 100% for the first production of a Belgian adaptation; 150% for the production of a classic play in French or the adaption of a foreign classic; 250% for the production of an original Belgian play (*création*). Unhappily these awards are made from within the overall budget available to the theatre. Thus the more *créations* there are, the less money is available for general subsidy (18).

The size of these subsidies emphasizes the importance attached by the government to original creative work and the necessity for inducements to encourage such work. This pattern of supplementary subsidy for *créations* is not unique to Belgium, nor is the procedure of granting additional subsidy to the theatre rather than to the playwright. It is an inducement to recalcitrant directors to stage more new plays. This is of indirect benefit to the playwright. But should nothing be done to help him directly? In any case the policy of encouraging new plays is sometimes in opposition to the need to win new audiences, since new audiences do not on the whole like new plays.

A Belgian correspondent makes an interesting point that is also applicable to the situation in Great Britain. Years ago the Flemish Repertory theatres in Brussels and Antwerp played a different play every week for 36 weeks of the year. This means that a new or unpopular play could be slipped into the programme without great financial risk. But now that each production runs for three or even four weeks, with a very much higher standard of presentation, the financial risk is far greater. The longer run provides an opportunity for the play to be 'nursed' but the financial risks are greater.

There has been a long history of help to authors in the French theatre. It began with the pioneer work of André Antoine and Aurélien Lugné-Poe in staging worth-while new plays. But it was not until 1947 that there was established a governmental policy of *'aide à la première piéce'*, largely through the inspiration and insistence of Charles Dullin. It was initially decided not to limit the number of plays that might be supported; not to embarras the author with official patronage; not to interfere with the natural workings of the theatre.

Plays reveiving favourable report at first reading were to be read by all members of the commission. When the play came to be staged the choice of *metteur en scène* was also to be approved by the commission. When the entrepreneur had produced a balance-sheet for the production, the commission would agree on a subsidy of not less than one-third of production costs. Various changes in procedure were made as a result of predictable difficulties: some members of the commission did not pull their weight, there was public criticism over choice of some of the plays, and so on. But between 1947 and 1967, 92 plays by young authors were subsidized and presented: 60 of them have vanished without trace. Critics consider that the commission with all its limitations did valuable work but was never a crucial factor in the creation of a new theatre. It is illusionary perhaps to think that this might ever have occurred.

In 1967 a new procedure was established by M. André Malraux, then Minister of Culture. The decree *'Aide à la première piéce'* was replaced by a *'Commission d'aide à la création dramatique'*. The responsibility for this commission was to examine applications for subsidy from theatrical companies not regularly subsidized. There was no longer any question of the selection of a certain play, new or otherwise, but of supporting the director with sufficient initiative. The new regulation read:

> In order to encourage the writing of plays in French, subsidy is available, on the advice of a consultative *ad hoc* committee... to the animateurs of independant dramatic companies and to the directors of private theatres who take the risk of staging new plays.

And the same benefits apply for the first translation of a foreign play into French.

There are two points to be made. The allocation for 1979—80 was 1,947,000 F. (£200,000) from a total theatrical budget of 188,588,000 F. (£20 million) or almost exactly 1%. The second point is that the subsidy for new plays takes the form of a contract between the Ministry of Culture and the director of the company which intends to stage the play. It is therefore hardly surprising that French playwrights are

247

demanding as a requirement a minimum royalty when one of their plays is staged by a subsidized company; bursaries for playwrights, and integration of the playwright into the theatrical ensemble.

It is fair to say that although a Ministry might be expected to make some provision for the first two complaints, the third is a professional matter which the theatre itself must work out.

In defence of the directors it must be pointed out that they have divided responsibilities. They are not in a position, financial or artistic, to risk alienating a public on whose support they critically depend. But they also have their artistic responsibilities towards their company. We discussed briefly the theories of M. Jean-Paul Vincent who is in charge of the Théâtre National de Strasbourg. He has his problems: that of working with young playwrights did not appear to be among them. Nevertheless, as we have made clear, there are *metteurs en scène* and *animateurs* who take no greater pleasure than in working closely with a playwright with whom they have discovered some natural affinity. The only trouble is that for many French animateurs in 1978 the only congenial playwright appears to have been Brecht.

As a further means of helping playwrights, the organization known as ATAC, whose activities were described in pages 106-110, established in 1969 a Bureau d'Auteurs (19). This bureau not only acts as a kind of agency between playwrights and the subsidized theatre, duplicating copies of plays and bringing them to the attention of theatre directors, but is attempting to deal with the loneliness and isolation of the playwright to which we have already drawn attention. The staff, having read a play and agreed that it has merit, organizes seminars in which a group of actors and directors read the play aloud in the presence of the playwright and then discuss it with him. Once again it is a question, say the organizers of the Bureau, of bringing writers, directors and actors into contact with each other. And what has surprised them has been the increasing interest of actors in new plays. It seems as if actors, almost intuitively, have been making common cause with playwrights to discover a new or renewed source of theatrical creativity in new forms of collaboration.

Another important project which has been in existence since 1971 is Lucien Attoun's Théâtre Ouvert. This involves a *metteur en scène* being invited to choose an unpublished and unacted play and to stage it, with the collaboration of the author and a number of actors, without scenery or costumes, and in the simplest possible manner, for three of four performances in front of an audience. This is done with the object of involving an author in the procedures of staging a play, to let him feel the impact of his words upon a public, and to bring actors into living contact with contemporary texts, all without going to the lengths and the expense of a full-scale production (19). Théâtre Ouvert has spread from Paris through the country, and has been closely associated with the Avignon Festival.

We are indebted to Christoph Campos for up-to-date facts about the Théâtre Ouvert.

By the end of 1977 Théâtre Ouvert was presenting four rehearsed readings, a dozen author's readings, and a workshop every year. It had also begun to expand beyond the (Avignon) festival. The readings now go on tour to provincial arts centres and playhouses — other readings by local playwrights are organized in provincial towns during the winter; and the organization has begun to sponsor full-scale productions two or three times a year. From 1971 to 1977 there were 47 rehearsed readings, 116 (author's) readings, and four workshops. About 120 playwrights had had their work presented, 31 for the first time. 30 plays that had begun their career in Théâtre Ouvert had later been produced on stage.

During 1978 Lucien Attoun's kingdom has expanded again with five new schemes; a series of cheaply produced photoprinted playtexts . . ., of which 50 copies were given to the author . . . and 450 circulated to managers, directors, actors, critics and foreign literary agents; a bi-monthly newsheet called 'Ecritures'; a series of sponsored closed workshops . . . where actors and a director, hired for a week, work on a text with an author . . . ; a weekly evening gathering for playwrights every Tuesday at the offices of Théâtre Ouvert (21, rue Cassette, Paris 6); and an occasional conference of playwrights in Paris and Avignon.

It was suggested by M. Campos himself at the Theatre Quarterly Conference (see below) that the proliferation of playreadings can lead to a trivialization of the plays and the creation of a para-theatrical experience. There is a great danger, he suggested, in extracting playwrights from the total theatrical experience. There was no general agreement on the issue, but the warning may be a salutary one.

To turn now to Great Britain, the Arts Council provides the following schemes to encourage new writing in the theatre.

The Council's Theatre Writing Schemes are designed to help dramatists directly and to encourage theatre companies themselves to stimulate and support new writing.

There are five schemes of assistance:
1 *Bursaries* are available to help writers to work in temporary isolation from the theatre.
2 The *Contract Writer's Scheme* is designed to enable theatres to

offer realistic sums to writers working for them on a wage, fee or commission basis.

3 The *Royalty Supplement Guarantee Scheme* aims to ensure that writers who might otherwise only be paid low royalties on the production of a new play receive a supplement to ensure fair payment for their work.

4 A limited number of *Resident Dramatist Attachments* will be available to enable theatres to apply for considerable financial help in employing a resident dramatist for long-term periods of 6 to 12 months.

5 *Writer's Workshops* will be helped by means of a joint arrangement with the Council's Training Committee. Contributions towards a deficit will be considered.

In the autumn of 1978 an exploratory conference to examine new ways of encouraging and supporting theatre writing took place at the University of East Anglia, Norwich. The conference was conceived jointly by the newly formed British Associate Centre of the International Theatre Institute and the Calouste Gulbenkian Foundation. The organization was provided by TQ Publications (Theatre Quarterly) which is how we shall now refer to it.

While sessions were planned to provide opportunities for discussion of various ways in which playwrights might be helped, the conference was also concerned with the assessment of the desirability of creating a British equivalent to the O'Neill Centre's National Playwrights Conference in Waterford, Connecticut. The Conference meets once a year and within a week stages some 12 to 14 productions of new plays selected from well over 1,000 which are submitted annually. Certain scripts are referred to regional theatres and universities who are encouraged to stage not only first productions but second productions for which there tends to be less enthusiasm (20).

In Britain an interesting scheme known as New Theatre Workshops was initiated in 1979. A team of some thirty or more writers, actors, directors, designers and technicians are provided with accommodation for a fortnight and set to work on a series of projects. The Workshops are intended to emphasize the creative process rather than 'the manufacture of theatre products' (or plays). It is rather typical of the contemporary British approach to these things — the whole project is known rather whimsically as 'the Tring Thing' from the country town where the first two courses took place — that there should be a good deal of opportunity for work in mixed media, finding a creative tension from the interplay, for example, of dance, masks, visual design, music and the spoken word. In view of what has been said above on the isolation of the artist the following passage from the report on the 1980 course is of special interest.

All progressive tendencies, with concern for the writer, have, over the last decade, sought his or her integration with the process (of encouraging all members to find their creativity). This proves to be no threat to the writer... Similarly the director should feel no threat when working collaboratively. Experience reveals that all goes well until a conflict arises because the common objective has been lost or was too insubstantial. It is very easy for these conventional relationships to re-assert themselves: the actors feel they are 'serving the writer'... while directors are left to mop up frustrations and the writer feels isolated, taking the blame.

In Italy the Ministry provides an additional subsidy for new Italian plays of 20% on receipts for commercial companies with a maximum of 1,500,000 L. (£1,000) a performance, or 2 million L. for every 30 performances, and 4 million L. for every 60 performances, which in the case of plays of exceptional interest can be increased to 10 million L. (£7,000) (20).

Subsidized companies in the Netherlands are encouraged by the government to produce two or more original Dutch plays a season but few of them do so. Dutch plays are said (by the Dutch) not to be popular, the audiences stay away, so the theatre refuses to stage them and the authors make no progress. Article 41.7 of the 1978 budget for the arts allocates an approximate sum of 209,000 G. (£25,000) for the development of dramatic literature, a sum which in terms of population compares favourably with the Arts Council's £67,000 (21).

The vigorous determination of the Swedes to create an integrated democratic society expresses itself in a widespread tendency to form unions and associations, artistic as well as industrial. Those of the writers and the playwrights are said to be efficiently run and lively in debate. In these congenial circumstances the Swedes find it difficult to understand why the country does not produce more outstanding playwrights. There are various possible explanations: a post-war backlog of British and American plays, the Swedish theatre having been in a somewhat debilitated state until revived in the early 1960s by Ingmar Bergman and Alf Sjöberg; a tendency to rely on translations, and unhelpful conditions pertaining in the regional theatres.

Various proposals to help creative artists, including playwrights, are being pressed forward by the Swedish Arts Council with considerable energy. The sum of one million SKr. (£150,000) is available for the encouragement of new Swedish plays at the rate of 7,000 Skr. (a little less than £1,000) a time; while a variety of other schemes provide income for Swedish artists for five and seven year periods and under some conditions, a lifetime (22).

Awards are made on the recommendation of a committee (Konstnarsnamnden) on which both artists and their professional organizations are strongly represented. It is too early to be able to report on the success of this encouragement but a speaker at the TQ conference said that the Union of Swedish Playwrights has 341 members of which 195 are active and 10 are able to live wholly by writing plays.

The situation in Switzerland is uneasy. Although certain theatres such as the Stadtebundtheater of Bienne-Soleure have considered the problem of how best to foster new plays, there is a feeling that not enough is being done on a national level. (We have already expressed our doubt whether this is the kind of thing on which any effective action can be taken at national level). In 1977 10 towns got together to fund a competition for new plays; individual efforts in the direct commissioning of new plays have been made by, for example, Werner Duggelin at the Basler Theater, and by a number of Kleines Theater/Petits Théâtres; but results hitherto have not been encouraging (23).

The Swiss semi-governmental Foundation Pro-Helvetia concentrated its activities in 1975-76 on helping young authors by supporting a project to put new playwrights into contact with *metteurs en scène* and professional theatre companies, rather on the lines of the French Bureau d'Auteurs. 'The experience should allow young authors', states the rubric, 'to become better familiarized with this difficult art (of playwrighting) and above all to move from writing simple pieces (monologues) to more complex plays'.

There are two further points to be dealt with. The first concerns the appointment to a theatre of a dramaturg or literary adviser (or editor). It is traditional in many theatres for the artistic director to choose his own repertory. In some respects this is no great labour. A subsidized theatre will mount some eight or nine productions a year. These will include a judicious balance of classics, contemporary classics, and new plays. The hard-pressed director will tend to choose plays that he knows, that have been successful elsewhere, or that are by writers with whom he is familiar. The Board of Directors, if there is such a body, may press him to be more or less adventurous, which is where the necessity for a policy becomes essential. By the time he has made his choice there is little hope for the manuscripts of new plays that are piling up in his office. When pressed to appoint a dramaturg, reader or adviser he may well question whether it is economically viable to appoint a full-time member of his staff to choose at best a couple of plays a year. Yet so important might these plays be that an argument should perhaps be made for all theatrical subsidy to be increased to include such an

252

appointment. Once again perhaps we should follow the example of the German theatres and appoint as dramaturg someone who can play a part in the whole running of the theatre, as an assistant director perhaps as well as an advisor on the extent of the theatre's repertory.

The final point concerns Festivals. Festivals have become a feature of the European artistic scene. Their prevalence has established the fact that people like to visit certain towns and cities for a short period to enjoy some kind of specialized artistic activity. The suggestion falls attractively within the argument of this book since a festival is a local activity and must look for a large part of its support to local funding. But festivals of new plays are understandably infrequent. A new play will have a short run and probably a not very productive one. A more generous fee will unbalance a realistic budget unless there is some special grant or subsidy available. The best hope is that a festival production will act as a 'shop-window' or 'try-out', and that a successful preview will lead to a subsequent production under more financially favourable conditions.

The playwright in broadcasting

Such a considerable employer of labour as one of the larger broadcasting organizations has to make many decisions as to its relationship with the artists it employs. Broadly this means a decision between permanent contracts, long term contracts, for three years, for example, contracts for a certain amount of work rather than for a specified length of time, or the exploitation of the market on a freelance basis. There seems to have been a certain tendency for television companies especially to avoid the longer contracts, largely on the grounds that artists prefer a certain freedom of manoeuvre, and to work for whom they will according to the nature of their material. But while this freelance status guarantees that freedom which is traditionally associated with artistic expression it also leaves the writer in a state of extreme economic insecurity. There is of course no definitive answer to the problem.

Lord Annan's report on British Broadcasting (24) gives an interesting picture of the pressure by the unions for greater commitment towards artists by the broadcasting companies. The report quotes the Writer's Guild of Great Britain as being dissatisfied with their treatment by the broadcasting companies. It is 'in the interests of broadcasting', the Guild is reported as saying, 'that the producing companies should have access to a body of professional freelance talent for the maintenance of high standards....' The existence of such a body they believed to be essential to ensure a continuation of variety, originality, and artistic independence. The Guild thought that in many respects they had been treated 'as little better than casual labour in terms of future economic security and participatory rights in relation to decision-making'.

British Actors' Equity was similarly anxious that the employment of artists in television be stabilized, although this is a slightly unrealistic objective. Younger members of the BBC drama department are mostly on long-term contracts; but as they develop into producers, directors, or script-editors they tend to 'go freelance' because they wish to work right across the field of television, BBC and ITV, film, theatre, and even commercials; while in the same way nothing would be more limiting for an actor's development than permanent commitment to a single company, broadcasting or theatrical.

In another passage of the report Lord Annan refers to the dangers of 'formula writing haunting and daunting talented innovators. The imperatives of broadcasting — the need to work fast, to keep costs down, to fill many hours and to schedule in an orderly way — operate against the survival of the single play'. And, it might be added, the single play of originality. For it is the very economics of the medium and the huge anonymous structure within which television broadcasting all too often takes place, that provide generous opportunities for artists but tend to press them into a structured and conforming role.

From this point of view the series, a largely American creation, manufactured with extreme professionalism, is the enemy of the individual and original play which pertains to the status of a work of art. The series can overstretch its material and constrict its writers to a bland and predictable conformity.

In view of the strictures that have been made on the state of playwrighting in the Netherlands it is encouraging to note that between 1959 and 1974 the number of drama productions on Dutch television rose from 19 in Dutch and 48 in translation, to 170 in Dutch and 16 in translation. It is curious that this talent has not transferred itself to the stage (25).

It is always difficult to know on what basis to pay an artist when the market mechanism is not in operation. We know that the laws of supply and demand as well as other social tastes of a remarkably quirky kind have put a price on paintings out of all proportion to any rational value. But in the same light it could be argued that the playwright in broadcasting is seriously underpaid.

We have noted that an original play, one hour in length, broadcast by the BBC is likely to draw an audience of some millions. For this the author will be paid around £2,000. On German television he would be paid 25,000 DM. (about £6,000); on Swedish radion 17,500 S.Kr. (about (£2,500). How long does it take to write a play? The subject was discussed on page 241. The Germans are not far wrong in suggesting that 10 months is a reasonable time for the composition of a full-length play, whether for stage or TV.

In English terms, £2,000 for a year's work rates at about £38 a week which is a good deal below the minimal national wage. In realistic terms it is reasonable to suppose that at the same time the playwright could be turning his hand to other sources of revenue; but it would be quite wrong to trade upon the possibility. For it must be accepted that playwrighting, whether for stage or television, is a high skilled and professional occupation.

There is considerable argument then that the television playwright is underpaid. Unfortunately we have also noted a tendency for the broadcasting companies to decrease their output of drama. The Société Suisse de Radiodiffiusion et Télévision states that it broadcasts few plays on television but rather more on radio, which is contrary to usual practice. Swedish television has tended to give up the encouragement of native dramatists in favour of importing telerecordings. In 1976 41% of the television drama broadcast by Swedish radio was of British origin and 25% in the other categories. West German television on the other hand in the same year broadcast over 200 plays by 185 authors of which only 25 were British, and BBC radio claims that it initiates between 400 and 500 scripts a year. Nevertheless the fact of the matter is that if a broadcasting organization has established productive links with other countries which is ready to take its telerecordings, it can spend far more money on production costs knowing that it is going to recoup a considerable amount from foreign sales. This is highly satisfactory for the playwright at the producing end of the transaction; a good deal less satisfactory for the one at the receiving end.

Those countries that receive a high proportion of imported programmes tend to be expert at 'dubbing', which is a valuable source of employment for actors. The Swedish public, on the other hand, with an enviable and impressive international outlook, prefer to view programmes in their language of origin.

Of the immense opportunities offered by broadcasting companies for the employment of artists there can be no doubt. This is particularly true of the Federal Republic of Germany where it is estimated that some 100,000 people live or at least partly depend on freelance earnings in German radio and television. The tendancy for the broadcasting authorities to accept rather than to initiate freelance work is a reflection of their anxiety both to circumvent the hierarchical nature of their own administrative structure and to reflect the democratic ideals and ideological demands of contemporary German society.

In recent years, however, with the purchasing power of freelance earnings declining, it has become apparent that the freelance, now working in opposition to market forces, has become more vulnerable to institutional pressure than the staff man. The issue of the security of employment for freelance workers has become inseperable from the problem of freedom of expression for all creative workers in broadcasting. It is a problem that has considerably exercised Actors' Equity in their dealings with the BBC. The freelance is sometimes all too free!

These representative figures for the proportion of native and foreign television programmes tell their own story: United Kingdom 86:14 (with pressure from the unions to reduce the figure for imported programmes which in any case are mostly American); France 50:50; Sweden 30:70 (26).

The principle involved is a serious one, that of the free flow of information and the sovereignty of states. Broadcasting is as much a cultural manifestation of society as the arts themselves. In view of the increasingly important position it is rapidly assuming in the leisure of European society, broadcasting and television broadcasting in particular is perhaps the dominating element in our cultural life. If, therefore, as has been argued, a society must create its own living culture, even though the quality of that culture may vary and not depend upon imported books, American television series and an anonymous and faceless environment, it is clearly of the greatest importance that a broadcasting organization shall provide a balance between an expression of native culture and an open door to the contemporary world. Cultural imperialism can operate as maleficently in terms of broadcasting as of the theatre, and more effectively.

Organizations of writers

Such organizations emerged in the nineteenth century when the rapid development of a commercial theatre made it necessary for authors to create a platform for the discussion of outstanding professional problems. Developments in Germany were typical of what happened elsewhere. The first organization of German playwrights, the Allgemeine Deutsche Schriftsteller, took place in 1878. Others quickly followed. General unification took place in 1967 when Herr Friedrich Karl Fromm, writing in *Der Autor*, pointed out that both playwrights and composers writing for the theatre enjoyed many common interests. This led to the formation of the Dramatiker Union of playwrights and composers for stage and film, radio and television, which established close relationships with all writers using the German language in the rest of Germany, Austria and Switzerland. It now has more than 500 members and a secretariat based in West Berlin. It publishes two periodicals, *Dramatiker Union Mitteilungen* which appears four times a year and deals with many matters of technical interest to its members, and *Der Autor* which appears irregularly and deals with various themes of a specialist nature.

An interesting development has recently taken place in Britain. Dramatists have traditionally belonged to the League of Dramatists or the Society of Authors, but a feeling among the younger playwrights that these organizations were no longer fully in touch with or representative of the contemporary theatre led to the foundation in 1975 of the Writers' Guild on which authors of all kinds were represented. The powerful Federation of Theatre Unions, which includes Actors' Equity, the Musicians' Union, and the National Association of Theatrical and Kinemetograph Employees accepted the Writers' Guild beneath its umbrella. But in 1975 a group of young playwrights who considered that the Writers' Guild did not adequately represent theatrical interests and who were particularly associated with the *fringe*, formed the Theatre Writers' Union. This now has a membership of 150. The existence of what virtually amounted to rival organizations became an open issue when the Theatre Writers' Union challenged the National Theatre over its contracts with dramatists. It emerged that the National, in common with most other theatres, was paying a derisory commissioning fee. The TWU demanded not only that this should be considerably increased but that writers should be paid additionally for attendance at rehearsals and other services in connection with the production of their plays. The union is now negotiating contracts with the main managerial organizations.

There was in fact considerable discussion at the TQ Conference on the desirability of playwrights banding together. It was noted that the Italian playwright's conference, held in September 1978, had been notable for the absence of practising playwrights; but on the other hand both the Scottish Society of Playwrights and the Northern Playwright's Society had had some success in putting pressure on local theatres to pay proper attention to new plays and foster the needs of local playwrights.

Publishers

There is no clear pattern for the publishing of plays. In the bigger countries there are a number of publishers ready to publish plays and in the smaller, very few. This is simply a matter of economics. There is no general readership for plays in any country such as there is for fiction; but in most countries there is a small but steady specialist group of readers. Most classic texts remain in print, especially if they appear on the examination syllabuses of schools and universities; but contemporary plays tend to be published in small editions and reprinted only if the writer achieves some more stable success and there is demand for his works in permanent form.

The size of the reading public in most European countries is not a source for much satisfaction. Figures published in France in January 1976 showed that 27% of the population owned no books at all and only 37% more than 50. The figures of most immediate concern is that while the more popular books are contemporary novels, chosen by 35 out of every 100 readers, plays, together with books on art and religion, attract only 2 in every 100 readers, coupled with the extraordinary fact that contemporary plays are least popular among regular theatre-goers. (27). There was an 'explosion' of interest in the publishing of plays in the early 1970s but now there is an unhappy lack of confidence in publishing as a link between playwright and audiences.

In Britain there is a substantial section devoted to plays in the catalogues of Methuen, Heinemann, Faber, Evans, Oxford, French, and most publishers will handle individual plays if their author is sufficiently well-known or the play has some distinctive quality.

In the Federal Republic of Germany there are sixty publishers, the Verband Deutscher Bühnenverleger, interested in handling new plays. Leading publishers such as S. Fischer Verlag, Surkamp, Verlag der Autoren or Rowohlt, print 200-300 copies of new plays in very simple format and send them to any intendants, dramaturgs or artistic-directors they think may be interested. They usually act as agents for their own authors as sometimes happens in other countries. The system is a convenience to the theatres and a source of profit to the publishers, who have taken a certain gamble in having printed the play, if it proves to be successful. But they must pay translators in advance and if there is further income it will be distributed in the proportion of 70% to the author and about 15% each to translator and agent (28).

British and French publishers also sometimes act as agents for the plays they publish but it is beyond their capacity to market such plays as energetically as agents do.

In publishing a play a publisher does not look in the first place for big sales but for dissemination. Further productions will lead to further sales. A printed play is more readily available for production, and easier to handle, than a manuscript. To cope with this need for the availability of texts, the Society of Flemish Authors places duplicated manuscripts of unpublished plays in public libraries for use by amateur groups, though copyright regulations would prohibit this procedure in larger countries.

A speaker at the TQ Conference drew attention to the policy of the Norwegian government of protecting the native culture 'against the inroads being made by English, French and German works'. Every work of value is guaranteed an initial minimum sale of 1,000 copies which the Government purchases for free distribution to all lending libraries, while generous subsidies ensure that authors receive 20% of the published price. Two to three hundred titles are published in this way annually.

Agents

The increasing complexity and interrelationships of the European theatre, particularly within the context of the Council of Europe and the EEC, makes some kind of system of agents obligatory. In principle many authors would favour a direct relationship with his publisher or a theatre director. In the case of the former this is possible. The author of a novel can enjoy such a direct and lasting relationship with his publisher who can deal with television, film or translation rights as they arise. But a publisher will not usually press an author's work in the field of performance. He will not take energetic action to get it filmed, translated, serialized and otherwise promoted. This is the task of the agent.

The playwright can hardly avoid the use of an agent, whether he be the publisher or an independant organization, since in West Germany, for example, the play agencies keep in close touch with the theatres and know their special requirements and interests. No theatre will fail to read a manuscript from an agency of repute or one whose standards they have learnt to respect.

The work of an agent is more complicated with a playwright than with a novelist, for a play which is even reasonably successful may have a number of different productions and each has to be separately negotiated; and within the complex structure of the subsidized and commercial theatre, such negotiations can be complex. The playwright, in short, can hardly dispense with the services of an intermediary to place and sell his play and to handle the complex procedure of advances, royalties, rights and possible publication.

Moreover it is the job of an agent not only to sell but to buy. One of the better markets for British plays is the German. German agents keep a sharp watch on all new productions in the British and in particular the London theatre, largely through dramatic criticism in the daily and Sunday press. The same procedure takes place in the smaller countries where dependance on foreign plays is considerable even though the financial returns may be small.

Antipathy towards agents is expressed on two counts: one is based on a kind of moral resentment against anyone who lives on 10% of an artist's earning; the other is against the intrusion of a mercenary element in what some people see, with the increasing involvement of public money in theatrical enterprise, as a public responsibility that should be regularized by government decree.

The answer can only be that so regularized a system might be possible within a centralized economy; but that in the mixed economies of Western Europe we must expect to find an infra-structure of theatrical organization reflecting that complexity. It is clear that the present system of rewarding playwrights on a royalty basis is one that leaves a great deal to be desired. Much thought is urgently needed. The whole immense structure of the contemporary European theatre ultimately rests on the creative ability of a very small number of people who have a gift for spinning dialogue in dramatic form. Neither central nor local governments who are responsible for subsidizing the theatre seem to have found a way of nurturing the individual artist with anything like the sensibility and flexibility his precarious role in society demands. Whatever criticisms are made of the Arts Council of Great Britain there is evidence that its non-governmental status enables it to develop more flexible procedures than are sometimes possible in more centralized organizations.

There are no literary agents in France. Authors deal direct with publishers and theatrical managers. Their rights are effectively laid down and safeguarded by the powerful Société des Auteurs et des Compositeurs but the more reticent are inhibited from selling their work or singing its praises.

Copyright

The laws of copyright and those which are aimed at protecting an author's or performer's control over his own work are of supreme importance to every creative artist but far too complex to be dealt with in a book of this kind. Dr. McFarlane's history of the subject makes this clear (15). The laws of copyright have tended to derive from industry which explains why protection is more often accorded to the company that has produced the product than to the artist who created it. In Britain the rights of the author were first established by the statute of Queen Anne in 1709 but the right of performance was not covered until the Dramatic Copyright Act of 1833.

Every country established its own laws in a similarly erratic and piecemeal fashion. But the complexity of the problem was compounded with the invention during the present century of many forms of mechanical reproduction. Only the utmost vigilance by such organizations as the Performing Rights Society prevents an indiscriminate and widespread recording or rerecording and production of any performance anywhere. The rapid growth in the last few years of cable and satellite television systems, which can pick up any broadcast emanating from anywhere in the world and beam it to anywhere in the world, or transmit it by cable into the home of anyone who has subscribed to the system, has virtually destroyed all existing forms of legal control of performance. The only possible comment is to express modest satisfaction that the EEC has accepted responsibility for harmonizing the copyright laws within the Community and, together with the professional organizations concerned, for considering how the artist is to be paid and his work safeguarded as a result of prodigious technological developments in all forms of discourse and communication (29).

Notes and Sources

(1)   Especially *Extra-territorial* - Faber and Faber, London 1972
(2)   Quoted by John Arden (see Chapter 10 noted 1 above).
(3)   Alfred Simon - *Les Diverses Possibilités d'Aide aux Auteurs Dramatiques* - Paris, 1973, unpublished.
(4)   Harmut Lange - *Die Theater, der Tod der Aktuellen Dramenproduktion* - Der Autor, May 1973.
(5)   Jean Dasté (see Chapter 5 note 14 above).
(6)   Denis Gontard (see Chapter 5 note 11 above).
(7)   Much useful information has been provided by M. Christoph Campos, director of the British Institute in Paris.
(8)   Jean-Paul Delsemme - *Decision et Programmation Theatrale* - Direction Generale de la Jeunesse et du Loisir du Ministère de l'Education Nationale et de la Culture Francaise, Brussels, 1977.
(9)   Dieter Hadaszik, Jochen Schmidt, Werner Schulze-Reimpell - *Was Spielten die Theater?* - Deutscher Bühnenverein, Cologne, 1976.
(10) R. H. Tawney - *Religion and the Rise of Capitalism* - John Murray, London, 1944.
(11) Published by A. and C. Black, London.
(12) *Rilevazione* (see Chapter 6 note 18 above) and *Lo Spettacolo* (ditto).
(13) *Nederlands Theatre-en-Televisie-Jaarboek* - Staatsuitgeverij, 's Gravenhage, 1978.
(14) Maria Teresa Benedetti - *Il Teatro di Giovanni Testori* - Milan,

undated.

(15) Gavin McFarlane - *Copyright: the Development and Exercise of the Performing Right* - John Offord Ltd., 1980.

(16) Lüder Wortman - *The Situation of Playwrights in the Federal Republic of Germany* - West German Centre of the ITI.
also
Information from Dramatiker Union (see page 80).
and Joachim Werner Preuss (op. cit.)

(17) Swedish Centre of the I.T.I., Stockholm.

(18) Ministry of Dutch Culture, Brussels.

(19) ATAC Informations Nos. 87 and 89, Paris.

(20) Theatre Quarterly No. 33

(21) *Nederlands Theater en Televisie Jaarboek*, 1976-77.

(22) Swedish Centre of I.T.I., Stockholm.

(23) Pro Helvetia

(24) Lord Annan - *Report of the Committee on the Future of Broadcasting*, - H.M.S.O., 1977.

(25) See note 21 above.

(26) *Le Développement des Activités Théâtrales* - Journal Official de la République Francaise, 1977 No. 20.

(27) *Developpement Culturel: le Livre et la Lecture* - Bulletin d'information du Service des Etudes et de la Recherche du Secretariat d'Etat et de la Culture, Paris, January 1976.

(28) Personal interview.

(29) An interesting discussion on the subject is reported in *Arts and EEC*, the report of a conference that took place at the I.C.A. in May 1978.

11. The Educational Background

A policy of cultural democracy

This chapter has been written in the spirit of the first resolution passed by the European Ministers of Culture meeting at Oslo in 1976. The resolution stressed the importance of every society having a cultural policy, embodying governmental responsibility worked out in conjunction with policies for education, leisure and recreation. This policy must make provision for cultural minorities, the disadvantaged and the underprivileged. It must include people in sparsely populated areas and encourage new ways of allowing children to express their collective talents: and it must encourage a critical understanding of the products of the mass media. Discussions at Oslo centred around not only the above proposals but the quality of life in cities as well as country communities, problems of decentralization, the place and function of the professional artist in our society and the increased provision of cultural and artistic resources for all sections of the population.

A number of papers have been issued by the Council of Europe which provide a useful background to this chapter. Although references have been given in the text it might be helpful to make more detailed note of them here (1).

Finn Jor's *The Demystification of Culture* plunges vigorously into the whole subject of cultural democracy and gives examples of the many hundreds of socio-cultural centres, something rather more than arts centres, now established all over Europe. It is a description of the facilities that are now being almost universally provided for everyone, irrespective of age, sex, class or even the payment of fees, to participate in some kind of artistic or cultural activity. Artists participate both in their own right and as 'animateurs'. There is a cultural process as well as a cultural product. The amateur not only receives but also participates.

Stephen Mennell's *Cultural Policy in Towns* gives an account of the cultural life, policy, and the administration of cultural policy in 14 European cities. The importance of every government and every local authority having an explicit cultural policy is strongly underlined.

J.A. Simpson's *Towards Cultural Democracy* analyses the problem to which frequent reference has been made in the present report. In the reassessment of cultural values that has taken place throughout Europe during the present decade, 'élite' culture has come to be recognised as one of many sub-cultures. A wider concept of culture now includes a variety of activities which together may be regarded as valuable forms of expression. The problem of traditional cultural policy is that its encouragement benefits only those who are already privileged. Its unquestionable virtues should not be lost in the process of democratization.

J. Goldberg and P. Booth's useful paper is entitled somewhat long-windedly, *Decentralization of Cultural Promotion: The Role of National and Regional Organizations in the Supervision and Co-ordination of Policies for the Decentralization of Culture*. It discusses clearly and realistically in general terms many of the policies that have been described, with particular reference to the theatre, in the present report.

Stephen and Barbara Mennell's *Explorations in Cultural Policy and Research* is a most useful collection of papers showing the attitudes to cultural problems that are being adopted by contemporary sociologists.

The Democratic Renewal of the Performing Arts is another useful collection of papers delivered at a Symposium on the Performing Arts that took place in Athens, 1-3 March, 1976.

The present chapter, to which these pages provide a background, will be devoted to a discussion of the ways in which, and what happens when, the drama leaves its theatre and enters the schools, the marketplace, the arts or cultural centre, and mixes with the people.

Drama in schools

The word 'drama' rather than 'theatre' is used because there is a widely held belief that whereas the practice of drama can play a significant part in the education of a child, the concept of theatre and theatrical performance is a more sophisticated and less relevant aspect of the process. It is not a controversy in which there would be any purpose in entering at this point (2).

The emergence of drama as an acceptable educational activity is the flowering of a tradition that goes back to the very roots of European education. But it is not the tradition of classical education which has tended to be Cartesian and overacademic but that which has been built up by the great educational innovators and reformers from Rabelais and Erasmus to Montessori and A.S. Neil. *'Fais ce que tu veult'*, wrote Rabelais. 'Remove from the work of the school all that is toilsome and give to learning the quality of freedom and enjoyment'; that's Erasmus. And here's John Locke: 'And I doubt not but one great reason why many children abandon themselves wholly to silly sports . . . is because they have found their curiosity baulked and their enquiries neglected'. 'Curiosity', wrote Rousseau, 'is the means of development . . . The notion of things acquired for oneself is clearer and much more convincing than those acquired from the teaching of others'. And Froebel: 'It is not enough that we show the child objects . . . He takes delight in constructing; he is naturally geometrician and artist'.

We have singled out a handful of examples from the work of the more celebrated to establish both a chronology going back 400 years and a European breadth for educational reform. It is a conviction that places extreme importance on the process of self-discovery, on tactile experience, on self-discipline, on personal involvement and on the nature of sensory experience. The Swiss psychologist Jean Piaget has written penetratingly on the importance for personal growth of what he calls the 'sensory-motor' process, and that exploration by the child of the external world in a form that is known as play. Possible play upon the two words 'play' and 'a play' is not fortuitous. Drama can be educationally justified on the grounds that it provides opportunities for particular kinds of subjective exploration of the external world, not only of the objects that compose it, but of the people, with their thoughts and feelings, that shape it. Art provides a means for the transformation of reality: dramatic art provides a means for this transformation to be carried out in terms of personal involvement, with the body functioning both as artist and artefact.

The dramatic element in play has been seized on by the educationists to contruct a variety of techniques to deal with a variety of teaching situations. These have been analysed by a Swiss teacher in the following terms: (3).

Play as a teaching method can be used to make educational problems intelligible through sensory, perceptual, physical performances. A widely conceived policy can lead to the possibility of the collaboration of specialists and an improvement in the whole teaching situation.

Training in interaction is intended to develop the sensibility of one person towards another and to alleviate 'man's inhumanity to man'. The very nature of dramatic activity involves this network of relationships on many social levels. These 'preparatory exercises' lead to, *Role play* in which a chosen role is played in an agreed situation and the relationship of this role to other characters is explored.

Project-playing (planspiel) is used to define the area of a dispute and the limitations of an emotional conflict.

Psychodrama offers opportunities for the participants to analyse their emotional/psychic disagreements, advance their private roles and so unravel their own emotional conflicts.

Sociodrama seeks a practical unravelling of group conflicts by enabling participants to live through their own situations.

The *lernstück* provides opportunities for a group to present the resolution of their conflicts to a public; it is a form that was used by

Brecht in his younger years.

At a *School theatre performance* pupils give their production in front of an audience. The performance is an end in itself and may have little relation to process.

In a contentious field there will be many who would differ in their definition of these categories but they have been given here as an indication of the complex sub-divisions to which educational drama has given rise.

An aspect of the subject, however, that will be of particular interest to the readers of this book, is the close relationship of such educational developments with new theories pertaining in the professional theatre. They stem very largely from the work of Constantin Stanislavsky who, if not the first to conceive of a new approach to the art of acting, was responsible for rationalizing the technique. Stanislavsky looked for ways of releasing the creative potential of the actor; the teacher tries to find ways of releasing the creative potential of the child, which is only another way of speaking of the ability of a child to learn. The actor is now encouraged to find his way into a character; the child is encouraged to find his own answers to a question. Actors and children are no longer told what to do in the process of acting or learning: the director or the teacher provides a situation, a structure in the form of the play or the lesson within which the actor and the child must work; and the actor and the child make their own discoveries, and do their own creative work not only in isolation, but also as part of a group in which personal interaction plays a large part. Both are relating their work to the environment, their society, to life outside the theatre and the school. Even in terms of architecture the old forms have been abandoned: the theatre is looking for new actor-audience relationships; the proscenium arch has given place to the open stage, the thrust stage, theatre-in-the-square, the round, and whatever name is given to the theatre where the audience sits in the middle. Primary schools are now designed not as a series of closed class-rooms but on an open plan, as a series of spaces or areas, perhaps on different levels, certainly with differing environments for different kinds of work or study.

An enquiry into the place of the arts in the curriculum of secondary schools has recently been carried out in Britain by the Gulbenkian Foundation (4). No educationalists will any longer be surprised at entering a school and finding children or the young people deeply involved in drama, in music, in painting, or almost any creative or artistic activity. We have known for long that children have a strong visual sense and can paint what an adult would call 'a beautiful picture'; but the ability of children to compose, to write poetry, to carve wood, to improvise plays all to a very high degree of imaginative accomplishment

266

is perhaps less widely understood. Timetabled drama is now to be found in many schools in the Netherlands as well as Great Britain; and among the *activitiés libres* to which the headmaster of French secondary schools may devote 10% of the timetable, drama is becoming increasingly popular.

Theatre-in-Education

It is not perhaps in every country that a visitor might find a school a company of professional actors working with children in the hall or even in their classrooms. It could happen in the Netherlands and the Scandinavian countries; it is a fairly common experience in Great Britain.

It is difficult to penetrate the origins of what has become a national movement, although it is clear that it was the result of a synthesis between theatre and education brought about by people who had had experience of both. It was an emergent movement in the 1960s, encouraged by a decision late in the decade on the part of the Arts Council of Great Britain to make a special allocation to Children's Theatre, to which TIE, as it has come to be called, is closely related. But it was also given impetus by the rapid development of Fringe companies with which many TIE companies made common cause.

The *Theatre-in-Education Directory*, published in 1975 (5), provides details of 22 Theatre-in-Education companies, 22 Community Theatre companies, most of which express an interest in playing to children, seven Community/Young People Theatre companies, 13 other Young People's Theatre companies, eight Children's Theatre companies, four theatre-based companies, and two companies closely associated with local education authorities, 78 companies in all. But many are as ephermeral as the Fringe itself, and although they are unlikely to have declined in numbers, their composition and constitution are likely to be unrecognisably different.

They are variously financed, though not generously, even by the standards of the mainstream theatre, by the Arts Council of Great Britain, local education authorities, and various charities among whom the Gulbenkian Foundation has been an outstanding benefactor. Those that work closely with education authorities benefit from their members being paid as teachers, for whom level of payment is very much higher than for actors. In 1976-77 local authorities in Great Britain paid out £503,626 in salaries to Theatre-in-Education groups, £150,330 in fees to Theatre-in-Education and Young People's Theatre groups, and £256,944 for professional performances to schools (6). More recent figures are not available.

Their work is sharply educational; they work with children in schools and in school hours. They usually choose such subjects as, to quote from the Directory, 'the Parliamentary system, symmetry, or the conservation of natural resources by making them so vivid through . . . theatrical skills and techniques that the experience becomes a trigger mechanism for subtler and deeper intellectual recall'. While there is no need to dispute such claims, it should be made clear that the success of dramatic techniques in helping the actual learning process has not been fully established, but it is therefore very much to everyone's credit that uncertainty as to effectiveness has not led to any evident limitation on the work of the companies.

Another contributor to the Directory writes,

TIE is an attempt to aid children to come to terms with themselves and the society in which they live, in order that they may understand that society and be able to make of it what they wish. This is clearly a difficult aim when our society does its best to ensure that children see it on its own terms - and at their expense.

The passage is quoted as an example of an attitude that underlies a great deal of this kind of work. The purpose of drama is seen as both sociological and psychological in that it makes a contribution to personal development, whatever is meant by that commonly-used expression, to interpersonal relationships and to group dynamics. Its purpose is very rarely seen as introducing children to one of the great art forms of Western Europe. This is yet another example of that centrifugal tendency of both dramatic art and education to which we have already drawn attention. The focus is predominantly outwards, towards society, no longer inwards, towards the individual, that creature in whose future society holds decreasing confidence.

Animations and animateurs

The words have been in use, especially in France, for many years. They caused considerable anxiety in Britain until it was realized that they describe an activity that the British had also been doing for some time without knowing what it was called - like M. Jourdain and his prose.

What the words have done is bring into focus an extremely wide and varied area of education in the arts and especially in drama. The 'animateur' is really a teacher, but in adult education rather than in schools. It is a useful term with which to describe, for example, a professional actor working with children in the manner described above, for he is not strictly speaking a teacher, although he is teaching. To describe him as an 'animateur' responsible for creating 'animations', which in the past have been variously and loosely described as 'improvisations', *'jeux dramatiques'* or 'creative drama', is to define his function in a useful manner.

268

Here is an example of an 'animation' in a French school (though the attempt to be specific has been frustrated by the discovery that the French have begun to refer to the 'animateur' as the 'réalisateur'). It was conducted by a member of the Théâtre de Tournemire, a professional group established in the Maison des Jeunes of Lyons. Teachers were invited from local primary and secondary schools for one, two or three sessions of an hour-and-a-half each. The *'réalisateur-animateur'* decided to use the single session to create and act a story by and with the children. He requires the utmost skill in soliciting the ideas of the children, helping them to structure their contributions into a consecutive narrative, rejecting with the utmost sensibility those that clearly 'wouldn't work', finding roles for as many as possible, and keeping the interest of those not actively involved by supplying sound effects or just quietly waiting for their turn. Subsequent sessions attended by older children were progressively more complex and moved from a world of fantasy into such realities as parental relationships (7).

Madame Josette Coenen-Huther, to whose work we have already referred, provides further useful documentation and examples of the use of drama to develop both creativity and the critical spirit in children, though one sometimes wonders who or what it is they are being encouraged to criticize.

As an example of a company that plays with children rather than for them, she cites the Théâtre de la Ville of Brussels and the Dutch Jeugd en Teater Werkgroep. The latter has the advantage of its own theatre where it organizes regular afternoon performances for children, which their parents may attend. Other companies such as Proloog, with strong radical tendencies, conduct sessions in schools with the purpose of encouraging the pupils to question the whole structure of education and indeed of society itself.

Children's theatre
There is a clear distinction to be made between Theatre-in-Education and Children's Theatre. The former is usually identifiable for its educational emphasis. Such companies normally play in schools, involve the children, and aim to cast light upon some topic or to enrich some aspect of the educational process. Children's Theatre or Theatre for Children takes many different forms. Many private theatres stage plays for children especially at Christmas and many subsidized theatres encourage school parties for 'suitable' plays and offer reduced prices for students and young people at their evening performances. Sometimes they offer various kinds of *animations*, demonstrations or workshops.

In most countries there are Children's Theatre companies which play

Professor Crump entertaining children in the street, London 1981.

A performance for children by the Free Theatre Barn Group, Stockholm, 1981.

almost exclusively for children. Their performances can take many different forms from the most loosely structured *animations* to plays of a more or less conventional kind but specially written for children.

Most countries offer variations of this pattern. In French-speaking Belgium, for example, there are nine 'recognized' children's theatres (*théâtres de l'enfance et de la jeunesse*), five in Brussels and one each in Wavre, Namur, Charleroi and Liège. They receive an annual subsidy of 200,000 B.F. (£3,500) to cover 50% of their costs together with 200,000 B.F. for each artist, technician or 'animateur' engaged for a year. Other companies and amateur groups receive smaller subsidies. In Flemish-speaking Belgium there is the distinguished Royal Youth Theatre of Antwerp (Koninklijke Jeugdtheater) founded in 1942, then the first of its kind in Europe, receiving 19.3 million B.F. (£350,000); the Jeugd en Theaterwerkgroep, Brussels, and the National Jeugdtheater, Gent, with 9.6 million B.F. (£165,000) between them (figures for 1976-77) (8).

Children's theatre in France has a distinguished origin in the celebrated Théâtre de l'Oncle Sebastien founded in 1929 by Léon Chancerel, a pupil of Copeau's. It lead a charmed existence until the beginning of the 1939-War. Apart from a small number of companies, of which Miguel Demuynk's Théâtre de la Clairière was one of the more notable, there was little development until 1969 when a decree of the Ministry of Education gave authority to primary school teachers to devote six of the 27 weekly teaching hours to creative activities. Pupils may now visit the theatre during school hours on three afternoons in the year. The companies providing these performances can receive subsidy both from the Ministry of Culture as well as from the municipalities and the Conseils Généraux.

Since 1976, companies in Caen, Lille, Lyon, Nancy, Saint-Denis, and Sartrouville have been designated by the Ministry of Culture as Centres Dramatiques Nationaux pour l'Enfance et la Jeunesse. In 1980 they received a total subsidy of 3,960,000 F. (£400,000). All companies playing for children can benefit from the fund for the first production of a new play. In addition to these specialist companies, the Centres Dramatiques, Maisons de la Culture and Théâtres Privés all give a certain number of performances for children (9).

But subsidy is inadequate and companies come and go. They often compose their own plays, using classic children's stories. Maurice Yendt with his Théâtre des Jeunes Années presents to children a poetic image of reality, giving a symbolic interpretation to stories and adding something of the marvellous to the action. Catherine Dasté has involved children particularly in the visual side of productions, and now that this kind of thing has been taken up by other companies she has moved towards a theatre in which music is integrated with the action. Henri Degoutin with *La Comédie de Lorraine* has picked up the tradition initiated by Léon Chancerel of basing his work on the methods and the characters of the Commedia dell' Arte.

In 1980 there were 46 children's theatre companies based on Paris, most of them committed to touring both in the Paris region and throughout the provinces. They play largely to children between the ages of 6 and 12 and many of their productions are *créations collectives*. There were 42 companies in the Isle de France, and a further 76 companies in the French provinces.

French children's theatre companies are represented by the Association de Théâtre pour l'Enfance et la Jeunesse which provides an annual register of the companies, their repertory and their requirements (10). The Ministry of Education is not involved in any theatrical activities, and if a relationship between the companies and the education authorities takes place it is at local level. The division between education and culture was made by André Malraux and General de Gaulle when the former detached certain services from the Ministry of Education to create the Ministry of Culture.

In the Federal Republic of Germany there is a predictable variety of children's theatres. Some are the work of gifted individuals such as Eberhard Mobius's Das Schiff in Hamburg; some, such as the Nürnberg Children's Theatre are predominantly traditional and literary and present a succession of operas, operettas and plays to audiences of young people. The Münich Children's Theatre is an example of the private commercial enterprise of an older tradition, independant and largely unsubsidized, playing in a converted cinema a repertoire based on fairy stories and the stock-in-trade of children's literature - robbers, witches and giants.

The new movement in children's theatre takes its tone from Grips, a Berlin company that established itself in the 1960s and acquired its own theatre in 1972. It achieved its first big success in 1970 with *Pfeiferling* by Volker Ludwig, who is the director of the company. In recent years Grips seems to have found a way of mastering all the imponderables of children's theatre with plays that combine strong social, educational and even political content with a highly entertaining manner of presentation, appealing equally to bourgeois and working-class children, supported by parents, teachers and social workers (11).

A strongly didactic and social note in the German Children's theatre is one of its more notable characteristics. An interesting example is the company which calls itself Rote Grutz, the name being a pun on the German words for 'jelly' and 'brains'. The origins of the company go back to 1973 when two members of the Grips company decided to work

272

together on a programme for 7 to 10 year olds on sex education following an example that had been set in Sweden. Their first production was called *Darüber Spricht Man Nicht* (*One does not talk about it*) and its success was such that several members of the company broke away to pursue the subject in greater detail and in 1977 staged *Was Heist Hier Liebe?* (*What do you mean by love?*) Both plays were created after discussions, games and role-playing with children and young people (12).

Following the success of Grips a number of state and municipal theatres have made renewed attempts to establish children's and youth theatres, often with considerable success; and what is perhaps even more important is that a number of young companies have begun to work in the field with little or no subsidy, occasionally, as with Ommes und Oimel in Levershussen, being taken over by the municipality and subsidized. In West Germany there is no category for subsidized children's theatre, but in 1976-77 the state and municipal theatres gave 1,876 productions (Stücke), to well over 1½ million children and young people. Figures for attendance by children at the subsidized theatres show that the professional theatre is underpinning a movement that is becoming notable for the quality as well as the variety of its work. Nothing is more encouraging in this respect than the number of theatres that are employing a full-time and specially-trained member of staff to develop contacts between theatres and schools, to organize or conduct 'animations' in which actors collaborate with teachers, and to help or advise, when invited, with school productions.

In the later 1970s the movement began to loose impetus. The reasons were partly financial, partly the difficulty of finding an appropriate form and style for this kind of work, and partly political restrictions. Several companies had been in trouble as a result of their overtly social material.

The Clottu report laments that the Swiss professional theatres have been slow to realize the importance of involving their staff in 'animations' with children; only the Zürich Schauspielakademie appears to have been aware of the need to train specialists in educational drama along with existing specialist teachers of art and music; but sources suggest that such instruction amounts to only two to three hours a week.

Nevertheless following a state-funded symposium on educational drama in 1972 there has been renewed activity throughout the country and a number of cantons such Aargau, Zürich, Baden, Basel and Bern have run seminars for teachers in middle- and folk-schools on the subject of the school play, and this had led to proliferating discussion by public and private educational establishments of all kinds.

It is increasingly the practice of subsidized theatres to offer a variety of services to children and young people. These may take the form of a variety of 'animations', season-ticket schemes, reductions for student cards and special productions for different age-groups, and include seasonal entertainments such as the egregious English Christmas pantomime or special productions of plays on the examination syllabus.

The history of theatre for young people in Great Britain goes back to the early years of the century, but the movement gathered no great momentum until the years following the 1939-45 War when the Old Vic company and the Glyndebourne opera both sponsored children's theatre companies. The future, however, lay with more modest groups which played largely in schools. The practice became popular and a large number of companies were formed and organized under the British Children's Theatre Association. In the late 1960s the Arts Council of Great Britain began an annual allocation of funds for children's theatre and the movement bifurcated into more or less identifiable children's theatre and Theatre-in-Education companies with a good deal of over-lapping.

In 1976-77 an Arts Council working party on children's theatre received 127 replies to a questionnaire revealing that between them the companies had given 14,070 performances (an average of 112 each) of 559 productions (four each) over an average of 12 weeks of the year to audiences totalling 2,638,276 (under 50% of the total age group in the country), an average of 187 each. 7,428 performances were given in schools, over 4,500 in theatres, and 1,940 in 'other venues'. The price of a seat varied between 82p. in theatres and 10p in other venues (13).

Of these 127 companies between 60 and 70 were independant professional companies, 25 without subsidy, and another 25 were attached to regional theatres. Two of the most notable are the Unicorn theatre, London, with a subsidy of £127,470 in 1979-80, and the widely acclaimed National Youth Theatre.

There are some eight professional dance and ballet companies playing wholly or in part to children, about 20 puppet and marionette companies, and nearly 50 amateur groups, composed mostly of teachers, playing almost wholly to children.

For the situation in Italy we must turn to an early number of Scena in which there appeared an article which the author claimed was intended to initiate a debate on the subject of theatre for children. He sees the present state of children's theatre as a kind of confrontation between traditional concepts and contemporary *animazione*. His approach, as in so much current writing about the Italian theatre, is intensely political, and one regrets that he finds it necessary to use such terms as *squallida tradizione* to describe pre-1969 children's theatre which he claims to have been a prerogative of the private theatres. There are now at least 14 collective and cooperative companies working for and with children.

In another number of Scena (14) the same author, in discussing the production of a play for children by Giorgio Strehler at the Piccolo Theatre in Milan, suggests that the theatrical vision of a master *regista* can stand in the way of the spontaneous imaginative response of children. Strehler himself on the other hand claims that children's theatre is for 'little adults' (15). It is probably true to say that the experience of theatre-going for children and young people is one of which we have very little real understanding.

On a less contentious level, however, it can be recorded that in 1975-76, for example, the Piccolo Theatre of Milan gave 49 performances for children of a poetry recital on the life and work of the Russian poet Vladimir Mayakovsky. The Teatro di Roma visited many schools where the company worked with and for the children with a programme of *animazioni*. The Trieste Stabile arranged a programme of school visits; the Teatro Stabile di Catania toured Sicily with a lesson-performance on the work of the Sicilian dramatist Luigi Pirandello, and the Teatro Stabile di Bolzano went on a short didactic tour.

In the Netherlands there is a growing amount of theatre for children but, as in England, it is as much directed towards personal and social development as the theatre arts. It is by the alternative theatre groups that the most vigorous efforts are being made for the creation of theatre for children and it is therefore not surprising to find, as also occurs in England, a pronounced radical slant in the content of the performances. The comments of Madame Coenen-Huther have already been quoted.

In 1976 the Minister of Culture presented Parliament and the Dutch theatre with a White Paper on the subject of a national policy towards drama. He proposed that Theatre-in-Education, especially of the politically-committed variety, should be increasingly the responsibility of local authorities. He bluntly resented the fact that theatre groups should demand and receive subsidy - 13 groups were at that time being subsidized to the extent of 6 million G. (about £2 million) - to present plays critical of the society that supported them. Local authorities would be free to make their own choice of company.

As a result of the political slant in so much of their work, the Dutch Theatre-in-Education groups have found themselves increasingly in conflict not so much with the teachers, whom they see as victims of the system, but with the education system itself. The spiritual freedom of children, which artists see as the basic right of the individual, is claimed not to be possible within the context of a state-controlled education. The issue is an extremely complex one; for a young man or woman does not have to be of a violently political turn-of-mind to question what is meant by such concepts as 'discipline' and 'freedom' in what is bound to be the somewhat constricting structure of a national system of education. And in an increasingly competitive world it is difficult to envisage a realistic alternative. The answer would seem to be that with the introduction of the arts into the curriculum children have an opportunity to cultivate that sense of inner- or self-discipline which satisfies elements in these two conflicting concepts (16).

Children's Theatre in Sweden, published by the Swedish Centre of the ITI, Stockholm, 1979, gives a fascinating picture of how, during the 1970s, some of the Free Theatres and companies specializing in performances for children, began to tackle the real problems of how to play to young audiences, styles of acting, use of language, methods of presentation, and how to handle fantasy, fairy story and myth with the younger children and social problems with the older. Most surprising and challenging is the description of how the Unga Klara (Young Clara) Ensemble, an independant off-shoot of Stockholm's City Theatre, composed a play on the subject of, and entitled, *Medea's Children* based on Euripides, and tackling, quite deliberately, for audiences aged seven to twelve, such themes as death and divorce and the relationship of parents to their children. There can be little doubt of the value of such experiments when responsibly conducted under the close supervision of teachers and psychologists, but it is a pity that the results have not been more widely propagated and discussed.

The development of theatre for young people in Switzerland has been described in *Le Théâtre pour les Enfants et les Jeunes en Suisse*, no. 4, published by the Association Internationale du Théâtre pour l'Enfance et la Jeunesse, Paris, 1977.

Until the 1960s theatre for young people was limited to afternoon performances of the classics for school parties, and a rapidly declining tradition of school productions. First indications of an attempt to give teachers a form of drama training came from the German part of the country but a radical change was brought about from 1967 when the Théâtre Populaire Romand of La Chaux-de-Fonds staged its first performance for children and established theatre groups and clubs for young people. There followed an increasing number of productions and animations, conferences and exhibitions.

Children's theatre companies have now been established in a number of Swiss towns but the situation is particularly promising in two regions: Neuchâtel and Jura in French-speaking Switzerland and Argovia in German-speaking. Collaboration between professionals, amateurs, teachers and cultural centres is developing. But the report makes clear that the situation is 'fragile'; that working conditions are difficult and subsidy inadequate.

As far as we have been able to ascertain the subsidized theatre in every European country offers a variety of services for children and young people. These may take the form of season-ticket schemes, similar in operation to those for adults, reductions for young people with student cards, and special productions for children. These can be seasonal entertainments such as the celebrated British Christmas pantomime or special productions of plays on the educational examination syllabus.

Particularly interesting information has come to us from French-speaking Belgium where a considerable amount of theatre-visiting in school hours is organized by Rendez-vous Jeunesses Théâtre. This is a season-ticket scheme offering young people 18 productions a year in professional theatres. In the autumn of 1976, for example, the productions included *Volpone*, *Béjart's Ninth Symphony*, *Dr. Knock*, *Pelléas et Mélisande*, Tom Stoppard's *Dirty Linen*, *Macbeth*, Strindberg's *A Dream Play*, *Kennedy's Children* and *Requiem for a Nun* (Faulkner) (16). Most theatres offer season-ticket schemes or reduced prices for parties of children.

The country also provides an impressive programme of *'animations decentralisées'* organized by the Ministry's *Les Tournées Art et Vie*. Small groups of professional artists gave a total of 379 performances of many different kinds of music and drama largely in small towns and villages, 50% paid for by central government, 25% by regional government, 25% from the box-office.

In conclusion we will turn to some interesting statistics of theatre-going by French children compiled in 1975 by the Service des Etudes et Recherche which reveal similar demographic patterns to adults. In 1973, 28% of all young people between the ages of 12 and 20 had been to the theatre at least once, 72% not at all. Regular theatre-goers in this age-group numbered 4.4%. They were older students with professional parents (44%), living in the larger towns (48%), with a preference for modern drama over classics, comedies or musical comedies. Those who go to the cinema (82%) in preference to the theatre (28%) do so far more often, 7% going once a week. Many more girls (33%) go to the theatre than boys (21%).

The attitude of children from poorer homes to the theatre is often that 'its not for us', 'its of no interest to me', or 'its too much like school'.

Amateur Theatre

Reference to Chapter one will remind readers that the practice of the-atre-going is usually established, like many other practices, in children of school age. The responsible people are therefore parents and teachers. If neither party is interested children 'miss out' on what may be an enriching experience. It is therefore arguable that subsidy should carry with it a certain educational obligation. This does not mean that the programme of every subsidized regional theatre should include a certain number of school matinées and a Christmas pantomime but that, in contemporary idiom, a dialogue should be established between theatre directors and school-teachers in the locality. If there is to be any reality in the policy that has been argued throughout this book that there must be a constant democratizing of cultural activities, a living relationship between artists and their community, and an involvement of one with the other, such a dialogue cannot be deferred.

Such discussions, moreover, should be widely initiated, not in accordance with some abstract political democratic principle, but because it is not at all clear of what a theatre's educational policy should consist. School matinées or reduced prices for children at evening performances are something; so are *animations* or practical classes taken by members of a professional company; so are all the practices that have been described in the foregoing pages. But it is not a matter of either/or. An educational policy can be evolved only by discussion between theatre workers and teachers based on respect for and on understanding of the nature of the other party's contribution. An important element in a child's education is his introduction to theatrical art both as participant and audience: it is a subject that still requires investigation jointly by actor (or director), teacher and parent. But it may be necessary for the authorities to initiate, encourage, or focus such discussions.

Theatre-going and a zeal for participation in dramatic activity does not necessarily stop, any more than education itself, when the young person leaves school. Amateurs may take it amiss to find their favourite leisure activity described as further education, but that is because education itself has come unhappily to be associated with various kinds of academic 'slog' instead of as an entry into a variety of new worlds and experiences. Nor, it is to be hoped, will this important section be ignored by professionals who take the limited view that the amateur artist is one who lacks the drive, the gumption, the skill to make a profession of his enthusiasms.

If it is agreed that it is essential to introduce children to the arts while they are still at school, it follows that it is similarly important to provide opportunities for adults to follow the art or arts of their choice. Many of the arguments for subsidizing the professional theatre apply with significant force to the amateur theatre especially in an industrial society. That society has obligations to ensure its own survival, its vitality. Culture can neither be taken for granted nor left to individual caprice. Opportunities to read good books, and even poor ones, must be provided for those who cannot afford to buy them. (In passing we might note that while the United Kingdom makes a poor showing in subsidy for the theatre, it provides impressive subsidies for public libraries). Opportunities to act or play in an ensemble must be provided for groups that cannot afford the high cost of a rehearsal room.

It may very well be that the flame of commitment burns less strongly in the amateur than the professional. On the other hand it is arguable that the somewhat constricted conditions in which the theatre so often operates might persuade the genuine enthusiast to earn his living at a bread-and-butter job and reserve his passion for a company which, though lacking perhaps a highly developed expertise, approaches the art of the theatre with sensibility and circumspection. It is unfortunate that such companies are not as commonly found as one would have hoped.

A commonly noted scepticism or lack of interest in the work of the amateur theatre derives from the belief that most amateur companies function as a kind of pale reflection of the professional theatre, staging almost exclusively its proven successes and imitating its techniques. It is therefore satisfactory to be able to state that this dispiriting picture is no longer true. The will for artistic independence, which led to the creation of an alternative professional theatre, has found its parallel in the world of amateur theatre. In the Scandinavian countries, the Netherlands, and to a certain extent in West Germany, 'the amateur theatre is motivated by a determination to make a public statement'. Assiduous readers of this book will no doubt realize what is meant by this: it is the outcome of seeing the theatre in a social context so that the production of a play becomes not merely an exercise in technique, in which of course artistic and aesthetic qualities may play a considerable part, but an opportunity to reflect or project certain socio-political problems on both local and national level. In most European countries, the amateur theatre has set its face rigorously against imitating professional models and concentrates on creating its own material and its own methods of work. The 1981 Festival of Amateur Theatre held at Monaco was notable for the variety, the freshness and the vigorous individuality of performances many of which were given by groups from village communities having little contact with the mainstream professional theatre. It may well be argued that in its virtual freedom from destructive financial constraints and with its present artistic dynamic the amateur theatre is likely to play an increasingly significant role in the developments of the theatre.

It is therefore not surprising to find a growing involvement of the amateur theatre in the field of education. An increasing number of amateur theatres have their own children's and youth groups, which are not, strictly speaking, making theatre but engaging themselves more generally in creative drama activities. In some countries, notably the Scandinavian countries and the Netherlands, and in a decidedly educational context in Great Britain, the work in creative drama can be seen as a movement in itself. It has been suggested that as much as 20-30% of the international activities of IATA/AITA are concerned with educational drama.

So we find that in some countries the amateur theatre is a highly organized national movement. Some Swedish companies and the influential Nederlands Centrum voor het Amateurtoneel receive generous government subsidy and are fully committed to the idea of amateur theatre as a distinct form of artistic/social expression. In Belgium and Switzerland the situation is a little more complex owing to varied cultural and linguistic structures.

Support for the amateur theatre by local education authorities is also fairly common in France and Great Britain in the form of a tutor's, or director's salary, or provision of premises where the group meets. Subsidies from central, only very occasionally, and local, very much more often, government are sometimes available to groups which can be seen to be broadly educational in aim and achievement.

In Belgium the amateur theatres of the two cultures, French and Flemish, have come together to form the Belgian National Committee of Amateur Theatre (Comité Nationale Belge du Théâtre Amateur/ Belgisch National Comite voor het Amateurtoneel), with government subsidies for study conferences, weekends and courses. Training courses have been established in some 20 centres in Dutch-speaking Belgium, increasingly well-attended. There is a National Competition, the Koninklijk Landjuwel, and a variety of festivals for groups that do not care for a competitive element. There is a vigorous interchange of amateur theatre groups between Flanders and the Netherlands under a specially formed joint-organization (17).

The amateur theatre in Belgium depends on a fairly traditional international repertory but is making special efforts to introduce work by contemporary Flemish playwrights. That and the training of directors is the responsibility of the Interfederaal Centrum Vlaams Amateurtoneel.

Experimental work does not play a large part in its activities since that is largely the concern of the Jeunes Théâtres and the semi-amateur companies; but the amateurs are greatly interested in new concepts of creativity as developed by some of the country's professional directors. There are thought to be some 750 amateur groups in the French-speaking area of Belgium though the figure could go a good deal higher. These groups are represented by a loosely structured federation called Les États Génèraux du Théâtre Amateur on which are represented the Ministry of French Culture and a number of regional and national cultural organizations covering the provinces of Brabant, Hainault, Liège, Namur and Luxembourg and including the Belgian National Theatre and the Belgian Society of Authors, Composers and Publishers. Early in 1977 all the amateur groups in the country were sent a questionnaire from the answers to which an interesting picture of the amateur theatre emerged.

They had an average of about 18 actors per company, an interesting difference from the professional company which usually numbers about six; 65% between the ages of 20 and 35, a predictable preponderance of young people; a proportion of men to women of 60:40 with the male majority increasing with age; the director a member of the company; 65% of companies include their own technician but a similar percentage lack adequate equipment; most companies design and construct their own scenery but appear neither to make nor to hire their own costumes, largely depending, it appears, on non-theatrical apparel which must limit choice of play; few of them own their own premises; most rehearse in premises they describe as 'rudimentary' - dirty, inadequate and preventing a serious study of direction or decor, which they rent for an average of 500 B.F. an evening; ideally they rehearse where they are to perform, usually in some kind of public or communal hall, with a capacity of some 200-300, usually described as 'bon' which they hire for anything between 1,000 (£20) and 4,000 B.F. (£70) a performance with an additional 100 to 3,000 B.F. for light, heat, cleaning etc. Audiences are composed mostly of adults with a 60% preponderance of women.

For repertoire, the number of Belgian and French authors has tended to decrease in favour, in this order, of English, German, Russian, Spanish and Italian plays. Each production is given between 15 and 20 performances at the rate of about two a week, the one respect in which Belgian practice differs strongly from English where amateur productions are usually given for a small number of consecutive performances.

Figures for satisfaction are both high. Reasons for the former are clear; amateurs would not participate if they did not enjoy the work; but 43% are dissatisfied because of limitations imposed by the authorities, high cost of production, inadequate organization, unsatisfactory repertoire etc.

The leading organization of the German amateur theatre is the Bund

Deutscher Amateurtheater, founded in Berlin in 1892. In 1978 there were 401 member companies, 31 with indoor stages, 70 open-air, together with 236 puppet stages. Active personnel numbered 24,590, 13,971 working on stage, 10,691 behind stage. They were drawn from a great variety of professions though there is little evidence of a working-class membership. A majority of members were between 30 and 40 years old and had been members of a society for 15 years (18).

The member companies gave 4,318 performances, 3,154 in theatres, 1,164 in the open-air, and 262 of puppets, each production being rehearsed between three and four months and played for between 4 and 7 performances to 1.3 million spectators with an average capacity of 78.6%.

The most surprising fact is that by far the largest number of groups is to be found in Bavaria which in 1965 had a population of just over 10 million, while North Rhein-Westphalia with a population of 16 million had 16 groups; Baden Würtemberg (8 million) 79 groups, Lower Saxony (7 million) 17 groups.

Most of the groups receive some kind of help from Land or City Council. In the papers accompanying these statistics there is considerable emphasis on the provision of training courses for amateur actors and the spiritual values that are established by work in the amateur theatre.

As to repertory, the most frequently performed authors of the past are Shakespeare, who as in the professional theatre tops the list, Shaw, Goldoni, Hoffmannstahl, Ostrovsky, Kleist, Molière and Nestroy. The two most popular playwrights of the present century are, somewhat surprisingly, Curt Goetz and Ephraim Kishon. The most frequently played authors in the open-air theatre were Carl Zuckmayer, August Wanner, and Otfried Preuszler.

Curt Goetz, with whose once popular work some readers may not be familiar, was a doctor who wrote many comedies largely debunking the bourgeoisie and acted in them with his wife. Such plays as *Der Hahn im Korb* and *Die Hochzeit in Montevideo* have been very popular in schools.

Ephraim Kishon is a Jewish satirist whose popular and extremely amusing anecdotes, largely centering on the state of Israel, appear to have been the subject of dramatization.

A certain amount of subsidy is provided in most countries by regional or municipal governments, rarely the central government.

The amateur theatre in France is represented by the Fédération Nationale des Compagnies de Théâtre et d'Animation which was founded in 1907 and which in 1976 merged with the Fédération Catholique and now represents many of the non-professional French theatrical companies.

The structure, objectives and audiences of the member companies are as varied as elsewhere, comprising theatre groups of Les Maisons de Jeunes; socio-educational section of schools and colleges; theatre companies of large national organizations; university theatre groups; large schools; young workers clubs; rural clubs; independant groups.

The Federation organizes courses and educational programmes, national and regional festivals, conferences and discussions as well as the Grand Prix Charles Dullin awarded for the best interpretation of a full-length play. The magazine *Théâtre et Animation* provides a link between the Federation and its member groups. In 1978 the Federation organized important regional meetings and Festivals at Epinal, Vannes, Challons, Istres, Pontoise, and Saint-Quentin.

Traditionally, the amateur theatre in Britain, which has a long ancestry, has been social and recreative rather than political and educational; but although there are still many companies of a comfortably bourgeois nature there is a growing interest in social issues. (It was probably in the 1930s when under the political threat of Fascism and the unacceptable reality of three million unemployed that the amateur political theatre showed itself at its most vigorous).

There is a kind of first division of amateur companies that own their own theatre and stage a succession of productions for a few nights each throughout the year. There are over forty members of the Little Theatre Guild of Great Britain and although on the whole their work is not socio/political, it is often of a high artistic standard, fulfilling a useful social function, and keeping alive the best elements of the traditional theatre.

A survey of the amateur theatre in Great Britain has recently been carried out by the Central Council for Amateur Theatre. The overall figures are impressive - about 8,400 groups in England alone; a total membership of 479,000 of whom 258,000 are acting members (0.57% of the population) and 135,000 interested in backstage and front-of-house. In 1976-77 they sold 14.5 million tickets and took £10.3 million at the box-office. The average seat-price was 61p. Each group has about 30 acting members and gives about three productions a year, each for about four performances. Operatic societies tend to give fewer productions but more performances of each. About 50% of the groups receive some kind of financial aid, sometimes in the form of provided facilities, 32% from the district or parish council, 17% from the Local Education Authority, 7% from the Regional Arts Association. Most groups manage to store their own scenery and costumes. They perform in a variety of venues but it is unusual for groups to own or rent permanently their own premises. It is understandable that music groups are far readier to employ professionals than the drama groups.

We are strongly supportive of the proposals made in the postscript to the report that local authorities should be more generous in the provision of working spaces; that there should be a closer relationship between the amateur and professional theatre; and that the amateurs themselves should do more to attract the interest of school-leavers who have shown an interest in the theatre.

In the Netherlands the amateur theatre is represented by the vigorous Nederlands Centrum voor Amateurtoneel, supported by a central government grant of two million guilders a year which enables it to employ 18 full-time advisers based in different parts of the country, and housed in splendid premises in Maarssen, a town adjacent to Utrecht.

The NCA provides all the usual services to its 2,000 individual and group members; but perhaps the most unusual feature of its work, and the one of greatest interest to readers of this book, is its publication of a variety of text books and plays which it prints itself in clear and elegant format. The script of a new play is distributed free to all members along with the organization's bulletin-magazine. (Other publications are sold at little above cost price.) The authors of published plays receive a small emolument equivalent to about £125 and authors of commissioned plays an honorarium of 2-3,000 Guilders. The editor of the series works closely with professional theatre companies like Centrum that are interested in contemporary plays.

Proposals for the decentralization of the organization have produced certain anxieties at headquarters. Present subsidy comes direct from central government. Proposals for community art would be subsidized, if accepted, by the provinces under a new 'welfare plan'. It is the problem being raised at every level: the balance between central control and local initiative.

In the early years of the century the amateur movement in Sweden was associated with the national labour and temperance movements; artistic standards were not high. It was from 1948 onwards that the amateur movement began to assume the importance it enjoys today. New groups were established, many of them acquiring their own venues, often with the help of the local authority, developed their own training schemes and gave regular performances.

After a period of negotiation the present umbrella organization *Amatörteaterns Riksforbund* (ATR) was founded in 1977. By the autumn of 1978 it represented some 100 member groups all 'with serious intentions'. Many have their own stage, employ an artistic director, teachers and other members of staff. Perhaps most interesting of all, ATR is establishing its own publishing company to represent Swedish dramatists who write for the amateur theatre, and to negotiate royalties for amateur productions with established dramatists. Its magazine, now in its eleventh year, is *Teaterforum*.

The report provides a fascinating picture of the development of the Swedish amateur theatre. In the 1950s the groups experimented with stage forms (arena, open stage), theatrical styles and the training of actors. In the 1960s it experimented with group productions (collective creations and similar activities). Since 1975 it has been increasingly concerned with social and political subjects, the working-class and aspects of local history. A production of considerable significance was *The Play about the Norberg Strike* in 1977. It was played by a cast of over 100 amateurs, many of them descendants of those who had participated in the strike (1891-92). Similar productions were written and staged in other parts of the country and considerable interest was raised in the professional theatre (19).

The most recent development has been in the direction of education. An increasing number of groups are collaborating with secondary school pupils, with children and pensioners, and with trade unionists investigating the history and current problems of local communities.

There are perhaps at present some 200-250 well organized groups in addition to several thousand groups of a less identifiable kind working in a great variety of contexts. This rapid extension of the amateur movement is difficult to analyse but is generally attributed to the industrial crisis the country is experiencing, the increasingly technocratic quality of life which pushes people to discover personal form of creativity, and the increasing willingness of central and local authorities 'to support the development of a popular independant folk culture alongside an institutionalized culture'. In 1980-81 the Swedish Amateur Theatre received a central government subsidy of 720,000 SKr.

Some 60 Swiss amateur French-speaking theatre groups are represented by the Fédération Suisse des Sociétes Théâtrales d'Amateurs. Founded in 1926 with four companies, it now aims to create 'fraternity among its members' and to provide the kind of services that we have noted in the case of other countries. It is financed by contributions from member groups with a small addition from the communes.

In the season 1977-78, 41 societies gave 312 performances of 69 works of which 13 were by Swiss authors. The artistic enterprise and standard of performance of a majority of groups is said to be steadily improving. The amateur theatre is looked upon as an indispensable support and extension of the professional theatre. The dividing line between the fully amateur companies and the 'Petits Théâtres' of which we have already spoken, hovering uncertainly between amateur and professional status, is far from clear.

The categories are also blurred in the German-speaking areas. The *Kleintheatervereinigin* is a union of some hundreds of little theatres. Experimental work does not play a large part in its activities since that is largely the responsibility of the Jeunes Théâtres and the semi-amateur companies; but the amateurs on the whole are greatly interested in new concepts of creativity as developed by some of the country's professional directors.

Summary

May we refer to the metephor of the pyramid that was used at the end of Chapter five, and to the passage from J.M. Synge, quoted in Chapter seven, in which he spoke about the quality of life that must invest a whole community if its members are to produce masterpieces. There seems to be no way at all in which an artist can dissociate himself from society. The very act of dissociation is a very powerful statement of what it is, an act of dissociation. And society, however much it may be analysed, arranged and dissected into groups, classes, minorities, infrastructures and sub-cultures by the sociologists, can only remain a whole and living entity. The Renaissance ideal, though one that we tend to regard as a charming but out-moded foible, makes a statement that we cannot disregard.

The implication of this is a truth so evident as to hardly require stating. The sickness of any part of society can lead to the impoverishment of the whole. The sickening and inhuman face of industrial Britain and the lives of the millions who are caught up in this evil parody of a decent society produce the debilitation from which we all now suffer. It is clear indeed that a society cannot built cathedrals when it consigns its millions to living in the insensitive environment of most housing estates; nor produce poetry when it pays little regard to the quality of its vernacular language; nor theatrical masterpieces when the men who built the National Theatre rarely attend a performance at it.

Although a recurrent theme of this book has been that of taking Shakespeare to the masses or inducing more people to support their regional theatre, this is a mere gloss on the real issue which is nothing less than the creation of a new culture; and that means starting from the bottom, with children, with a generous and continuing system of education, with amateur creativity in all its forms, with the lives of ordinary people. It is not a question of trying to 'improve' anybody by the imposition of moral or artistic standards, but simply of recognising that the language we use and the houses we live in and the work we labour at are all a part of life itself and as such are expressive 'of our total sensibility. We ignore such simple truths at the risk of forfeiting humanity itself. Each of us can only play his modest part in a continuing evolution and this book has attempted to suggest the part the theatre might play in the development of a vigorous democratic society.

Notes and Sources

(1) All available from the Publcations Department, Council of Europe, Strasbourg 67006.
(2) See John Allen - *Drama in Schools: Theory and Practice* - Heinemann Educational Books, 1979.
(3) Joseph Elias, Teacher in the Ober-seminar of Zürich and the Theatre-in-Education section of the Zürich Schauspielhaus Akademie.
(4) *The Arts in Schools: Principles, Practice and Provision* - Calouste Gulbenkian Foundation, 1981.
     See also
     Actors in Schools - Education Survey No. 22 HMSO 1976.
(5) T.Q. Publications
(6) *The Arts and Museums Statistics* - Chartered Institute of Public Finance and Accountancy, 1978.
(7) Journal of the Théâtre Populaire Romand, La Chaux-de-Fonds, No. 108 June 1977.
(8) Ministry of Dutch Culture, Brussels.
(9) *Théâtre en France* - Association du Théâtre pour l'Enfance et la Jeunesse, Paris, 1977.
(10) See note 9 above.
(11) *Programmheft des Grips-Kindertheater - Treffens* - Berlin, 1979
(12) Karin Gartzka in SCYPT Journal, No. 4, 1979
(13) Drama Advisory Panel's Children's Theatre Working Party Report, February 1977 - April 1978, Arts Council of Great Britain.
(14) Maya Cornacchio - *Dal Bambino al Teatro e Riterno* - Scena, Milan, March-April 1977.
(15) Giorgio Strehler, Scena, See Chapter 6, note 19 below
(16) See Chapter 7, note 12 above
(17) Information supplied by the Bund Deutscher Amateurtheater - Richard-Wagner-Strasse 13, 7500 Karlsruhe 1
(18) Einar Bergvin - unpublished paper

Jean Dasté, and a mask belonging to the Comédie de Saint-Etienne.

Shakespeare's 'King Lear' at the Comedie de Saint-Étienne, one of the French Centres Dramatiques Nationaux.

12. Some Final Thoughts

The wide range of material that has been considered in this book makes it difficult to conclude with a tidy summary of events or a neat list of recommendations. In the latter, in any case, we have no great faith. Action can only validly be taken on the basis of considered judgement. To recommend that governments should do this and theatre directors that would be not only arrogant but supererogatory. Those involved in the theatre know a great deal better what's afoot or what remains to be done than an outside investigator. But what an investigator might be allowed to propose is that what is needed in the theatre by and large is not more action but more thought. It has been surprising to find how little evidence exists of serious thought having been given to the theory of public subsidy for the theatre. The practice of subsidy has grown, particularly since the 1939-45 War, without ever having been effectively underpinned with a body of theory. Pragmatists may congratulate themselves on this escape from theoretical constraints; but the need for economising throughout the public sector of industry, as well as the arts, has made theatres vulnerable to cuts in Arts Council subsidy and the Council itself to inadequate funding by the Treasury. In neither case is there a tradition of public debate and once again it seems necessary to insist that a total cultural policy implies a total area of debate. This is not to be so unrealistic as to suggest that the smallest decision be subject to the biggest debate but that the schedule be a declared policy and a democratic debate of that policy, and how it is to be applied, so that there can be no question of decisions being made at any level disingenuously or without a declared reason.

The debate must be concerned with not only amounts of money thought to be both available and necessary but the manner in which it is to be provided and the precise uses to which it is to be put and for what purposes. The awarding and acceptance of subsidy must be as much a subject of artistic strategy as political decision. This is the more important since there are indications that in the foreseeable future neither central nor local governments are likely to increase contributions significantly except to keep pace with inflation.

It is also evident that the theatre has likewise failed to do some of its homework. Audiences are tending to languish. With certain notable exceptions there are few theatre directors who would not rejoice at the creation of a new public for the theatre. But apart from a better under-standing than hitherto on what is meant by marketing the product, a subject that is not within the scope of this book, directors and their publicity team tend to rely on traditional forms of publicity - 'spreads' in the local paper, chatty items of news, advertising stunts and commercial gimmicks. But what was established clearly in the first and final chapters of this book is that we know very well the nature of the potential audience for the theatre and where it is to be found - in schools, colleges, polytechnics and universities. The failure of the theatre to win the greater and more substantial support of this potential audience goes along with the failure of Ministries of Education and Culture to see the educational-cultural process as a single responsibility which, far from changing radically in nature as children become young people and move from school to higher education and then into full citizenship, simply becomes richer and more diversified. (Chapter 11).

We are of course acutely aware that higher education affects only a small proportion of the age-group. The stubborn and intractable fact remains that in demographic terms few theatres have succeeded in creating a popular theatre in the sense of having won a more or less permanent broadly-based audience. The problem is not easy; but the means of solving it are at hand. Children and young people must have experience of the theatre both as participants and audiences while they are still at school, irrespective of social class. This is not that they may help to swell bourgeois support for divertissements and lubricity but because the arts, just as much as the sciences, are an aspect of human intelligence and sensibility.

The last thing we would wish to do is disparage in any way the established theatre. It would be as lamentable an act of philistinism to close our great opera houses and national theatres because they are expensive to run as it would be to draw shutters over the windows of Europe's palaces and mansions because they are expensive to maintain. Nevertheless these great establishments, the anachronistic survival of former cultures, must not be allowed to dominate or stifle contemporary art. It is very tempting to argue that an attractive and comfortable theatre providing consistently excellent productions of the classics of dramatic literature, past and present, gives pleasure to audiences and a peaceful life to the administrator. But culture, of which art is an important element, is both a projection of our communal sensibilities and the scene within which we act out, for better or worse, our lives. Culture breathes and changes. It is as much a part of human life as the human body itself. Culture, and the art within it, cannot be viewed as a sustained, Virgilian, unchanging platitude.

Perhaps the most significant pages of this book are those in which we described the attitude of young actors to the theatre (pages 153-55).

The group at Gennevilliers claimed that what concerned them was not a question of democracy and authority within a company but of the creation of a new type of theatrical organization, in which the problems related to division of labour in the present sense no longer exist. Actors today are not at all the same kind of people they were a hundred years ago. Still less directors. And the playwright? If he is in danger of losing his identity it is for two reasons. One is that many actors have discovered within themselves what the Italian director (page 203) described as 'creative phantasy'; and the other is that society has lost faith in the spoken word and the ability to use it poetically.

But there is an even deeper reason than this. Insofar as the theatre is a social phenomenon, an aspect of society, it must respond inevitably to changes in society. One of the dangers of this argument is that in speaking about theatre we tend to lay excessive emphasis on bricks and mortar. But the theatre is least of all a building. The venue is a physical necessity and a well-designed theatre building is both more convenient and more comfortable than the street. But it has only limited capacity, however skillfully designed, for adaptability. So when we talk about the theatre we are really talking about the ensemble of performing artists for whom the architect and designer have created a scene and the play-wright a text. But the job of the playwright is to project in dramatic form the values of his society. Sometimes he confirms those values, more often he challenges them. And society questions why it should support, or subsidize a man or woman for challenging its fragile stability (page 185).

Now all this may be very annoying for the administrator and the politician who want things cut-and-dried. But it is the stuff of which a living theatre is made. It would be totally unwarrantable to criticize the tremendous achievement of the German theatre since the war. But it might be permissable to speculate whether its formidable theatre buildings, questioned in fact by the President of the Republic himself (page 108), the tremendous subsidies that support it (page 98), the limitations imposed by its organizational structure (page 61) are al-together in the best interests of theatrical art. It is impossible to escape the fact that with a subsidy about seven times higher than that pertaining in Great Britain it produces one seventh (or some incon-siderable fraction) the number of playwrights. And the whole impressive structure is sustained by an educational system that places considerable emphasis, in words that are becoming the bane of those who believe in the importance of the arts in education, on 'things that matter'. These 'things' tend to be the skills of reading, writing and arithmetic. Splendid! Who wants an illiterate generation? But the so-called academ-ic skills, too often in practice a 'slog', are crucial, not only for increasing

291

the Gross Domestic Product, but in providing a passport to the world of the spirit and the imagination. Education is barren if it fails to provide young people with the forms through which we celebrate the rituals by means of which society recreates itself, the opportunity to become artists and audiences.

When we have decided upon the theory, then we can take action. Buildings, of course, we need but not too substantial. We have suggested (page 96) that there should be a theatre in every town with a population of 100,000, but theatres have flourished in towns much smaller than this (page 95). So let us have smaller theatres for smaller companies of professionals and for use by the amateurs (page 238), and arts centres where artists can work and audiences rejoice in their work. And then we must recognise that artists and audiences present us with two, not unrelated, sets of problems. For the artist have a problem which only they can solve, that of their relationship to each other, as was discussed above, and this is one to which administrators can expect no easy solution. But is is extended, as we found in discussing the work of the director of the Strasbourg theatre (page 178), into the relationship of the theatre artist with his community. For actors, directors and playwrights are no longer interested only in the size of their audience and box-office receipts, but in its quality, nature and composition. The whole of the popular and alternative theatre movements are based on a passionate interest of theatre workers in their social responsibilities.

Against this background there are a number of comments that might be made:

The procedures and mechanisms of subsidy that have been developed in recent years seem to be adequate enough to preserve a traditional structure of the theatre. A direct contract between central or local government and a theatrical organization assumes that the former, though insisting on its respect for the freedom of the artist, does not expect any serious deviations from an undefined but generally acceptable conventionality; while the latter is not in a position to argue the artistic justification for new approaches to the art of the theatre.

Insistence on the accountability of the theatre must be recognised. But accountability cannot be taken to justify certain prescriptions that specify number of performances or number of productions and the size of venue where they shall take place. There is no justification in spending public money to support further creative work if conditions are attached of an artistically limiting kind.

That the politician has neither time nor experience to investigate the unaccountability of artistic procedures is to underline the argument that has been made repeatedly in this book, that the democratization of cultural activities must be accompanied by constant and vigorous democratic debate.

It is also on account of the insufficiency of the politician in artistic matters that argument arises in favour of the 'buffer state', the professionally-manned executive that carries out in detail the general legislative policies of government, whether central, regional or local. This is not to suggest that any such existing organizations, the Arts Council of Great Britain or the Swedish Cultural Council are ideal models of their kind; but they are models; and though subject to the perennial weaknesses that flesh is heir to, they are structured to meet the demands that are made on them.

But if the policy of decentralization has any meaning at all, it is in the field of culture that its justification will most vividly be found. The 'buffer state' in the form of the Arts Council of Great Britain may serve admirably to carry out the policies of central government; but it is questionable whether a centralized organization is in a position to respond to local needs down to parish level; and there seems to be a powerful argument in favour of the Regional Arts Association, or its equivalent, whatever it may be called, to function in a similar executive capacity in carrying out the general policies of the local town hall. It requires no very great powers of perception to lament the haphazard provision of subsidized theatres in countries such as France and Italy: 19 regional theatres in the one, eleven in the other, both countries with a total population in excess of fifty-five million.

But it seems to us that by far the most striking fact to have emerged from this survey is the changing nature of the theatre. It has been unequivocally established that the main support for the theatre comes from young people. What is not confirmed statistically but which is evident to anyone with the opportunity to observe the interests of the young, whether as theatre-goers or theatre-workers, is their passionate concern for what is new and contemporary. It seems to be abundantly clear that young theatre workers, actors, directors and playwrights, are earnestly striving for new methods of work, new relationships, and a new social context, not only within the acting area but in relationship with their audiences. This is a profoundly important and significant struggle, for it involves the way in which future members of European society think and feel even if it does not directly impinge upon that great platitudinous imponderable, the Gross Domestic Product. The implication appears to be that those who grant subsidy must develop sufficiently flexible procedures to keep pace with the changing attitudes of their clients. For in the last resort we can only revert to a paraphrase of what J. M. Synge so clearly expressed, that a national theatre will not maintain, let alone improve its standards if the country takes no pleasure in its amateurs, its young theatre workers and its regional theatres. No national theatre is an island. But any community must have regard for the cultivation of its cultural soil. Nevertheless there is evidence (page 10) the expenditure on the theatre, as a proportion of the total expenditure on cultural and recreative activities, is decreasing. When this fact is set beside the inroads being made into control by an artist of his own work by advances in technological reproduction, we begin to see the real nature of the problem and how critical it is that society should evolve the structures that preserve its spiritual vitality as well as its economic independance.

List of Illustrations

The Author as Director of the Glyndebourne Children's Theatre with a party of schoolchildren backstage at the Toynbee Hall, London 1947.

Appendix 1
Sources of Information

Belgium

Neither details of subsidy nor more general theatrical statistics are issued either privately or publicly. In our case detailed information has been generously provided by both the Ministries of Flemish and French Culture.

Ministère de l'Education Nationale et de La Culture Francaise,
158 Avenue de Cortenbergh,
1040 Brussels.

Ministerie,
Rue des Colonies,
Brussels.

Information on the amateur and youth theatre in the French sector has been provided by:

Service de l'Animation et de la Diffusion Culturelle,
Galerie Ravenstein 4,
1000 Brussels.

Other useful addresses:

Belgian Centre of the ITI,
c/o Mark Hermans,
Rudolfstraat 33,
B 2000 Antwerp.

Belgian Embassy,
103, Eaton Square,
London SW1.

The British Council,
Galilee Building,
Avenue Galilee 5 (Galileilaan),
B 1030 Brussels.

France

The Ministère de la Culture et de la Communication issues details of theatrical subsidy:

53 Rue Saint-Dominique,
75006 Paris.

The Ministry also issues an admirably produced monthly periodical - **Les Cahiers de la Culture et de l'Environment** - in which there are informative articles on all the activities in which the Ministry is involved with relevant statistics when appropriate.

The information and statistical research department of the Ministry is the Service des Etudes et de la Recherche du Secretariat d'Etat à la Culture - 4 rue d'Aboukir, Paris 2.

Details of activities in the Centres Dramatiques are to be found in the monthly **ATAC Informations, Magazine d'Action Culturelle et Théâtral** - 19 Rue du Renard, Paris 4e.

Some of the Centres Dramatiques and the Maisons de la Culture issue their own magazines, bulletins or periodicals. These are referred to in the text.

For children's theatre:

Association du Théâtre pour l'Enfance et la Jeunesse,
98 Boulevard Kellermann,
75013 Paris.

Other useful addresses:

The British Council,
9 Rue de Constantine,
75007 Paris.

Centre Francais du Théâtre/Association pour le Soutien du Théâtre Privé,
7 Rue de Helder,
Paris 9e.

French Centre of the International Theatre Institute,
UNESCO,
1 Rue Miollis,
75732 Paris.

297

French Cultural Councillor,
22 Wiltin Crescent,
London SW1.

Federal Republic of Germany

There is no aspect of the German theatre of which the most detailed statistics are not available. The most comprehensive collection of statistics is to be found in **Theaterstatistik** published every year since 1965-66 with two volumes of **Vergleichende Theaterstatistik** for 1949-68 and 1949-74, by the Deutscher Bühnenverein/Bündesverband Deutscher Theater (Quatermarkt 5,5000 Cologne 1). There is a charge for this of 17 DM (1981).

Details of expenditure by the Länder are to be found in **Die Ausgaben der Länder für Künst und Kulturpflege 1970-1976** published by the Sekretariat of the Kulturministerkonferenz, Narssestrasse 8, 5300 Bonn 1.

Statistics are also provided in the **Deutsches Bühnen-Jahrbuch** published in Hamburg and in the **Deutscher Stadtetag** published in Cologne. Certain slight inconsistencies in all these figures are accounted for by the use of different statistical methods and the inclusion or exclusion of certain variables.

An overall view of the German theatre with selected statistics is to be found in Werner Schulze-Reimpell's **Development and Structure of the theatre in the Federal Republic of Germany** also available from the Deutscher Bühnenverein.

A detailed study of the theatre in the Federal Republic of Germany has been written by Herr Joachim Werner Preuss available from the Federal Republic of Germany Centre of the International Theatre Institute, Zentrum Bundersrepublik Deutschland des Internationelen.

Theatre Institute E.V.,
Bismarckstrasse 17,
D 1000 Berlin 12.

Help is usually available from:

Inter Naciones, Kennedy Allee 91-103,

D 5300 Bonn/Bad Godesberg.

Other useful addresses:

The British Council,
Giselestrasse 10,
8000 München 40.

and

Hahnenstrasse 6,
5 Cologne 1.

Bund Deutscher Amateur Theatre E.V.,
Richard-Wagner-Strasse 13,
7500 Karlsruhe 1.

Dramatiker-Union (the organization of writers),
Bundesallee 23,
D 1000 Berlin 31.

Embassy of the Federal Republic of Germany,
23 Belgrave Square,
London SW1.

Great Britain

Figures of subsidy are to be found in the annual report of the Arts Council of Great Britain. The Council has detailed figures of expenditure and receipts of all the theatres, companies and activities it subsidizes, but they are treated as confidential information and not generally available - 105 Piccadilly, London W1V 0AU.

It is extremely difficult to get any figures relating to activities of the private/commercial/independent theatre. The headquarters of the managerial association is:

Bedford Chambers,
The Piazza,
Covent Garden,
London WC2E 8HQ.

Detailed figures for local authority spending on theatre and the arts are to be found in **The Arts and Museum Statistics 1976-77** and **Leisure and Recreation Statistics 1980-1** published by The Chartered Institute of Public Finance and Accountancy, 1 Buckingham Place, London SW1E 6HS.

298

Details of most British theatres and theatrical organizations will be found in the British Theatre Directory, published annually by:

John Offord Publications Ltd.,
P.O. Box 64, Eastbourne,
East Sussex BN21 3LW.

Other useful addresses are:

Association for the Business Sponsorship of the Arts,
12 Abbey Churchyard, Bath BA1 1LY.

The British Council,
65 Davies Street, London W1.

Calouste Gulbenkian Foundation,
98 Portland Place, London W1N 4ET.

Contact with most British Theatrical organizations can be made through:

The British Theatre Association,
9 Fitzroy Square, London W1.

Italy

Lo Spettacolo in Italy: annuario statist-icho anno published annually by the Societa Italiana degli Autori ed Editori (SIAE), Rome, has been particularly helpful in supplying figures, in some cases over the last 40 years, for the theatre as well as a variety of other entertainments. Comparative figures are given not only for each province but for the larger and smaller towns within each province.

The **Annuario del Teatro Italiano** also published by S.I.A.E. provides details of all the plays produced each year and where they were staged. It is possible from this book to follow the course of tours.

Analysis of performances, attendances etc. of the various categories of companies, regional, private, cooperative etc. are to be found in **Rilevazione Statistiche sulla Stagione Teatrale di prosa** 1975-76 published by the Associazione Generale Italiana dello Spettacolo (AGIS), Via di villa Patrizi 10. Rome.

Useful information of a more general kind is to be found in **Il Teatro di prosa in**

Italia published by the Servizi Informazioni e Proprieta Letteraria of the Presidenza del Consiglio dei Ministri, Rome.

Other useful addresses:

The British Council,
Via Manzoni 38, 20121 Milan.

Pallazo del Drago,
Via IV Fontane, 00184 Rome.

Ministerio dello Turismo e Spettacolo,
Via dello Ferratella 51, Rome.

Italian Institute,
39 Belgrave Square London SW1X 8NX

The Netherlands

Details of subsidy and general theatre statistics are not issued by the government; but in this case detailed information has been provided by the Ministry of Culture, Recreation and Social Welfare, (Ministerie van Cultuur, Recreatie, en Maatschappelijkwerk, Rijswikj, Steenvoordelaan 370.

An important discussion document, **Toneel ter Zake (Theatre as Business)** was published in 1976 by the Ministry. Even then its figures were some years out-of-date; but it is useful in showing the general direction of governmental policy for theatre.

Information on the Dutch theatre is usually available from the Netherlands Centre of the International Theatre Institute, Herengracht 166-8, Amsterdam.

Other useful addresses:

The British Council,
Keizersgracht 343, Amsterdam.

Netherlands Embassy,
38 Hyde Park Gate, London SW7.

Sweden
Admirably set-out statistics are to be

found in **Kulturstatistik 1970-75** publish-
ed by the National Council for Cultural
Affairs (Kulturradet) and the National
Central Bureau of Statistics, Stockholm.
The figures are brought up-to-date on
stencilled sheets.

Information may also be available from:

Svensk Teaterunion (ITI),
Birger Jaalsgatan 53, 111 45 Stockholm.

Statens Kultuuradet,
Master Sammuelsgatan 42,
103 40 Stockholm.

Central Bureau of Statistics,
100 Kaslavagan, S-102 50 Stockholm 27.

Other useful addresses:

British Council,
c/o British Embassy, Skarpögatan 6,
S-11527 Stockholm.

Swedish Embassy,
23 North Row, London W1.

Switzerland

The admirable report of which we have
made considerable use, **Elements pour
une Politique Culturelle en Suisse,
Berne 1975**, the Clottu Report, provides a
detailed and often candid analysis of the
Swiss Cultural scene. But figures for
subsidy are not published and have to
be derived from the individual theatres.
Hence we have detailed figures only for
what the Swiss consider to be the most
important theatres. For these figures we
are grateful for the intervention of the
Federal Office of Cultural Affairs,

**Thunstrasse 20,
3000 Berne 6**

The semi-government Foundation **Pro
Helvetia** is generous and expeditious in
supplying information about its activities
in the arts:
**Hirschengraben 22,
CH-8001 Zürich.**

There is also a great deal of useful
information to be found in **Theater in der
Schweiz/Théâtre en Suisse/Teatro in
Svizzera**, the Swiss Theatre Yearbook,
Theaterkultur Verlag, Zürich, 1979.

Other useful addresses.

Société des Auteurs et Compositeurs
Dramatiques,
1204 Geneva.

Swiss Embassy,
Montague Place, London W1.